VICTORIAN WORKING WOMEN

VICTORIAN
WORKING WOMEN

An Historical and Literary Study of
Women in British Industries and Professions
1832-1850

WANDA F. NEFF

NEW YORK
THE HUMANITIES PRESS

Published by
FRANK CASS AND COMPANY LIMITED
67 Great Russell Street, London W.C.1
by arrangement with George Allen & Unwin Ltd.

First published
in the United States of America 1967
by Humanities Press Inc.
303 Park Avenue South
New York 10, N.Y.

First edition   1929
Reprinted with a new bibliographical note   1966

Library of Congress Catalog No. 67-13855

Printed in Holland by
N. V. Grafische Industrie Haarlem

BIBLIOGRAPHICAL NOTE TO
THE 1966 EDITION

The social and economic background to Mrs. Wanda F. Neff's pioneer work is largely provided by the following (in chronological order):

Ivy Pinchbeck, *Women Workers and the Industrial Revolution, 1750–1850,* 1930. Second edition in preparation with a new introduction by O. R. McGregor.

C. Willett Cunnington, *Feminine Attitudes in the Nineteenth Century,* 1935.

Dorothy Marshall, *The English Domestic Servant in History* (Historical Association Pamphlet), 1949.

Marjorie Plant, *The Domestic Life of Scotland in the Eighteenth Century,* 1952.

J. Jean Hecht, *The Domestic Servant Class in Eighteenth-century England,* 1956.

Margaret Hewitt, *Wives and Mothers in Victorian Industry,* 1958.

Victorian businesswomen, who appear to have been more numerous at all levels than is generally supposed, still await a general study.

PREFACE

FOR assistance in the preparation of this book I wish to express my gratitude, first of all, to the American Association of University Women for the opportunity their European fellowship gave me to study British civilization. The courtesy and constant helpfulness of the officials of the British Museum, Bodleian, New York City, Columbia University, and Vassar College Libraries considerably lightened my labours of investigation. For aid in economic materials I am indebted to Mr. E. Lipson, of New College, Oxford; for general supervision and guidance in literary materials to Professor A. H. Thorndike, of Columbia University, whose wisdom and original viewpoint have inspired so many of his students; and to Professor Emery E. Neff, also of Columbia University, who read and corrected my manuscript. I wish also to thank, for help given in various ways: Mrs. Graham Wallas; Professor Caroline Spurgeon, Bedford College, University of London; Miss M. J. Tuke, Principal of Bedford College; Miss Christine Burrows, Principal of the Society of Home Students, Oxford; Professor Louis Cazamian, University of Paris; Professor Albert Feuillerat, University of Rennes; and Professor H. M. Ayres, Mr. C. W. Everett, Professor R. H. Fife, Professor G. P. Krapp, Professor R. L. Rusk, Professor H. R. Seager, Doctor H. W. Wells, all of Columbia University.

WANDA FRAIKEN NEFF

1929

CONTENTS

VICTORIAN WORKING WOMEN

CHAPTER I

INTRODUCTION

THE working woman was not, like *Punch* and Free Trade, a Victorian institution. The word *spinster* disproves any upstart origin for the sisterhood of toil. Nor was she as a literary figure the discovery of Victorian writers in search of fresh material. Although Mrs. Anna Jameson in 1846 wrote: "After all that has been written, sung, and said of women, one has the perception that neither in prose nor in verse has she ever appeared as the labourer,"[1] she was not borne out by the facts. A goodly number of working women appear in literary annals from the days of Chaucer, and a few of them are vividly unforgettable figures. Nevertheless, Charlotte Brontë, in *Shirley*, when she gave to Caroline Helstone the reflection that Lucretia spinning at midnight in the midst of her maidens "kept her servants up very late", was representing the new attitude. To the Victorians belongs the discovery of the woman worker as an object of pity, and in the literature of the early nineteenth century one first finds her portrayed as a victim of long hours, unfavourable conditions, and general injustice, for whom something ought to be done.

This belated consciousness of long-standing evils must be attributed to a variety of causes. Not only were working women regarded as a problem. All women were a problem. When W. R. Greg wrote an essay, *Why are Women Redundant?* he was not trying to be facetious. There were too many women in England, he gravely announced. What was to be done with them? Mrs. Jameson in 1851 proclaimed from the lecture-platform that there was an excess of half a million women in England.[2] The census figures allow 365,159. The Napoleonic Wars could be held directly responsible for only a small part of this disproportion* which the census had recorded since 1801. The rank and file of the Army in those days, moreover, furnished little substantial matrimonial material. The Empire with its need for a large number of men in the Civil Service was a far more disrupting factor. The settlement of new lands attracted adventurous young males to Canada, Australia, Tasmania, New Zealand, as well as the criminal and the destitute forced to leave England.† In quiet villages women continued an existence unchanged through the ages, and for many of them there were no husbands. Census figures in 1851 show that 24·86 per cent. of the women in England and Wales at the age of 30 were unmarried; 17·89 per cent. at the age of 35; 11·88 per cent. at the age of 50. When the census figures are subjected to the cold eye of a later age, it is not the proportion of 100 women of all ages to 96 men which is disturbing, but rather the proportion of mature men who remained bachelors. Out of every 100 men in 1851 in England and Wales, 25·89 were unmarried at the age of 30; 18 at the age of 35; 10·74 at the age of 50. Women were "redundant", then, not because there were too many of them, but because the men did not marry.

In the middle of the nineteenth century, a period when the only suitable profession for women was marriage, no eloquent pens berated such elegant celibates as Major Pendennis or Joseph Sedley. Even Mr. Pickwick was not blamed for not marrying Mrs. Bardell. There was no tax on bachelors. They had their excuses for avoiding the responsibilities of marriage. The Napoleonic Wars, if they had not cut down the flower of English manhood, had been responsible for much financial confusion. Business became a gamble. One man was a profiteer, another a bankrupt.[3] After peace was declared, trade

---

* Trevelyan, G. M., British History in the Nineteenth Century, p. 129, states that the seven years of the Peninsular War cost less than 40,000 British dead out of a population (Clapham, J. H., An Economic History of Modern Britain, pp. 53, 54) of approximately 17,000,000 in the United Kingdom, a proportion very similar to the American dead in the world war.

† In the year 1832, 50,000 emigrants went to Canada alone.

suffered the usual after-war deflation. England no longer enjoyed a monopoly of commerce with America. Her manufacturers had European competitors.[4] Hundreds of firms failed. Factory hands had no work. Farmers went bankrupt with the drop in the price of corn. Rural labourers became paupers. The Corn Law passed in 1815 benefited the landowners at the expense of the rest of England. Between Waterloo and the passing of the Reform Bill unsettled conditions persisted. Young men on the brink of matrimony faltered. They could not afford to marry poor girls. They must marry wealth or remain bachelors, with the usual solaces of an age which still nodded over the wild-oats theory. Experienced business men like Mr. Sedley went under. The unmarried daughters of a ruined father were thrown upon the labour market without warning, untrained and helpless.

If women had not obtruded upon the sympathies of Victorian reformers, they might have been left alone for a longer period. Their enforced celibacy, unpleasant as it might be for the women who wanted to marry—there were always some who did not—would find the consolations of piety and charity. As Emma Woodhouse wisely remarked: "A single woman of good fortune is always respectable."[5] It was women in the aspect of wage-earners, labourers, who aroused suddenly indignant defenders. Two million women, according to Mrs. Jameson's uncertain figures, had to be self-supporting. The vision of delicate females trying to earn their daily bread moved journalists, lecturers, novelists. These women did handsewing, like Harriet Martineau after her father's failure, or they advertised in The Times their qualifications as governesses. In the lower classes there was the same spectacle of working women in increasing numbers. During these unsettled years had come the dramatic changes of the Industrial Revolution, with machinery demanding the labour of women and children. Mothers and daughters, forced by the widespread misery of the times, snatched at any work they could get. They left the cottages where they had worked hard but in obscurity and flocked to the mills, those gaunt structures looming above the once pleasant rural landscape. And for the first time the sleepy Tory gentlemen who believed in the Corn Laws experienced a twinge of discomfort.

Women as workers did not harmonize with the philosophy of the Victorians, their deification of the home. Women ought to marry. There ought to be husbands for them. Women were potential mothers. Then the moral earnestness of a generation feeling the belated results of Methodism and Evangelicism was torn by the spectacle of human sufferings. Christian gentlemen had the courage to try to reform long-standing evils. They had attacked slavery, the vicious prison system, the lack of education for the poor. They had discovered the sanctity of childhood. Classing women and children together as helpless creatures needing the protection of strong men, they were indignant at the knowledge that women had to support themselves, that they suffered degrading wrongs as working women.

This moral seriousness manifested itself not only in such philanthropists as Lord Ashley, but also in writers like Charles Dickens, who used the novel more and more for the correction of abuses. The tone of Victorian literature became serious. Even Thackeray could not entirely escape a pulpit manner. One would expect a further intensifying of this moral literary quality in the fact that women were finding increased opportunities for writing. The *Edinburgh Review*, the *London Quarterly Review*, and the *Westminster Review* with the convention of unsigned articles opened their columns to women. Lady Eastlake reviewed *Vanity Fair* and *Jane Eyre* for the *Quarterly*. Hundreds of women's magazines, with the editors and contributors largely women, sprang up in the early years of the nineteenth century.[6] The society Annuals such as the *Keepsake* and *Friendship's Offering*, edited by women of social and literary prominence, were also a flourishing innovation. Not all women writers showed the high seriousness which was later to be commended in poets. They wrote to make money, and some of them earned large sums. They had the wisdom to study their public. The demand for fiction was greater than it had ever been before. If the manufacturers and business men who had come up from humbler rank with the new industrial regime had no time to read, their wives and daughters had the leisure and the inclination for the lighter varieties of literary food. With the increase of schools and more general ability to read among the lower classes, recruits were further added. Lady novelists helped to serve this new public. They wrote stories of high life for the young ladies outside the charmed circle of the aristocracy. The Countess of Blessington, to support an extravagant style of existence and an expensive husband, earned £2,000 a year for twenty years by writing novels and tales dealing with the fashionable world. Mrs. Marsh, Mrs. Crowe, and Julia Pardoe varied the same kind of fiction with the historical and supernatural romances which added colour to the monotony of a machine age. Catherine Gore, who preceded Thackeray in writing social satires, published two hundred volumes of novels, plays, and poems. Mrs. Frances Trollope, the mother of Anthony Trollope, to support her husband and children, wrote one hundred and two novels, dealing with a variety of subjects likely to attract the popular mind.

But other women writers were not satisfied to amuse a half-educated reading public. Many an authoress had a serious purpose in wielding her pen. She had in large measure the earnestness of her age, and she wanted her books to be powerful weapons for worthy causes. Lady Morgan took upon herself the defence of the oppressed Irish, and wrote novels dealing largely with their wretched past. Maria Edgeworth gave a picture of the Irish estates owned by absentee landlords. Harriet Martineau preached the evils of the Poor Laws and the inevitable improvement of England if society were governed by the principles of political economy. Novels with a purpose so strongly reflected the reforming spirit of the age that they were in heavy demand. Mrs. Trollope, with a careful finger on the pulse of her public, responded by writing *Michael Armstrong* to circulate the abuse of factory children. Charlotte Brontë apologized for *Villette* because it took up no "philanthropic scheme".[7] By 1850 fiction was in a harness of moral obligation.

In all this bulk of philanthropic writing by women, one would expect a concern with questions relating to their own sex. The most cursory examination reveals a wealth of such material. Mrs. Gaskell and Charlotte Brontë are the great champions of the women of their generation. George Eliot is their most intelligent critic. But with these came women less in fame, but equal to them in their eagerness to make the lives of women more endurable. Charlotte Elizabeth Tonna (1790–1846), so popular in her own day that a complete edition of her works was published in the United States with an Introduction by Harriet Beecher Stowe ranking her above Dickens as a reformer, was a strict Evangelical with the conviction that the reading, and even more the writing, of novels was a sin. But after she was deserted by her adventurous and unstable soldier husband, she had no way of supporting herself except by writing. She saved herself from the evils of fiction by composing a species of tales, not novels, because they were based upon the truth. She took the unwieldy Blue Books of Parliament reporting the suffering of factory women and children, selected the most harrowing facts, and made them the experiences of imaginary characters. As editor of the *Christian Lady's Magazine* she printed articles showing the necessity of women's informing themselves in politics and economics, and used even simpler methods than Harriet Martineau to explain the changes made by industrialism. She was as conscious of the new age in her magazine as Dickens in *Household Words*. Mrs. Anna Jameson (1794–1860), remembered now as the author of *Characteristics of Shakespeare's Women* and several pleasant volumes on Italian Art, urged by painful memories of "governessing", waged a tireless campaign for working women. Mrs. S. C. Hall (1800–1881), who wrote sketches of Irish life strongly influenced by Mary Mitford's general manner, also composed stories illustrating a long list of the sufferings of governesses, and later used the pages of the *Saint James Magazine*, of which she was editor, to expose the wrongs of women toilers.

The most interesting result from reading many of the dull books which grew out of a consciousness of sex oppression is the discovery of the interest of women authors in working women. One turns from them to men to find similar material. Disraeli, Dickens, Thackeray are equally conscious of the changed conditions of existence for women. Female characters who are wage-earners are introduced, especially in the novels of Dickens. From fiction one proceeds to verse, and then to the outer borders of literature, the magazines, the pamphlets, and finally to the parliamentary Blue Books. From all these miscellaneous data the working woman emerges.

The primary object of this study is to build up a complete picture of the working woman in England between 1832 and 1850. These dates, loosely set, mark her emergence as a definite social problem presented to a large reading public. In 1832 the Sadler report began the exposure of the wrongs of factory women. This was quickly and steadily followed by Government investigation of other female toilers. By 1850 the factory legislation of 1847 was showing results, the Children's Commission of 1842–43 had achieved an extensive notoriety for a wide diversity of women's employments, and the agitation for the relief of the governess had a definite programme. The term *working women* will include only those classes of labour which received special investigation and definite reform during the years under observation. Such hopeless slaves as the hand-loom weavers and the immortally toiling agricultural labourers and domestic servants have, of necessity, been omitted. In examining the literature of that period* for material concerning

* Not only are the fiction and verse published between 1832 and 1850 included in this study, but also that of the next generation dealing with conditions of this period. Consequently the novels of George Eliot and the novels of Dickens and Mrs. Gaskell published after 1850 are used.

the kinds of work woman performed, the conditions of her labour, her pay, her way of life, the term *literature* has been stretched to its widest limits, with no separation of strictly literary and non-literary matter. This method has considerable advantage. From such a mass only can the investigator estimate how much the writing of the day was concerned with those women who supported life by their daily labour. Furthermore, with the journalism and parliamentary reports side by side with *bellse-lettres* one is enabled to test the accuracy of fiction and poetry dealing with social questions, to determine what of fact and what of fancy the artist has combined for his purpose, and how much he, as compared with the philanthropist, the magazine writer, the Government official, has devoted himself to the question of working women.

A second purpose of this book concerns a definitely literary problem. One is conscious almost at once that certain classes of working women immediately attracted novelists and poets and were given detailed and fervent attention; others were neglected or dismissed with summary or general treatment. What is the explanation? Does the answer lie in the nature of fiction itself, the limitations of the writer's equipment, or the class of labour under consideration? One must decide whether any generalizations can be made as to what is available fictional fabric and what is not; whether the novel and poetry can be employed for certain kinds of subject-matter only. Were writers in the Victorian era limited in their choice of scenes and character by their own education, training, outlook, or by established literary traditions from which they could not escape? Does the solution of the problem lie, finally, in the workers themselves? Were some in greater need of the help of publicity from authors than others? An answer to these questions may help in explaining an obvious fact: that certain working women were largely neglected by literary agencies and that others formed a new class of heroine, compelling both sympathy and interest.

The total result of the investigation of the subject of working women from a great variety of sources is a discovery of the function of *belles-lettres* in handling social questions. This is a consideration with which any student of the nineteenth century, a period when Art came to grips with complex contemporary struggle, is especially confronted. If literature is a primary source, if it precedes the findings of Government officials and keen-scented journalists, why does it thus come first? If it is secondary material, its *raison d'être* ought to be examined: does it bring facts before the public in more dramatic form than an obscure pamphlet; does it offer an interpretation of the facts by means of application to a concrete case; can one look to its leisurely reflections merely for proposed solutions to problems already presented by the Press, lecture-platform, and pulpit? In this specific problem of the working woman one goes even further in weighing the literary use of social material. Here an important inquiry is the outcome of female authorship. With more women writing, and writing on social questions, the student wants to know whether the cause of the working woman was helped. Or has the feminine contribution been essentially emotional, concerned with grievances, not their remedy, a preoccupation with the individual at the expense of the group, or acceptance of religious evasions and sentimental moralizings instead of a scientific examination of actuality and a courageous weighing of general considerations? One must compare Thackeray with George Eliot, Disraeli with Mrs. Tonna, Dickens with Mrs. Gaskell and Charlotte Brontë. Men may have succeeded where women have failed, or possibly both have demonstrated the ineptitude of the Arts when they are too close to social tangles. In the study of Victorian working women, then, lies hidden a new appraisal of nineteenth-century literature.

CHAPTER II

THE TEXTILE WORKER

1. Introduction

"GROUPS of merry and somewhat loud-talking girls, whose ages might range from twelve to twenty, came by with a buoyant step. They were most of them factory girls, and wore the usual out-of-door dress of that particular class of maidens; namely, a shawl, which at midday or in fine weather was allowed to be merely a shawl, but towards evening, or if the day were chilly, became a sort of Spanish mantilla or Scotch plaid, and was brought over the head and hung loosely down, or was pinned under the chin in no unpicturesque fashion.

"Their faces were not remarkable for beauty; indeed, they were below the average, with one or two exceptions; they had dark hair, neatly and classically arranged, dark eyes, but sallow complexions and irregular features. The only thing to strike a passer-by was an acuteness and intelligence of countenance, which has often been noticed in a manufacturing population."[1]

The mill women thus described by Mrs. Gaskell have come to stand, in popular opinion, for the Victorian working woman. Appropriated by the social scientist as they have been, studied minutely from a variety of sources, and presented to the public with a wealth of detail in numerous important books dealing with the industrial development of nineteenth-century England, they have received the notoriety achieved by no other class of women workers. Such emphasis they have entirely merited. They have had an indissoluble connection with some of the most momentous changes to be recorded in history, and are without doubt the most important Victorian working women. But, because their condition has been investigated with so much care, it seems feasible in this study to make no more than a brief summary of the available economic materials and concentrate upon the neglected literary aspect of the woman textile worker.

For the history of woman as the spinner and the weaver *

* For a good historical summary of women in textiles see B. L. Hutchins·
Women in Modern Industry, ch. i.

one is carried back to the division of labour in primitive society, which assigned the clothing of the family to the female. The most ancient literature records her activities. In Greece Arachne and Penelope were the most industrious of weaving women. In Rome Minerva presided over the labours of women. The virtuous woman of Solomon made fine linen and sold it. Medieval pictures represent Eve with the distaff and whorl, as she was immortalized in the watchword of John Ball:

> "When Adam delved and Eve span,
> Who was then the gentleman?"

Queens and ladies appear in old prints busily employed in carding, spinning, and weaving.

In English literature the early references to women as spinners and weavers are scanty and for the most part pleasant. They were commended for their industry, never pitied for their overwork. The Wyf of Bath—of whom Chaucer wrote:

> "Of cloth making she had such an haunt
> She passed them of Ipres and of Gaunt"

—is the most familiar and the most robust figure among the first working women of literature. But her interest lies in her romantic adventures, and not in her industrial career, which may have been full of struggles for better pay for her good work and of determined resistance to the competition of men weavers. That her numerous husbands were pleasant interludes in a hard-working life is an interesting conjecture, though foreign to the fourteenth century. The spinners and the weavers in *Piers Plowman* are presented with equal indifference to their industrial well-being, as are those in the *Pleasant History of Thomas of Reading*, by Thomas Deloney.

The most important of women's occupations was connected with the making of cloth. An examination of social documents shows[2] that in the fourteenth century they were "wool-sorters and wool-wrappers, carders and spinners, dyers and weavers". One-fourth of the cloth woven in York at the end of the fourteenth century was the work of women. They were enrolled as apprentices and admitted to the memberships of the various crafts. Although later the jealousy of the men sought to restrict weaving by women, there were still many women weavers in the eighteenth century. They represented cheap unorganized labour. After the French Wars of 1793–1815 the men returned to find the women doing their work. Spinning, however, was the woman's portion before the days of the factory system.

The poets detached spinning from this industrial life of women as an occupation suited to literary treatment. Wordsworth in *Michael* and *The Brothers* follows the usual tradition in praising the never-idle wife before her wheel. In the beautiful sonnet *Nuns Fret Not*:

> "Maids at the wheel . . .
> Sit blithe and happy."

But even spinning before the cottage doorway in the sunshine has its hardships. Two shillings and sixpence was the average weekly earning of the woman spinner, and both poverty and the need of the weaver for her work compelled long hours.[3] The weavers commonly worked 14, 15, and 16 hours a day. A reading of the chronicles of the eighteenth century easily convinces one that in the widespread distress of the village and the town, the woman worker was involved in a painful struggle for mere existence. Grinding toil was her daily lot. The investigations of the hand-loom weavers between 1834 and 1840 reveal hardships that had long existed.[4] She had been trained in subjection in industry, and had experienced the jealousy and discriminating rules passed by men to restrict her activity in trade. From the Elizabethan period and on through the seventeenth century the common idea was widespread, that the husband and the wife were responsible together for the support of the children. Many wives and mothers, even though they worked at home, had to help their husbands with the financial burdens of the family.

Homes and babies were consequently liable to neglect long before women went to the factories to work.

But the cottage occupations continued a placid existence, outside the concern of the reformer. With the rapid development of the industrial system, especially of cotton, spectacular changes compelled the attention of everyone. The swift succession of inventions by Hargreaves, Arkwright, and Crompton in spinning, and Kay, Stell, and Cartwright in weaving, brought an influx of women into the textile industries of cotton, woollen, worsted, silk, and flax, where the power-machines could be operated by the cheap labour of women and children. At last the poets were aroused to another kind of verse. Wordsworth saw no glamour of romance in the age which found new uses for women's activity.

> "Then, in full many a region, once like this
> The assured domain of calm simplicity
> And pensive quiet, an unnatural light
> Prepared for never-resting Labour's eyes
> Breaks from a many-windowed fabric huge;
> And at the appointed hour a bell is heard,
> Of harsher import than the curfew-knoll
> That spake the Norman Conqueror's stern behest—
> A local summons to unceasing toil!
> Disgorged are now the ministers of day;
> And, as they issue from the illumined pile,
> A fresh band meets them, at the crowded door—
> And in the courts—and where the rumbling stream,
> That turns the multitude of dizzy wheels,
> Glares, like a troubled spirit, in its bed
> Among the rocks below. Men, maidens, youths,
> Mother and little children, boys and girls,
> Enter, and each the wonted task resumes
> Within this temple, where is offered up
> To Gain, the master-idol of the realm,
> Perpetual sacrifice."[5]

After 1832 women workers in the mills had a definite history. But for that history one goes first, not to the novelists and poets, but to the Blue books of Parliament. It began with the appearance of Michael Sadler's report in August 1832, and was continued by that of the Royal Commission the next year, and the series of reports of the factory inspectors between 1835 and 1855. From the debates in Parliament and the controversies which raged in the newspapers and the magazines, and more powerfully in the early books dealing with factory questions which the publication of the Government investigations inspired, one gets a wealth of material about factory women, bristling with conflicting facts and theories, but presenting every phase of their existence: their economic and social position, their moral, educational, and religious life, and the valiant attempts of reformers to rescue them from the misery which unchecked industrialism had brought.

2. The Economic Position of the Textile Worker

In 1832 women were to be found in almost every department of the cotton factories. They beat the cotton by hand. In the carding-room they were back-frame, bobbin-frame, and drawing-tenters. They were twist-winders and stretchers. They were throstle spinners, and before they were entirely replaced by men who could watch two mules and repair their machines, they were also mule spinners.[6] They worked at the power-looms in the weaving sheds. In the silk factories women were employed in every part of the industry, even acting as overlookers in one mill.[7] In worsted and woollen mills young girls were spinners as well as weavers. Too often writers were vague about the kind of work performed by the mill women they introduced into their novels. Dickens with Rachel in *Hard Times* (1854), and Mrs. Gaskell with both Esther and Mrs. Wilson in *Mary Barton* (1848), indulge in such unsatisfactory generality. But in *North and South* (1855) and in *Helen Fleetwood*, both Bessy and Mrs. Tonna's heroine are represented as employed in the carding-room. Mrs. Dixon and Anne, in Mrs. Gaskell's tale *Libbie Marsh's Three Eras*, are fine spinners. *Helen Fleetwood* (1841), first appearing as a serial story in the *Christian Lady's Magazine*, of which Mrs. Tonna was editor, illustrates the detailed information she offered to her readers, simple home-keeping Englishwomen ignorant of the changes the Industrial Revolution had brought. In the following passage she tries to make clear the kind of labour performed by women and children in cotton mills. Two girls are describing their first day of work at the mill:

" 'But only think, boys, what it must be to see ever so many great big things, frames upon carriages on each side of the room, walking up to one another, and then walking back again, with a huge wheel at the end of each, and a big man turning it with all his might, and a lot of children of all sizes keeping before the frame, going backwards and forwards, piecening and scavenging—why, we all stared yesterday, when that Mr. South said there was no sitting down; but nobody would even think of it. Move, move, everything moves. The wheels and the frames are always going, and the little reels twirl round as fast as ever they can; and the pulleys, and chains, and great ironworks overhead, are all moving; and the cotton moves so fast that it is hard to piece it quick enough; and there is a great dust, and such a noise of whirr, whirr, whirr, that at first I did not know whether I was standing on my head.' " The girls then described their work. " 'Why, you see, the frame goes sloping up so, and the bottom edge is not so high as this little table; and the upper edge has got two rows of little rollers, and over them several other rows, that stand up; and there are a great many cotton threads reaching from the bottom to the top of the frame; and while the machine moves about, the threads go running up, and twist round the little rollers above. Now the threads being thin and fine, they often break, and I have to keep a great watch, to get hold of the two ends when one breaks, and put them together, the same as in spinning.'

" 'It is spinning', said Helen.

" 'Yes, it is; but not a bit like Mrs. Barker's wheel and distaff, with only one thread to mind. The man at the wheel is the spinner, and when the frame comes up the room he has to set his hand against it and push it back, which is pretty hard work. The joining, or piecening, is easy enough when you get used to it.'

" 'And what is scavenging?'

" 'Oh, that made me laugh. You see, bits of cotton-wool will stick to the thread, and they mustn't go on the reels; so there is a little girl huddled up under the frame and she snatches off all the loose wool, and throws it down so fast! And when the machine runs back, if the little scavenger did not bob and duck, and get very low, she would have a fine knock on the head.' "[8]

Helen, the older girl, in describing her day's work, said: " 'My work is among much bigger machines than Mary's, in the carding-room, where the cotton is pulled out and prepared for the spinners.'

" 'Do you walk about?' asked Willy.

" 'Yes, a good deal. There is plenty of bustling, and crowding, and hurrying, but the work does not seem very hard.' "[9]

Satisfactory statistics concerning the proportion of men and women employed in the factories were collected because of the interest aroused by the increasing number of women in the mills. Dr. Andrew Ure in 1835 stated that of the workers over 18 years of age employed in the factories of Great Britain, 102,812 were women as against 88,859 men.[10] By 1839 the proportion of women had considerably increased. In cotton 56¼ per cent. of the workers were women, in worsted 69½ per cent., in silk 70½ per cent., in flax 70½ per cent.[11] Lord Ashley, in a speech in Parliament, March 15, 1844, stated that in 1839 in Great Britain the number of females of all ages in the factories had increased from 196,383 in 1835 to 242,296 in 1839, with 112,192 under 18.[12] Quoting figures from the report of the factory inspectors in 1843, he showed that in one district out of the increase of 6,040 persons in the factories from 1838 to 1843, there were, excluding young boys, only 785 males to 5,225 females of all ages.[13] A large part of this increase he attributed to the improvements in machinery, for as the power-loom replaced the hand-loom, women took the places of men. But the main reason was the Factory Law of 1833, which necessitated a reduction in the number of children employed, and their consequent replacement by women. In 1847 a definite statement of the number of workers in all textile trades showed the preponderance of adult women over adult males; in all but the woollen mills, where the power-loom was still little used.[14]

The supply of female labour to meet this new demand came from various sources. The wives and the daughters of men in the mills were naturally the principal element. Of 10,000 married women employed in 412 factories in Yorkshire and Lancashire, half had husbands in the same factory.[15] Mrs. Gaskell shows members of the Higgins family in *North and South* and the Dixon family in *Libbie Marsh's Three Eras*, Mrs. Tonna, the Wright and the South families in *Helen Fleetwood*, going to the mills together. Many women were the wives and the daughters of the hand-loom weavers, who, as they saw their craft falling into disrepute, were forced to send to the factories the women of the family, who had formerly worked at the looms at home.[16] The father of the mill girl Harriet in *Sybil*, Disraeli's novel of factory life, was a hand-loom weaver. Irish immigrants were another source of supply, as Mrs. Tonna informed the readers of *Helen Fleetwood*, especially for work in the flax mills.[17] To this class of workers both Peter Gaskell and Sir James Kay-Shuttleworth attributed much of the degeneration in living standards in the manu-facturing districts.[18] Furthermore, with the passing of the new Poor Law in 1834, many people began to migrate to the North from the agricultural districts of the South. Of these trans-ported workers Caroline in *Sybil* says: "Ah! them's the himmigrants . . . they're sold out of slavery, and sent by Pickford's van into the labour market to bring down our wages."[19] Poor-law commissioners often made arrangements with manufacturers in Lancashire to take the surplus agri-cultural population up to the North and bring down wages.[20] In this way large numbers were enticed to the North.[21] The whole tragedy of *Helen Fleetwood* hinges upon the situation of a widow who was persuaded by the poor-law commissioner, and by an agent hired by a Lancashire manufacturer to find fresh hands for his mill, to move her grandchildren and her adopted child Helen from their country home in the South to Manchester and a life to which they were totally unsuited. Many were no doubt miserable in their changed world. Other transplanted labourers were happier in their new homes. One woman, with six of her eleven children in the mills, declared that she would rather be transported to a penal colony than go back to the South.[22] Changed conditions in the country often turned the tide of labourers northward. The Enclosure Acts between 1700 and 1800 had already driven large numbers of the yeomanry, the country freeholders, and the labourers, formerly with a little land of their own, into the towns and into mills.[23] Agricultural reforms, such as the reclaiming of waste lands and peat bogs once used by small-holders, and the enclosure of the commons, where the cattle and pigs had been allowed to feed, created a large class of workers entirely dependent on wages. The custom of gleaning after the harvest was also taken away. After the Industrial Revolution had killed the domestic industries which had formerly helped out the earnings of farm workers, their condition had become pitiable. The North often gave the whole family employment. With the steady decline of the old village games since Puritan times, and with no other amusements taking their places, the monotony of life in farming communities encouraged restless people to flock to the industrial towns.

The subject of factory women's wages aroused so much interest that such books as Dr. Ure's *Philosophy of Manufactures*, with its elaborate tables,[24] and magazines like the *Edinburgh Review*[25] and *Fraser's*,[26] in briefer fashion gave a wide publicity to the Government statistics. Unfortunately, much of the investigation of wages was made in tantalizingly fragmentary fashion. In the cotton mills women were generally paid piece-rates, except for such rough work as picking (cleaning) the cotton, which received a set wage, about 8s. per week in 1833.[27] In 1833, with a thirteen-hour day, a woman's earnings ranged from 5s., which was the average for a piecer, to 15s., received by a weaver who looked after several pairs of looms.[28] In the woollen mills in 1833, when the power-loom was scarcely known, wages varied from 4s. to 7s. 7d. weekly.[29] In worsted fewer figures were given, but fixed wages were from 6s. to 7s. weekly,[30] and piece-rates for spinning averaged 9s. and 10s. weekly.[31] In the silk mills wages showed an average of from 7s. to 7s. 6d.[32] In flax mills women's earnings ranged from 6s. to 6s. 3d.[33]

In the Government returns in 1834 a detailed report was made comparing the wages of men and women at different ages employed in all branches of the textile industry. In cotton in Lancashire the highest average wage for men at the age of greatest efficiency was 22s. 8½d. as compared with 9s. 8¼d. for women.[34] In the woollen, worsted, flax, and silk mills there was a similar proportion.[35]

To one writer, at least, such figures were a subject for congratulation. Dr. Ure writes:

"Factory females have in general much lower wages than males, and they have been pitied on this account with perhaps an injudicious sympathy, since the low price of their labour here tends to make household duties their most profitable as well as agreeable occupation, and prevents them from being tempted by the mill to abandon the care of their offspring at home. Thus Providence effects its purpose with a wisdom and efficacy which should repress the short-sighted presumption of human devices."[36]

One wonders how this writer interpreted the conditions of 1844, when poverty and the power-loom attracted thousands of women to the mills.

The hours women worked daily became also an object of concern. These varied with the state of trade, so there was a great difference from year to year. The average working day in a cotton factory in 1833 was from 6 a.m. to 8 p.m. with an hour for meals, but with longer hours in busy times.[37] Disraeli represented Dandy Mick's mother working from 5 a.m. to 7 p.m.[38] In the woollen mills the Commissioners found in the finishing departments thirteen-, fourteen-, and even sixteen- and eighteen-hour days.[39] Before the 1833 restriction, women worked thirteen and fifteen hours daily in the worsted mills. With the operation of the Factory Bill of 1833, women were often compelled to work long hours after the children had

gone home. Fifteen and eighteen were frequent when trade
was brisk.[40] Again and again in the reports of the factory
inspectors attention was brought to the prevalent overwork
of women. They often worked at night. Charlotte Elizabeth
Tonna showed from Government reports such labour continuing for several weeks.[41]

Women were discriminated against by both their employers
and the men with whom they worked. Manufacturers preferred
them because they were cheap. In 1833 the owners of a Scotch
mill hired women spinners at wages one-thirteenth below those
of the men.[42] Although the association of spinners prevented
this reduction, eleven women at an average of 18s. weekly and
one woman, working a greater number of spindles, at 30s.,
were retained by the company in spite of the efforts of the
men. But their threats kept seven women from work, and
crowds of seven or eight thousand, throwing stones and
shouting after the insistent women, forced one of the partners
to accompany them to work and to give them temporary
living-quarters within the walls of the mill. Agnes Robertson,
a widow thirty-four years old with four children, was one of
the spinners employed. She testified that she was knocked
about by the mob crowded around her house, so that she
could not get in or out of it. They broke the windows and
kept up such tumult at night that she could not sleep. Her
piecer was seized by the men and beaten, and the mob trampled
on her feet. When the firm finally advertised the fact that
women would be paid the same wages as men, the rioting
ceased. Manufacturers also found women more docile to
manage. They were not restricted by the regulations of a
labour union, and could be used to break strikes. They did
not dispute the orders of the overlookers as did the men.[43]
They would work at night when men insisted on a decent
season of rest. One of the inspectors wrote in his report:

"A vast majority of the persons employed at night and for long
hours during the day are females. Their labour is cheaper, and they
are more easily induced to undergo severe bodily fatigue than men,

either from the praiseworthy motive of gaining additional support for their families, or from the folly of satisfying a love of dress."[44]

But employers insisted that women were preferred for other reasons. They were often better suited to certain work than men, especially to weaving, where a girl of eighteen was indispensable at the power-loom, a quick and skilful worker.[45]

Why men workers discriminated against their female competitors is not difficult to explain. Although they could not keep women out of weaving, they made a successful effort to force them out of mule-spinning by demonstrating their superior efficiency. In Glasgow the spinners' union was a close corporation that was strong enough to keep women out of spinning.[46] When women entered the mills in numbers far exceeding the men, the Yorkshire Short-Time Committee, alarmed by a period of bad times and great unemployment, in 1842, represented to the Government the necessity of limiting the proportion of women to men and of forbidding married women to work during the lifetime of their husbands.[47] Observers of factory conditions encouraged even more extreme measures. Francis Place in a letter to a cotton spinner in 1835 wrote that the cotton men who were thrown out of employment were to blame for their own misery:

"If, then, the men refused to work in mills and factories with girls, as they ought to do, as other trades have done, in workshops, and for those masters who employ women and girls, the young women who will otherwise be degraded by factory labour will become all that can be desired as companionable wives, and the whole condition of factory workers would soon be improved, the men will obtain competent wages for their maintenance."[48]

But fortunately for the women who did not marry or for the wives who would have been economically better off without the husbands they had to support, the operatives did not carry out the advice of such ardent reformers.

For self-defence women were not, like the men, organized in unions, and to this fact most of the warfare between them can be attributed. At various times they had made feeble attempts to protect themselves. In 1788 an informal union of hand-spinners in Leicester known as the "Sisterhood" had stirred up the men to riot against the use of machinery.[49] At Loughborough in 1811[50] a parson-magistrate was much alarmed by "a Spirit of Combination to dictate to their Employers and to raise the price of their Wages" shown by some daring women who held meetings, sent emissaries to organize and collect funds in neighbouring towns, and finally inspired the parson to issue a warning that they were breaking the law. Although these valiant rebels were lace workers, they show an early attempt at combination made by women. During the eighteenth century the Manchester Spinners' and Manchester Small Weavers' Societies had women members. During a spinners' strike in 1818 the men and the women drew equal strike pay.[50] Owing, apparently, to their failure to keep to trade-union rules, the women were excluded.[51] The women were condemned as "blacklegs", and made a breach in the strength of the men's unions. In 1829, at a meeting of the cotton spinners of the United Kingdom in Manchester, the spinners laid down the rule "that the union shall include only male spinners and piecers". At the same time they urged the women and girls to form a separate union and promised the aid of the whole federation in helping them to get men's prices for their work. But the women, unassisted, did nothing.[52] The *Leeds Mercury*, May 4, 1832, contained the following news item:

"The cord-setters in the neighbourhood of Scholes and Hightown, chiefly women, held a meeting to the number of 1,500, at Peep Green, at which it was determined not to set any more cards at less than a halfpenny a thousand."

To this is added the delightful warning:

"Alarmists may view these indications of female independence as more menacing to established institutions than the 'education of the lower orders'."[53]

The Glasgow Spinners' Association advised the women in reckoning up piece-rates and in trade disputes. In the early 'thirties they started a campaign to secure equal rates of pay for men and women, the employers protesting that the women turned out an inferior quality and quantity of work and refusing the request. In 1838 a representative of the Association in evidence before a committee on combinations of workmen stated that the object of his union was not to force women out of employment, but to protect them against being "paid at an under rate of wages if possible".[54] Women, however, played little part in the trade unions until 1834. Then, stirred by the great federation movement, they joined in large numbers the "Grand National Consolidated Trades Union";[55] and the "Grand Lodge of Operative Bonnet Makers", the "Grand Lodge of the Women of Great Britain and Ireland", and the "Lodge of Female Tailors" came into brief being. The influence of the union movement may have caused the activity of the "Female Gardeners" and the "Ancient Virgins" mentioned in The Times[56] in connection with a riot at Oldham demanding a ten-hour day. One woman was arrested. These organizations, however, were not unions, but were affiliated with the Friendly Societies to be described later, and they never again received public mention.[57] After the collapse of the Grand National the women were little heard of except when the men trade unionists complained against unfair female competition. In the Bolton association of cotton spinners, founded in 1837, women were admitted, the women belonging to the piecers' section only. In some districts, however, they were prohibited as piecers as well as spinners.[58] In weaving women were included in the unions from the start. Both sexes were paid at the same rate of wages, and there was no feeling about excluding women from the union. In 1824 eleven men and twelve women weavers struck because their employer had deducted a charge of 6d. to 9d. a week for artificial light.[59] During the 'fifties and the 'sixties the weavers' association became firmly established.[60]

Although they were unorganized, women could not be unaffected by the action of the men's unions. As sympathizers in the early strikes of the cotton workers in 1808 and 1818, they showed themselves more troublesome than the men.[61] But their position outside the union was full of danger for the men as well as for themselves. In 1818, during a strike of power-loom weavers at Stockport, the strikers held the girls who wanted to go back to work under the pump. Later, when women formed a majority among the textile workers, the situation became more serious.[62] Gaskell bases part of the strength of his attack on unions upon the extent of the sufferings of the women and children not in the unions who had no work while the mill was closed.[63] In *Sybil*, on the eve of a strike, Julia, one of the factory workers, welcomed the opportunity of an enforced rest and vowed to "lie in bed until sunset". But she and her companions showed none of the heroic spirit of the men. "As long as you can give us money," they said, "I don't care, for my part, how long we stick out."[64]

Their apathy toward the unions had one colourful incident in its history. Dickens, in his account of the Preston strike of 1854, in which the women not only failed to attend the mass meetings but refused to pay their part of the expenses, printed in *Household Words* the ditty inscribed to the Preston women by the strikers:

> "Within these walls the lasses fair
> Refuse to contribute their share
> Careless of duty—blind to fame,
> For shame, ye lasses, oh! for shame!
> Come, pay up, lasses, think what's right,
> Defend your trade with all your might;
> For if you don't the world will blame,
> And cry, ye lasses, oh, for shame!
> Let's hope in future all will pay,
> That Preston folks may shortly say:
> That by your aid they have obtain'd
> The greatest victory ever gained."[65]

The Friendly Societies formed among the women, which combined sick and burial benefits with provision for social meetings at public-houses, where the members, according to Lord Ashley and Mrs. Tonna, drank, swore, and smoked together, seemed to have resulted less in the beginnings of union organization, as was possible, than in the development of the independent female. Lord Ashley repeated the following conversation, later recorded by the faithful Charlotte Elizabeth in *The Forsaken Home*,[66] which took place between a club member and her husband.

"A man came into one of these club-rooms, with a child in his arms. 'Come lass', said he, addressing one of the women, 'come home, for I cannot keep this bairn quiet, and the other I have left crying at home.' 'I won't go home, idle devil', she replied, 'I have thee to keep, and the bairns too, and if I can't have a pint of ale quietly, it is tiresome. This is the only second pint that Bess and me have had between us; thou may sup if thou likes, and sit thee down, but I won't go home yet!' "

Baernreither in *English Associations of Working Men* (1889)[67] included some scanty information about these women's organizations. Friendly Societies exclusively for women existed, as well as such affiliated orders as the Female Foresters, Female Druids, Female Gardeners, Female Rechabites, Odd Females, Odd Sisters, Ancient Shepherdesses. In the north of England female burial societies termed "life-boxes" were common. The Commission of 1874 investigating both men's and women's orders reported general financial instability and mismanagement, which were not corrected until the publication of the series of yearly reports by the Registrar of Friendly Societies began in 1857 and the legislation from 1875 on brought about reform. With the reorganization of the men's societies resulting in provisions for the relief of wives, widows, and orphans, the societies exclusively for women became of less importance.

The interest of working women in the Chartist movement demonstrated their capacity for united action. In the first draft

of the petition, in 1837, William Lovett had included woman
suffrage, but this was dropped in the final form of the People's
Charter.[68] The Chartist outbreaks in 1842 enlisted girls and
women.[69] In the petition of that year, of every 100,000 names
signed 8,200 were the signatures of women.[70] *Punch* suggested
that female Chartists be dispelled by cockroaches, rats, and
mice.[71] Their connection with Chartism was even reflected in
one of the contemporary social novels. In *Sybil* Dandy Mick,
discouraged by the Chartist backsliders, says: "The girls is
the only thing what has any spirit left. Julia told me just now
she would go to the cannon's mouth for the Five Points any
summer day."[72] Caroline, Julia's friend, declared she would
not marry anyone who was not for the Five Points. In the riot
described in the story, women and children joined the men.[73]

Women could not keep aloof from the unions indefinitely.
But their effective organization lies outside the limits of
this period. The first union for women only was not
established until 1872,* and in the textile trades, as has already
been noted, women were ultimately combined in the same
unions with men according to the department in which they
were employed.[74]

So far as their economic position, then, was concerned, mill
women before the factory legislation of 1847 were employed
in large numbers at wages much cheaper than those paid to
men and for a stretch of hours that would have been ex-
hausting to strong men. Not only had they no means of
improving their condition, as the men had by their unions,
but they had the antagonism of workers and the greed of
their employers to fight against. To protection by the Government, the philosophers with their *laissez-faire* theories of
political economy were unitedly opposed. But even while both
the economists and the manufacturers were satisfied with the
general status of women in the textile factories, other forces
entered into the question. The sentimental prejudices of the
average Englishman were arraigned against a system which,

---

* The Edinburgh Upholsterers' Sewing Society.

in his opinion, attacked the institution of the home, ranked by him above scientific theories or private fortunes. It is, therefore, to the social aspect, rather than to the economic, that one looks for the literary treatment of women's employment in factories.

3. The Social Aspects of the Employment of Women in Textile Industries

All women were regarded in the first half of the nineteenth century solely as potential mothers. The worker with her own earnings was, accordingly, an affront against nature and the protective instincts of man. That the family was affected by the labour of girls and women in the mills was a consideration that roused general concern. The question of the health of human beings who were entrusted with the responsibility of the next generation, the conflict of factory work and long hours with domestic life and with a mother's care of her home and her children, the moral and spiritual degradation which might result from the employment of females outside their homes—with all this most of the literature dealing with the new industrial age was primarily concerned.

Concerning the health of mill women there was great divergence of opinion. One group contended that excessive labour where the temperature ranged from 84 to 90 degrees in the cotton-spinning department,[75] and to 120 and 140 degrees in the linen mills, where the air was vitiated by the fluff in the carding-room and dust in the picking-room of cotton mills, and the workers wet to the waist, in the wet-spinning process of flax, stood in bare feet on the wet floor in a steamy atmosphere, was a menace to health. Poor ventilation was common.[76] The older mills had too few windows. Those of the improved mills were often kept closed. In the usual airless workroom the smell of oil and gases further vitiated the atmosphere. The noise of machinery, which modern ingenuity has not yet conquered, added to the discomfort.

All of the work was done standing, and piecers, according to the calculations given by Lord Ashley to Parliament, travelled from seventeen to twenty-seven miles,[77] with the additional strain of turning the body round to the reverse direction four or five thousand times in a day. Meal-times before 1844 and later were often crowded out by the practice of cleaning the machinery at noon or by a rush of extra work. Food standing in the workroom and covered with fluff was eaten hurriedly, the workers often snatching a bit of it when they could. There were no proper rooms for washing, dressing, or eating. Toilet facilities were inadequate.[78] In many departments women worked where they had no protection from machinery, and their long hair and loose aprons exposed them more than the men. One girl who was caught by the clothes in a shaft revolving at great speed was given one hundred pounds damages when ten shillings would have paid for the enclosing of the machinery.[79] Women were scalped, arms and fingers were crushed, and legs were wounded by unboxed machinery.[80] In *Helen Fleetwood* Mrs. Tonna showed such a wreck of the factory in Sarah Wright, who had been pushed into the machinery by an angry overlooker. In *Mary Barton* Mrs. Gaskell recorded a similar disaster in the person of Mrs. Wilson, who had "cotched her side again a wheel. . . . It was afore wheels were boxed up." Even after a law was passed ordering the boxing of machinery, it was disregarded generally. Charles Dickens became so enraged by the neglect of the manufacturers to obey the law that he called their association "The National Association for the Protection of the Right to Mangle Operatives", and the series of articles appearing in *Household Words* on the necessity for boxing machinery, "Ground in the Mill", "Fencing with Humanity", "Death's Cyphering-Book", "Chips", and "More Grist to the Mill", are written in his most violent style.[81] In all these conditions the critics of the factories saw the direct causes of physical breakdown. Headaches, excessive fatigue, relaxed muscles, loss of appetite they traced to the long hours of tedious labour in a foul, hot atmosphere, and to lack of sleep from night work;[82] and fallen arches, pains in the feet, the turned-in ankles and knees, the swelled legs, the enlarged veins, and the general weakness were attributed to continuous standing.[83] Bad eyesight was an evil of many kinds of factory work;[84] wounds and ulcers on the legs, of others.[85] Certain diseases were attributed directly to mill work, such as asthma, chronic hoarseness, and consumption, brought on by breathing air choked with dust and fluff. Scrofula was also a frequent disorder. The workers were described as short and stunted in growth. Premature puberty among girls in the cotton mills and irregular menstruation among women in the wet-flax mills were also emphasized. In the contention that factory work was unhealthy these critics were supported by medical evidence,[86] and by figures from the report of the Registrar General for 1846, which admitted a comparison of city districts like Manchester, with a high birth-rate, and a country district, with a lower.[87]

The defenders of the health of the operative denied the bad effects of heated workrooms,[88] even going to the extreme in one case of showing the healthful effects of 140 degrees. The stove girls in the calico print works, who went from such an atmosphere to the open air, were represented as extremely healthy, with their colds cured by "going into the stoves".[89] They denied the excessive fatigue from standing, citing the evidence of a girl who stated that after standing for twenty-four hours she felt no pain in her knees or ankles, and contradicted the accuracy of Lord Ashley's figures concerning the exertions of piecers.[90] The better class of employers were indignant at the description of bad working conditions, irregular meals, the lack of necessary conveniences. They brought forward the testimony of doctors that no disease was peculiar to the factory,[91] and attributed the high death-rate in Manchester to its sudden growth and the consequent overcrowding and lack of drainage.[92] Consumption was shown to be equally disastrous in country and city districts. In Manchester in 1831 three out of nineteen deaths were from consumption, while in Essex, with an equal population, four out of twenty-one deaths were from the same cause. They insisted that other industries were far more dangerous than textiles, and that accidents were rarely fatal.[93] Harriet Martineau, whom orthodox political economy made the henchman of the manufacturers, in a pamphlet *The Factory Controversy* (1855), attacked the interference of the Government with the question of boxing machinery, and ridiculed the contention that accidents in the mills were frequent.

But the most bitter battle of diverse opinion raged around the subject of the effects of factory labour upon mothers. The group hostile to factory work for women quoted doctors who believed that the narrow pelves of women employed in the mills from childhood made childbirth difficult and dangerous. The practice of allowing pregnant women to remain at work was vigorously attacked. Night work was considered especially dangerous for them. Frequent miscarriages, varicose veins, ulcers on the legs followed the overwork of pregnant women.[94] That factory girls were not fit physically for motherhood was frequently stated. Martha, a factory girl before her marriage to Hudson, the reformer in *Helen Fleetwood*, died when her first child was born. The opposing side made no contention for health in all this phase of the subject. Both the mill-owners and some of the factory commissioners stated that married women were seldom employed in factories and that pregnant women never were.[95] That the number of women employed varied inversely with their age was explained by marriage. In New Lanark a list of married women consisting almost entirely of widows with children was sent to the Commissioners.[96] But with the exception of those given by John Bright,[97] who announced in Parliament that women generally left the mills upon marriage, all the data were for Scotland.[98] The conditions in Lancashire, especially in Manchester, were entirely different.[99] Married women commonly worked in the mills.[100] In 1833 one-tenth of the women employed in one mill were married.[101] Lord Ashley contended that married women were preferred.[102]

The health of the babies born to factory women was also a subject for debate. One class of authorities contended that they were stunted and shrivelled at birth.[103] The other side insisted that they were healthy.[104] But here again Scotch medical authorities were quoted. In such a case one confronts a typical kind of confusion. Country mills in Scotland and a hardy population could not be compared with the Manchester mills and the undersized Lancashire natives or the degraded Irish exiles. That the babies were neglected after birth was a belief supported by overwhelming evidence. The mothers as a rule went back to the mill about ten days or a fortnight after their confinements.[105] During the day they suffered pains in their breasts and their clothing was wet with dripping milk. The babies were nursed three times a day, and left for the rest of the time to the care of an old woman[106] or an older sister, and kept quiet on a mixture of laudanum and treacle called "Godfrey's Mixture", an ominous term that sprinkles the pages of many a novel. In *Sybil* Dandy Mick, scolded for his lack of thought for his mother, said that all she had done for him was to give him treacle and laudanum when he was a baby to stop his tongue and fill his stomach, and he could see no reason for gratitude.[107] The baby-soothing mixture is called "Daffy's Elixir" in *The Newcomes*. Perhaps no evil of factory labour brought so much heated writing as the neglect of babies, which accounted for the high death-rate among them.[108] Sibella Miles in her hysterical pamphlet *Essay on the Factory Question* (1844) suggested the formation of associations to hold meetings to agitate the relief of factory women from excessive hours of work and implored the wives of manufacturers to interest themselves in the babies of the factory "hands". That the unhealthiness of the generation of the early 'thirties in Lancashire was due to the employment of the mothers in the mills was the belief, however, of only part of those who studied the question.[109]

The difference of opinion about the healthfulness of factory workers depended largely upon the contradictory opinions held on the general hardships of such labour. John Roebuck, a Member of Parliament, wrote to his wife June 19, 1838 (during an interval when he was out of Parliament, it might be added):

"Amongst other things I saw a cotton mill—a sight that froze my blood. The place was full of women, young, all of them, some large with child, and obliged to stand twelve hours each day. Their hours are from five in the morning to seven in the evening, two hours of that being for rest, so that they stand twelve clear hours. The heat was excessive in some of the rooms, the stink pestiferous, and in all an atmosphere of cotton flue. I nearly fainted. The young women were all pale, sallow, thin, yet generally fairly grown, all with bare feet—a strange sight to English eyes."[110]

Indeed, the memory of the cotton mills was so powerful that Roebuck found it difficult to enjoy the beautiful scenery of Scotland. Yet this same man in 1844, in a speech in Parliament,[111] basing his conclusions upon the statements of Scotch in the Royal Commission of 1833, although the turning of the pages of the same report would have revealed bad conditions in Lancashire, said of factory labour: "It is indoor work, warm, and comfortable, and all that is required is continuous attention". But of the philosophy of Victorian parliamentarians more hereafter. Nassau Senior described mill work as mere "confinement, attention, and attendance".[112] A writer in *Fraser's* in visiting a mill had seen one woman with a book lying on a stool and another knitting.[113] Cooke Taylor observed mill girls leaving their work with so little weariness that he was sure none of them would refuse an invitation to a dance.[114] Dr. Ure broke out into rhythmic prose in his description of mill employment:

"Their light labour and erect posture in tending the looms, and the habit which many of them have of exercising their arms and shoulders, as if with dumb-bells, by resting their hands on the lay or shuttle bearer, as it oscillates alternately backwards and forwards with the machinery, opens their chest, and gives them generally a graceful carriage."[115]

The only shadow in the picture is the sermonizing which the writer added to his description of the charm of spending one's days in a cotton factory; for happiness, he warned his readers, is not in the present, but in a future state of existence.[115] Charlotte Elizabeth, reflecting the gloom of Lord Ashley's speeches, never saw the glory of cotton as Dr. Ure invariably did.

To explain the wide difference in opinion about cotton mills and the effect of factory labour upon women, it is not necessary to question the truth of either the cheerful or the discouraging witnesses. As has already been stated, Scotland and Lancashire in this early period presented different problems, so that generalizations made concerning mills in one section could not be applied to the other. Then, too, there was a great contrast in various mills. Cooke Taylor, after a visit to Henry Ashworth's mill, agreed by numerous witnesses to have been an admirable factory, could write with perfect honesty that the workrooms were "lofty, spacious, and well-ventilated, kept at an equable temperature and scrupulously clean"; and there was "nothing in sight, sound, or smell to offend the most fastidious sense".[116] That he could add: "I should be well contented to have as large a proportion of room and air in my own study as a cotton spinner in any of the mills in Lancashire", bears more the marks of hyperbole. One can imagine the rancour of intelligent employers like John Bright, with his sturdy regard for the well-being of his work-people, listening in Parliament to Lord Ashley's charges about the criminal neglect manufacturers showed their "hands". Furthermore, conditions varied greatly according to the department of the mill. The weaving-rooms, with their moderate temperature and good air, were far better places for the optimist than the cleaning- and the carding-rooms, full of dust and fluff, or the invariably hot spinning-rooms. Both Mrs. Gaskell and Mrs. Tonna, when they wanted to show the unhealthy effects of factory labour upon women, had the wisdom to choose the carding-room. It is true, also, that a second visit to a cotton mill is less disturbing than the first. Some writers who had never seen a cotton mill doubtless made melodramatic statements. Others, like Mrs. Trollope, who hurried up to Manchester on one of the first trains, made a rapid survey of conditions of which she knew nothing, and then wrote *Michael Armstrong* (1840), for a mass of readers who wanted to know the worst of mills, were unreliable. Conservative observers, prejudiced by the new industrial energy which was changing England, were unintentionally guilty of seeing only evil in factories. In the matter of accidents there was, perhaps, great exaggeration on both sides. But the reports of the factory inspectors show the danger from unboxed machinery, Harriet Martineau notwithstanding, and the safeguarding of employees by modern scientific appliances most powerfully demonstrates the superiority of the new factory over the old.

But for the final analysis of the divergence in the statements concerning the sanitary conditions in factories, one must go farther. Those who attributed the high death-rate in Manchester not to the unhealthiness of mill work, but rather to Manchester itself, overcrowded, lacking sewerage, helpless to take care of its sudden huge growth, were aware of what the rush of urban population had brought with it. Sir James Kay-Shuttleworth devoted pages of his book, *Four Periods of Public Education*, to the horrors of Manchester in 1832. Of the lack of sanitation, he wrote:

"The Irk, black with the refuse of dye-works erected on its banks, receives excrementitious matters from some sewers in this portion of the town, the drainage from the gas-works, and filth of the most pernicious character from bone-works, tanneries, size manufactories, etc. Immediately beneath Ducie-bridge, in a deep hollow between two high banks, it sweeps round a large cluster of some of the most wretched and dilapidated buildings of the town. The course of the river is here impeded by a weir, and a large tannery, eight stories high (three of which stories are filled with skins exposed to the atmosphere, in some stage of the processes to which they are subjected), towers close to this crazy labyrinth of pauper dwellings. This group of habitations is called 'Gibraltar', and no site can well be more insalubrious than that on which it is built. Pursuing the course of the river on the other side of Ducie-bridge, other tanneries, size manufactories, and tripe-houses occur. The parish burial-ground occupies one side of the stream, and a series of courts of the most singular and unhealthy character the other. Access is obtained to these courts through narrow covered entries from Long Millgate, whence the explorer descends by stone stairs, and in one instance by three successive flights of steps to a level with the bed of the river. In this last-mentioned (Allen's) Court he discovers himself to be surrounded, on one side by a wall of rock, on two others by houses three stories high, and on the fourth by the abrupt and high bank down which he descended, and by walls and houses erected on the summit. These houses were, a short time ago, chiefly inhabited by fringe, silk, and cotton weavers, and each house contained in general three or four families. An adjoining court (Barrett's) on the summit of the bank, separated from Allen's Court only by a low wall, contained, besides a pig-sty, a tripe manufactory in a low cottage, which was in a state of loath-some filth. Portions of animal matter were decaying in it, and one of the inner rooms was converted into a kennel, and contained a litter of puppies."[117]

Such regions, the writer showed, abounded in cholera. In 1834 more than 15,000 of the 200,000 inhabitants lived in cellar dwellings.[118] Gaskell in his description of the average factory house with its lack of drainage, cellar lodgings, absence of ventilation, sleeping-rooms used indiscriminately for both sexes, is not giving an extreme view.[119] One factory girl stated that in her home ten people slept in one room. In *Mary Barton* Mrs. Gaskell thus portrayed the home sur-roundings of a cotton worker:

"It [the street] was unpaved; and down the middle a gutter forced its way, every now and then forming pools in the holes with which the street abounded. . . . As they passed, women from doors tossed household slops of every description into the gutter; they ran into the next pool, which overflowed and stagnated. Heaps of ashes were the stepping-stones, on which the passer-by, who cared in the least for cleanliness, took care not to put his foot. Our friends were not dainty, but even they picked their way till they got to some steps leading down into a small area, where a person standing would have his head about one foot below the level of the street, and might at the same time, without the least motion of his body, touch the window of the cellar and the damp muddy wall right opposite. You went down one step even from the foul area into the cellar in which a family of human beings lived. It was very dark inside. The window-panes were many of them broken and stuffed with rags, which was reason enough for the dusky light that pervaded the place even at midday. After the account I have given of the state of the street, no one can be surprised that on going into the cellar inhabited by Davenport, the smell was so fetid as almost to knock the two men down. Quickly recovering themselves, as those inured to such things do, they began to penetrate the thick darkness of the place, and to see three or four little children rolling on the damp, nay wet, brick floor, through which the stagnant, filthy moisture of the street oozed up; the fireplace was empty and black; the wife sat on her husband's chair and cried in the dank loneliness."[120]

A stanza from Mrs. Norton's poem *Child of the Islands*, Mrs. Gaskell used as a heading for a chapter in *Mary Barton*:

"For us the streets, broad-built and populous,
For them unhealthy corners, garrets dim,
And cellars where the water-rat may swim!"

Engels' descriptions of the way the Manchester poor lived are perhaps even more terrible, but Mrs. Trollope in *Michael Armstrong* and Disraeli in *Sybil* (1845) introduced the filthy dens in which mill workers lived to an even wider reading public.[121] From the filthy courts a source of income was derived.

"Porkers, who feed pigs in the town, often contract with the inhabitants to pay some small sum for the rent of their area, which is immediately covered with pig-sties, and converted into a dung-heap and receptacle of the putrescent garbage upon which the animals are fed, as also of the refuse which is now heedlessly flung into it from all the surrounding dwellings."[122]

Even if the early mills had been provided with every device

for safeguarding health, as they were not, the workers lodged in such hovels would have profited little. Since the atmosphere of the poorest factories was probably superior to that of the homes, all the concern about pure air which filled the speeches of Parliament Members from the South seems somewhat ironic. To these terrible housing conditions were added the ignorance and neglect of the housewives who had been brought up in the factories.

Here again the whole subject of the new home conditions following upon the factory system was a complicated one that involved many questions. With the mother employed in the mills for twelve hours in normal times, and for much longer periods in seasons of good trade, the homes could not help being neglected. Most of them were filthy.[123] The food was poor and hastily prepared. Sir James Kay-Shuttleworth described the kind of meals served in the average mill family.[124] Breakfast

"generally consists of tea or coffee, with a little bread. Oatmeal porridge is sometimes, but of late rarely, used, and chiefly by the men; but the stimulus of tea is preferred, and especially by the women. The tea is almost always of a bad, and sometimes of a deleterious, quality; the infusion is weak, and little or no milk is added. The operatives return to the mills and workshops until twelve o'clock, when an hour is allowed for dinner. Amongst those who obtain the lower rates of wages this meal generally consists of boiled potatoes. The mess of potatoes is put into one large dish; melted lard and butter are poured upon them, and a few pieces of fried fat bacon are sometimes mingled with them, and but seldom a little meat. Those who obtain better wages, or families whose aggregate income is larger, add a greater proportion of animal food to this meal, at least three times in the week; but the quantity consumed by the labouring population is not great. The family sits around the table, and each rapidly appropriates his portion on a plate, or they all plunge their spoons into the dish, and with an animal eagerness satisfy the cravings of their appetite. At the expiration of the hour, they are all again employed in the workshops or mills, where they continue until seven o'clock or a later hour, when they generally again indulge in the use of tea, often mingled with spirits, accompanied by a little bread. Oatmeal or potatoes are, however, taken by some a second time in the evening."

Critics of the new factory age were shocked by the whole system of domestic economy.[125] They attacked the improvidence of mill women who hired the family washing, even that of their caps, a grave moral lapse in the eyes of worried factory inspectors who supplied much of such information.[126] The women did not know how to sew or to mend. Out of thirteen wives in one mill, only one could make her husband a shirt.[127] The average girl in the mill, like Anne Dixon in *Libbie Marsh's Three Eras*, knew nothing of housework. Wordsworth in *The Excursion* (1814) had earlier pointed out the neglect of the homes when the daughters left them for the factory.[128] Mrs. Gaskell portrayed Mrs. Wilson in *Mary Barton* as marrying with no knowledge of housework.

" 'If you'll believe me, Mary, there never was such a born goose at housekeeping as I were; and yet he married me. I had been in a factory sin' five years old a'most, and I knew nought about cleaning, or cooking, let alone washing and such-like work. The day after we were married, he goes to his work at after breakfast, and says he, "Jenny, we'll ha' th' cold beef and potatoes, and that's a dinner for a prince." I were anxious to make him comfortable, God knows how anxious. And yet I'd no notion how to cook a potato. I know'd they were boiled, and I know'd their skins were taken off, and that were all. So I tidied my house in a rough kind o' way, then I looked at that very clock up yonder,' pointing at one that hung against the wall, 'and I seed it were nine o'clock, so, think I, th' potatoes shall be well boiled at any rate, and I gets 'em on th' fire in a jiffy (that's to say, as soon as I could peel 'em, which were a tough job at first), and then I fell to unpacking my boxes! And at twenty minutes past twelve he comes home, and I had th' beef ready on th' table, and I went to take the potatoes out o' th' pot; and oh! Mary, th' water had boiled away, and they were all a nasty brown mess, as smelt through all the house. He said nought, and were very gentle; but, oh, Mary, I cried so that afternoon.' "[129]

Many of these ignorant wives never learned from their failures and some preferred to go back to the factories, where, at least, they performed labour that was familiar to them. The improvidence of the housekeeper working in the mill, Mrs. Gaskell also recorded:

"Mrs. Dixon rattled out her tea-things, and put the kettle on, fetched home her youngest child (boarded out on weekdays at a neighbour's), which added to the commotion. Then she called Anne downstairs, and sent her for this thing and that: eggs to be put to the cream, it was so thin; ham, to give a relish to the bread and butter, some new bread, hot, if she could get it. Libbie heard all these orders, given at full pitch of Mrs. Dixon's voice, and wondered at their extravagance, so different from the habits of the place where she had last lodged. But they were fine spinners, in the receipt of good wages; and confined all day in an atmosphere ranging from seventy-five to eighty degrees. They had lost all natural, healthy appetite for simple food, and having no higher tastes, found their greatest enjoyment in their luxurious meals."[130]

The same writer emphasized the fact that the women themselves saw the evil which followed the employment of married women. In a conversation, Mary Barton, Mrs. Wilson, and her old sister-in-law Alice brought out their view of the case:

" 'Father does not like girls to work in factories,' said Mary.
" 'No, I know he does not; and reason good. They oughtn't to go after they're married, that I'm very clear about. I could reckon up' (counting with her finger), 'aye, nine men I know, as has been driven to th' public-house by having wives as worked in factories; good folk, too, as thought there was no harm in putting their little ones out at nurse, and letting their house go all dirty, and their fires all out; and that was a place as was tempting for a husband to stay in, was it? He soon finds out gin-shops, where all is clean and bright, and where th' fire blazes cheerily, and gives a man a welcome as it were.' . . .
" 'I say it's Prince Albert as ought to be asked how he'd like his missis to be from home when he comes in, tired and worn, and wanting some one to cheer him; and maybe, her to come in by and by, just as tired and down in th' mouth; and how he'd like for her never to be at home to see to th' cleaning of his house, or to keep a bright fire in his grate, let alone his meals being all hugger-mugger, and comfortless. I'd be bound, prince as he is, if his missis served

him so, he'd go off to a gin-palace, or summat o' that kind. So why can't he make a law again poor folks' wives working in factories?' "[131]

The defenders of factory labour for women contented themselves by denying the truth of these accusations. They declared that mill women kept their houses clean, that they knew how to cook and sew, and that the family did not suffer from the employment of the wife and mother.[132] Cooke Taylor even instances the case of a woman transplanted to the manufacturing districts from the South who complained to him because she had to be too clean in her new surroundings to keep up with the high standards of Lancashire housekeeping. His rhapsodies about good housekeeping, however, could be true only in homes where the mother was not in the factories.

What neither side was aware of was the fact that a new system of home management had arisen as a result of the employment of women in factories. The home had lost most of its productive functions. Working women no longer ought to wash, cook, and sew after a long day at the factory. Too many conscientious mothers made the mistake of burning the candle at both ends. They did not realize that it was folly to make shirts at a time when such garments were being turned out more cheaply by the slop workers in co-operation with the manufacturers. Nor did they understand that their skilled labour was too valuable to be employed at the wash-tub. Effective machinery for relieving the housewife of her domestic labour not yet existed. There were no day nurseries for the numerous babies. Cheap canned food and shops supplying cooked dishes belonged to a later day. The wretched houses were difficult to keep clean. The critics, observing a transitional stage, were justified in their foreboding about the sacred institution of the home going fast to ruin. Neither could they comprehend the necessity of eggs, cream, meat, and butter to hard-working people. They were inured to a class of agricultural labourers subsisting upon a kind of food that was close to starvation.

The break-up of the home as a social unit was evident even to the most superficial observers. Under the system of domestic industry the parents and the children had worked together, the father the autocratic head, pocketing the family earnings and directing their expenditure. Here the home was the stronghold. But under the factory system the members of the family all had their own earnings, they worked in separate departments of the mill, coming home only for food and sleep. The home was little but a shelter.[133] The father found the labour of his wife and his children often more sought after than his. By 1844 the spectacle of men doing nothing or doing the work of children excited the indignation of the factory inspectors. Women and young girls were overworked when the husbands and fathers roamed the street aimlessly or tried in clumsy fashion to take care of the young children and the neglected house. Inspectors reported that parents sometimes shamelessly exploited their children. In *Helen Fleetwood* Tom South, living on the earnings of his children, gave his leisure to Chartism. Other unemployed men were less worthily occupied.[134] Even under these new conditions, then, the father generally remained the powerful head of the family. The children handed over what they earned to him. The daughter of Tom South was anxious to work overtime, because all of her regular wages went to her father and she had only the overtime pay for herself. This was a common situation among factory children. If a factory girl lived at home, she contributed generously to the household expenses. A silk weaver of eighteen, who was a witness before the Royal Commission in 1833, stated that out of her weekly wage of 13s. she gave 7s. to her mother.[135] Another, a reeler of twenty-six, out of 9s. gave her parents 7s. But in many cases the father lost his authority. especially when his children supported him. The children were disobedient. The Wright family in *Helen Fleetwood* is a powerful example of the family demoralization Mrs. Tonna believed to be the crop of tares of the factory system. The children showed no respect for their parents and no affection for one another. Even the mother was alienated from her children. If the daughters remained at home, they spent their money for fine clothes and amusements. Phoebe Wright was such a factory girl. Esther in *Mary Barton* saw too late her similar folly. "I might have done better with the money; I see now. But I did not know the value of it then. Formerly I had earned it easily enough at the factory, and as I had no more sensible wants, I spent it on dress and eating."[136] Working girls wore inappropriate finery, even silk dresses. Disraeli described them as "gaily dressed, a light handkerchief tied under their chin, their hair scrupulously arranged; they wore coral necklaces and earrings of gold".[137] John Barton pictured Esther, "dressed in her Sunday gown, and with a new ribbon in her bonnet, and gloves on her hands, like the lady she was so fond of thinking herself". Some mill girls went even further in throwing off family restraint and left home altogether for the independence of lodgings. Harriet in *Sybil*, the daughter of a poor hand-loom weaver, left her parents and the young children to starve, because she was tired of supporting them. She set herself up in lodgings with a friend, determined to drink only the best tea, and invited people to share it with her. In the evening she and her companion went to the "Temple" to eat and drink with Dandy Mick.[138] Esther left John Barton's house for lodgings when he tried to exercise authority over her. Of her he said:

"That's the worst of factory work for girls. They can earn so much when work is plenty, that they can maintain themselves anyhow. . . . You see, Esther spent her money in dress, thinking to set off her pretty face; and got to come home so late at night, that at last I told her my mind. . . . Says I, 'Esther, I see what you'll end at with your artificials, and your fly-away veils, and stopping out when honest women are in their beds; you'll be a street-walker, Esther, and then, don't you go to think I'll have you darken my door, though my wife is your sister.' . . . So says she, 'Don't trouble yourself, John. I'll pack up and be off now, for I'll not stay to hear myself called as you call me.' "[139]

It was not long before John Barton's prophecy was realized. Rachel in *Hard Times* lived by herself. The actual counterpart of these literary factory girls appeared in the records of Parliament. The daughters whose father tried to correct them for going into a public-house, left home. They said "they had their father to keep, and they would not be dictated to by him".[140]

The new girl of 1832 caused many a headshake. She was dangerously independent because she had her own money. Even a wife began to adopt grand airs unbefitting her position. Although her husband was entitled legally to her wages and could get drunk on them while she and her children went without food, as Barbara Bodichon pointed out,[140] still she often found a way of asserting her right to the money she had earned. But no writer of the period found anything but evil in the downfall of the old feudal family system. In these strange new ways the critics of the factory saw fresh evidence to support them in their position that women ought to be kept out of the mills. That both wives and daughters had worked even harder when they assisted the hand-loom weavers at home, without the satisfaction of an independent wage, was never suggested. Equally unthinkable was the possibility that a daughter of mature age had the right to spend her earnings as she pleased, if she paid for her board at home, or that lodgings for a working girl gave her a splendid independence. The economically independent wife who was a benefit to society because she was free, not a slave, was a figure of the future. The family has been covered with so much sentiment that even the twentieth century has not been able to show what a harmful and dangerous institution it can be. The Victorians must accordingly be excused for their blindness to its faults.

The popular opinion of the factory girl was that her morals were very bad, if we judge from the literature on the subject. Her degradation was traced, directly or indirectly, to her employment outside the home. Mrs. Tonna devoted much fervid writing to the unregenerate worker, "seemingly hardened past all fear or shame".[141] She has a man in her factory novel state that but one girl in fifty kept her character after she went to the mills. Phoebe Wright's virtue was gone. Helen Fleetwood's persecution by her fellow-workers was brought on by their hatred of her purity, which they attempted to besmirch. Indecent talk was common among the workers.[142] Mrs. Gaskell was less extreme in *Mary Barton*, but she makes John Barton unwilling to have his daughter in the mills, and she shows Esther going from the factory to become the mistress of a man who later brought her to life on the streets. Both Mrs. Tonna and Mrs. Gaskell represent the factory girl as too low to be taken into a lady's house as a servant. When Helen Fleetwood's health was threatened by the confinement in the mill, domestic service was thought of, unhappily too late, for "there isn't a small tradesman's wife would not think herself disgraced to take a factory girl for a servant".[143] Because Bessy in *North and South* wanted her younger sister to become a servant, she kept her out of the mills. In a story "The Miner's Daughters", published in *Household Words*, two studious girls of exceptionally good character are so stigmatized by having been employed in a factory that when one of them married a young farmer, none of his friends called upon them, and they finally emigrated to America.[144]

The basis for this literary gloom about factory girls is to be found in the report of Sadler's committee and other parliamentary papers, and such contemporary industrial books as those of Gaskell. A general looseness in morals was proved by the number of illegitimate children born to girls in certain mills.[145] An examination of the figures, however, indicates that they could be matched in any agricultural district, and surpassed among servants, as the Government records themselves proved.[146] But at the same time that immorality was being computed according to offspring born out of wedlock, the charge was made that the fact that no more unlawful children could be produced for the records was attributable to the wide circulation of books on birth control by Richard Carlile.[147] Under such disadvantages any accurate information about morals is not obtainable. Too much of the material is like that of Engels, a rough estimate that three-fourths of the factory hands between fourteen and twenty were unchaste, something impossible to prove. The opinions of midwives, of factory girls and their parents, of husbands, of employers, all result in a conflict of evidence that leads nowhere.[148] Along with this sexual laxity went such vices as theft, smoking, drinking, swearing, and filthy language.[149] The drinking was given special emphasis by the figures of a boroughreeve of Manchester, who counted the number of people entering a certain gin-shop in five minutes during eight successive Saturday nights and at different periods in the evening. The results of such computation were repeated with satisfaction by Gaskell, Engels, and Lord Ashley in Parliament,[150] though what they proved in a century when drinking was confined to no particular class or trade it is difficult to estimate. Women were accused of using drugs as well as men. Pawn-shops were frequently used by improvident work-people. Girls bought luxuries in dress on credit, and escaped debt and imprisonment by moving from place to place. When manufacturers and writers like Ure tried to meet these attacks they used the same inexact methods, which are little but contradiction of unsupported prejudices by others of like kind.[151]

But there was an honest attempt made to study the conditions which might lead to moral degradation, and here was more wisdom. The coarse surroundings of a young girl in the factory, the prevalence of indecent language, the absence of dressing-rooms, the necessity of working in scanty clothing on account of the heat,[152] the precocious sexual development which was believed to result from the heat and confinement, the long hours and the night-work which made it necessary for her to be out late on the streets alone, the exhaustion which led to thirst, and the monotonous labour which brought a craving for excitement, were all studied carefully in relation to their effect upon morals.[153] Mrs. Tonna gives an effective summary of the case in explaining the degradation of Phoebe Wright.

"Excluded from the free air, and almost from the pure light of day; shut up in an atmosphere polluted by clouds of fetid breath, and all the sickening exhalations of a crowded human mass, whose unwashed, overworked bodies were also in many cases diseased, and by the suffocating dust that rose on every side; relaxed by an intensity of artificial heat which their constitutions were never framed to encounter in the temperate climate where God had placed them; doubly fevered, doubly debilitated, by excessive toil, not measured by human capacity to sustain it, but by the power of machinery obeying an inexhaustible impetus; badly clothed, wretchedly fed, and exposed moreover to fasts of unnatural length even from that miserable fare; who can marvel if, under such a system, the robust adult speedily acquires a sickly habit of body and morbid state of feeling, leading at once to the most awful perversion of mind and corruption of morals?"[154]

Disraeli wrote of mill girls who wanted their liquor, although one of them declared: "If I was a lady, I would never drink anything except fresh milk from the cow."[155] Then, according to Dr. von Schulze-Gaevernitz, the first generation of industrial chiefs belonged to the uneducated classes, rough, coarse, strangers to etiquette, family traditions, and moral considerations.[156] Although the charges made that they frequently used the women in their mills for their amusement are probably exaggerated, they seldom had any interest in their "hands" except as sources of profit.[157] One of them says in *Helen Fleetwood*: "I protest, doctor, you are making out a connection between the office of a 'cotton lord', as you call us, and that of a spiritual lord or bishop that I never dreamed of. Why, according to your views, we should each regard his mill as a diocese, and preach in it."[158] Such men would not be likely to safeguard their women employees, dependent upon men in authority, the overlookers and the spinners,[159] nor place checks upon their behaviour. In the novels of the period all classes of manufacturers appear: rogues like the coarse and unfeeling Sir Matthew Dowling in *Michael Arm-strong*, and all the employers in *Helen Fleetwood*, ·indifferent employers like Mr. Carson in *Mary Barton*, and excellent men like Thornton in *North and South*, Trafford in *Sybil*, and Mr. Rouncewell in *Bleak House*. In *Mary Barton*, young Carson, and in *The Newcomes*, Barnes Newcome, who made a mill girl his mistress, were sons of the newly rich manufacturers who were demoralized by too much leisure and money. But the sons of the early mill-owners were, in many cases, university men, interested in social experiments and practical reforms,[160] and it was these men who were rapidly changing industrial conditions. Yet even the best employers, it was admitted, were helpless to improve the condition of workers as degraded intellectually and spiritually as the women in the mills were found to be. To education and the Church, then, reformers turned for their interpretation of factory conditions.

Since an almost unrelieved ignorance characterized the lower classes in 1832, it is not surprising that illiteracy, as well as congestion and absence of sewerage, were found in the mill towns which had sprung up all over the North. The general verdict was that factory children could neither read nor write. For girls this was not considered a disadvantage generally, since "learning to read made a woman discontented".[161] Gaskell's and Engels' estimates about the ability of mill workers to read and to write have, unfortunately, no information about women. But before 1833, when there was no compulsory school attendance, and afterward, when children under fourteen, who were compelled to attend school for two hours daily, had nothing but a mockery of education, no educational start could be expected. Even when a national appropriation for education was secured in 1833, the lower classes benefited little from it. Mrs. Tonna gives a picture of the kind of schools available for factory children in *Helen Fleetwood*. In the brief time taken out of the working hours for education by the Factory Bill of 1833, they were allowed to sleep or play while the ignorant old woman who acted as teacher devoted herself to the cleaner children of trades-people. Leonard Horner, reporting on the educational provisions made under the Factory Acts, found certificates of attendance signed by an illiterate teacher with his mark.[162] Sir James Kay-Shuttleworth reported ignorant teachers, schoolrooms in cellars and garrets, where children squatted on the floor, the absence of school-books.[163] A few good factory schools like the famous institution in Robert Owen's factory, or those in John Bright's, Thomas Ashton's at Hyde, and W. R. Greg's,[164] were illustrious exceptions to the general rule of almost total neglect of education. The Sunday schools with an inadequate number of teachers and interrupted instruction attempted to teach the reading of the Bible and religious tracts, and sometimes a little writing, but they could accomplish little.[165] Night schools were in general like that of Mr. Wopsle's great-aunt in *Great Expectations*.[166] Workers were too tired to gain much profit even from a superior kind of instruction. As one worker also explained, ragged clothes kept many children and adults from both Sunday and night schools.[167] It is not surprising, from all this conspiracy toward illiteracy, that "during the years 1839–41, in the counties of Chester and Lancashire, 40 per cent. of the males and 65 per cent. of the females signed the marriage register with a cross".[168] But such mental degradation was eventually to be used for the agitation of factory reform, as will be shown in a later chapter. Leonard Horner, who was opposed to Government interference with industry, favoured a ten-hour bill, if the additional leisure would improve the character of the workers, whom he described as "ignorant, prejudiced, and sensual".[169] Writers like Gaskell made eloquent pleas for a system of primary schools in the manufacturing districts. During the years while women and girls were veritable slaves, with no time to get the rudiments of education even if good schools had existed, schemes were being developed to bring some kind of cheap instruction within the reach of the children of labouring parents. But not until 1870 did an effective law for compulsory education and the provision for good instruction begin to lift the universal ignorance of the working classes.

Religion had no more place in the life of the average mill girl than education.[170] Old Mrs. Green in *Helen Fleetwood* was shocked at the desecration of the Sabbath in Manchester. Games were played, and groups of young people walked aimlessly up and down the streets while the morning services were going on. Mrs. Tonna represented the majority of the mill people as totally uninfluenced in their conduct by the precepts of Christianity. Mrs. Gaskell's novels dealing with an industrial population reveal the slight hold religion had upon the people.

Why had the Church failed to reach the thousands of workers crowded into the manufacturing cities? One powerful reason lay in the fact that the Industrial Revolution had come too swiftly for a conservative institution. There were too few churches and too few clergymen to meet the great increase of population in the Northern towns. As late as 1851, in the borough of Manchester there were sittings in the churches of all denominations for only one-third of the people.[171] Disraeli emphasized the inadequacy of a parish church, which remained the only one to take care of a community increased by manufacture from an obscure village to a city equal in size to "some European capitals".[172] The clergy in the Church of England were especially unfit for the new conditions, as Cooke Taylor recognized. Men from the universities who inserted long Greek and Latin quotations into their sermons and had no acquaintance with the Lancashire or Yorkshire dialect had little influence over the unruly mill girl.[173] They seldom took an interest in the public questions affecting their congregations, as Mrs. Tonna showed in the person of the Manchester clergyman who did not believe an interest in politics harmonized with his sacred calling and refused to interfere with glaring evils in the mills.[174] Men like the vicar in *Sybil*, who considered that he had done his duty if he preached two sermons each week, enforced humility on his congregation, and gratitude for the blessings of this life, could make little change in the prevailing manner of existence. This emphasis upon meekness and submission to existing institutions[175] definitely antagonized the manufacturing population. They charged the clergy with being in alliance with the manu-facturers. The Sunday schools, largely supported in some districts by mill-owners and conducted by teachers who taught obedience to one's superiors among the supreme spiritual graces, were not popular with the poor, who could not under-stand why humility and long-suffering should be practised solely by them. Mrs. Tonna came out boldly in her conviction of ministerial truckling to the wealth and the power of the manufacturers. The clergyman in *Helen Fleetwood* admitted that he did not dare to interfere with the mill-owners in their worldly concerns. "The quiet way", she wrote, "in which the clergy look on while the poor are destroyed around them, shows how little they care about them, bodies or souls."[176] The clergy in the North were compared unfavourably with those in the South by both Mrs. Tonna and Mrs. Gaskell. Mrs. Green's clergyman in the South was a father to his people, and their adviser in temporal as well as in spiritual matters. Mr. Hale in *North and South* was intimately familiar with the daily lives of his people in a Southern parish. But neither writer hinted that in the South as well as in the North the clergy were unpopular in the country districts, because they were tithe-owners and were connected with the adminis-tration of poor relief.[177] And other powerful factors led the people away from the Church. Scepticism, which in the eighteenth century had characterized only the gentleman, had now trickled down to the proletarian ranks. Both Gaskell and Sir James Kay-Shuttleworth[178] described the factory worker as a materialist. The free-thinker was introduced as a character in the fiction of the time. But how much such men as Higgins in *North and South*, Stephen Morley in *Sybil*, Tom South in *Helen Fleetwood*, and the young brasier in *The Wrongs of Women*, influenced the women around them is impossible to estimate. An easier explanation for the ecclesiastical backsliding lies in the overwork of the factory population. They were too tired to go to church on Sunday. Furthermore, they did not feel the social urge which kept an isolated agricultural population faithful in church attendance. They saw enough people during the week at the mills.

In spite of all the evidence of deterioration, religion had not lost its force. Methodism was strong in the North, and the Methodist Sunday schools among the most energetic in education. In 1851, of the 121 churches and chapels in Manchester, 53 per cent. belonged to the Dissenters.[179] Methodist ministers had not considered politics beneath their sacred calling. The Rev. J. R. Stephens, who took a prominent part in the early agitation for a short-time bill, was an ejected Wesleyan minister. He led a torchlight procession surrounded by followers wearing and carrying upon poles the red caps of liberty. He branded the manufacturers as a gang of murderers whose blood was required to satisfy the demands of public justice. The Catholic Church has always been a power in the North of England. The work of the Quakers in education was effective in reaching the lowest people. The Church of England, too, in spite of the heavy criticism directed against it, contained many earnest men like the Rev. Aubrey St. Lys in *Sybil*, who saw the need for a greater Church. The faith which still rested in the Church is curiously exemplified by a manufacturer, who entrusted the moral control of his silk factory to a clergyman.[180] But a most powerful proof that the clergy lacked neither knowledge of factory conditions nor moral and spiritual courage is the existence of a printed sermon by the Rev. Charles Gutch, delivered in Leeds in 1853.[181] A tragic catastrophe had struck the working population. The explosion of an overheated boiler had injured sixteen employees of Mr. Samuel Hammond, September 22, 1853. Three workers died on the day of the accident, three the next day, the seventh after fifteen days of agony. One of the women killed had been living in sin with a man who had deserted his wife for her. In the pulpit the clergyman, regarding the tragedy as a divine visitation upon sin, preached on the text from St. Luke xiii. 4 and 5 : "Of those eighteen, upon whom the tower in Siloam fell, and slew them, think ye that they were sinners above all men that dwelt in Jerusalem? I tell you, Nay: but, except ye repent, ye shall all likewise perish." Of the mill which had been visited with calamity the minister said:

"Many of you know what a character that mill bears for the vice and profaneness, the unchecked profligacy, the unblushing wickedness, of its work-people, both within and without its walls. . . . I have heard that mill spoken of as the lowest and the worst of its class. . . . Believing that God is of purer eyes than to behold iniquity, and knowing that no efficient steps had been taken, either before or after representations made by myself to the owner, to put down these scandals, to vindicate our outraged Christian decency, and to protect Christ's poor, I have indeed long trembled, that the God to whom vengeance belongeth, would show Himself."

The sermon is an exposure of the desecration of the Sabbath in Leeds, the awful housing conditions of the workers, the polluted atmosphere of the mill. He believed that the Church was inadequate to assume the duty of regeneration. Parishes in Leeds containing six thousand people had only one church. In a prefatory letter to the proprietor of the mill printed with the sermon, the clergyman reminded him of a conversation between them two or three months earlier, in which he had asked for the dismissal of a foreman who had seduced two mill girls, one of them now dead. He had then reproved the manufacturer for the sin committed in his mill and for his laxity in permitting mill girls to indulge in profane and indecent talk in the mill as well as out of it. He had urged the appointment of a woman overlooker of religious character in every room of the mill. He had tried to show the employer that other manufacturers had experimented successfully with philanthropic schemes. Nothing had been done to reform conditions, and finally disaster had come. In both the letter

and the sermon, in spite of the ecclesiastical clamour which
to a later generation seems out of harmony in a time of death,
the courage of the Church is an encouraging sign. "Why is
there so much wickedness in the mills, and foundries, and
collieries?" demanded the preacher. "Is it not because their
owners do not really devote their time, and money, and personal services to the education and religious control of their
work-people?" Such words are in dramatic contrast to the
documents and the literature which give the general impression
of clergymen afraid to interfere with manufacturers who
neglected the welfare of their "hands" and indifferent about
reproving mill workers for their sinful pleasures.

In their attitude to morals and religion, most writers
adopted the same critical viewpoint as they had toward the
new conditions of the home arising from the employment of
women in factories. They saw no good rising from a changed
way of life. It is highly probable that they gave the factory
girl a reputation for vice worse than the facts justified. She
was, it is quite certain, no worse than other girls of her class
and opportunity. But she was subjected to a scrutiny which
they escaped. Then, as has been earlier suggested, as a self-
supporting female she affronted Victorian prejudices. Nervous
gentlemen who did not like to contemplate the awful age in
which they lived, hearing that housewives did not want to
employ mill girls as servants, leaped to the conclusion that
these ladies were unwilling to pollute their homes with them.
The possibility that girls who knew nothing but factory work
were unfitted for domestic labour was never suggested.
Then, too, mill girls permitted themselves an independence
of conduct impossible in an agricultural community where
the squire acted as censor. So long as they did their work
well, their employers allowed them to use their scant leisure
as they pleased. They, unlike their superiors, were not
restrained by the ideals of Victorian conduct appropriate to
ladies nor by the precepts of religion. All this was an affront
to the accepted code of conduct of the time. Those writers

who were unable to make a disinterested attempt to get at the truth of the matter, unconsciously finding what they wanted to find, and who were incapable of the scientific use of the figures which fascinated and at the same time bewildered them, have made the social history of factory women a record of unrelieved degeneration. But in all the material lies hidden the germs of improvement, of steadily increasing opportunity, of dignity. This, contemporaries did not see. Yet they had the wisdom to realize that too many hours of work in factories which did not safeguard the health of women and girls coming from homes even more unsanitary, resulted in a steadily degraded population, ignorant and sodden in its pleasures. For improvement they looked first to fewer hours of work under conditions less inimical to health and life. Other reform would logically follow.

4. The Improvement of the Textile Worker through Legislation

That the problem of women textile workers was not recognized until after 1832 appears unexplainable only at first sight. Women at the spinning-wheel and the loom had the familiarity that brings indifference. Not until large numbers of women and children were massed in huge cotton mills did they receive the belated consideration which overburdened women in their homes or in small workshops had been denied. The cotton industry was too powerful to be overlooked. But even when an effort was made to improve long-standing evils through legislation, there was a great weight of custom to overcome. Of this Charlotte Elizabeth wrote:

"We used to think that what thwarts him (Ashley) is a hot opposition in the House of Commons. No such thing; it is like pleading with the deaf or preaching to the dead. Give him an adversary, and he can grapple with him; but who can grapple with a painted picture of a man that stares out of a frame without having either senses, or substance, or reality of any sort? This is just what the gentlemen become when our case is brought forward."[182]

In addition to this general apathy of the public there were also powerful agencies at work either to delay legislative action or to render it harmless. The mill-owners were the most formidable opponents to any Government interference with industry. The Reform Bill had been a great victory for the middle class, and manufacturers were well represented in the Parliaments which considered the passing of factory bills. The most admirable class of manufacturers were formidable foes to Lord Ashley's efforts to reform working conditions. Because they conducted their business with regard to the comfort of their employees, they refused to believe that conditions in all mills were any different from those in theirs, and they fought the idea of the necessity of Government interference. It must be added, however, that after effective laws were passed, and a system of thorough inspection was in force, the up-to-date factories of these same employers served as models for the inspectors in bringing up the others to an equal standard of sanitation and safety.[183]

Manufacturers, then, were able to present their arguments against factory legislation with great power in Parliament by members of their own order such as John Bright, and by theorists like Roebuck. Outside of Parliament, Nassau Senior, Dr. Ure, and Cooke Taylor were able assistants.

In the first place it was represented that the whole agitation for a ten-hour working day was a conspiracy of the cotton spinners to benefit themselves.[184] Their hostile interpreters suspected them of trying to raise their own wages when the decrease in production, following a ten-hour day, should advance the price of cotton cloth. They would thus earn as much in ten hours as in twelve. To achieve this diabolical purpose they had first invented monstrous tales of the cruelty practised upon children and had succeeded in deceiving Sadler and his associates, although that cruelty, if there were any, was practised by the cotton spinners themselves. With the passing of the Factory Bill of 1833, which limited the labour of children, they were not benefited, for women took the children's places. They then began a crusade to get a bill passed that would restrict the labour of women to ten hours, for then they, as well, would be similarly limited. Such a purpose behind their schemes was described by the Royal Commission, by Dr. Ure, and by Nassau Senior; but whether the cotton spinners were, in fact, using the children and then the women for their own ends is still a mooted question.

The danger that men as well as women would be restricted by a ten-hour bill applied to women was generally believed, although the solemn assurance that such was not the intention of the framers of the measure was frequently given.[185] John Bright showed that this result was inevitable.[186] The petition of the manufacturers in 1847 against a ten-hour bill contained the objection that the labour of men would be restricted.[187] It was also observed that promoters of the bill promised to the men the blessings of a shorter day.[188] It is true that, when the Law of 1844 was passed restricting women, as well as children, to twelve hours of work, it had the indirect result of restricting men also. The enemies of a ten-hour bill, in their arguments against it, all considered, then, that such a bill would limit all workers to ten hours.

The manufacturers prophesied immediate financial loss if a ten-hour bill were passed, and political economists and factory inspectors supported them in their fear.[189] Nassau Senior argued that long hours were necessary because a large amount of fixed capital could be made profitable only by a long working day.[190] He advanced the famous theory that all the profit was derived from the last hour, a conclusion Sibella Miles heartily ridiculed.[191] Ministers of the Crown and Members of Parliament listened more seriously.[192] Roebuck held similar views.[193] The small mills were represented as ruined by restrictive legislation.

Attempts were made to prove that the workers would suffer from a ten-hour day.[194] The workers were described as deluded in the notion that they would get twelve hours' pay for ten hours' work.[195] Numerous wise men did all in their power to

rescue them from such a delusion. It was also represented
that the majority did not want a shorter day. In one mill
where the men were offered a ten-hour day, they refused it.[196]

The greed of the manufacturers was a formidable foe to
beneficial legislation, but the theories of political economy
were equally hostile. This philosophy, which taught the evil
of all Government regulation of industry, could lead a well-
balanced woman like Harriet Martineau to oppose bitterly
all legislation enforcing the boxing of machinery. Dr. Ure,
writing of Althorp's amendment in 1833 to restrict legislation
to those who could not protect themselves, commented thus
upon the opposition:

"It will certainly appear surprising to every dispassionate mind,
that ninety-three members of the British House of Commons could
be found capable of voting that any class of grown-up artisans
should not be suffered to labour more than ten hours a day—an
interference with the freedom of the subject which no other legislature in Christendom would have countenanced for a moment."[197]

Milner Gibson, a Member of Parliament, had much to say about
the folly of Government meddling.[198] John Roebuck, the same
man who had written to his wife in 1838 about sights in cotton
factories that froze his blood, in 1843 deprecated interference
with adult labour, voted against the Factory Bill of 1844, and
made a speech in which he said: "It won't do to come down
to this House with exaggerated descriptions of misery, of
want, and of suffering. I deny them all."[199] Of the manufacturing population, he wrote that they were much better off
than any other portion of the population. When an economist's
private sympathies and his theories came into conflict, he
appeared sadly inconsistent. With Roebuck, the teachings of
political economy triumphed. Women were adults. Therefore,
there should be no laws passed to protect them. The reasoning
of political economy was as simple as a geometric theorem.
The reasoning of John Stuart Mill, though much more
subtle and humáne, led to the same conclusion. He feared
that legislation restricting women's labour would lend weight

to the system of tutelage under which they were held, and
thus delay their final emancipation as independent social units.

Among gentlemen with whom political economy was less
the rule of life, the pride in the industrial greatness of England
made the arguments of the danger of foreign competition
especially alarming. The references to it are innumerable.
Sir James Graham's predictions covered pages in Hansard.
The United States was considered the most formidable rival.
But Sibella Miles, among the women writers, had only scorn
for a competitive system based upon overwork and under-pay.
She argued that the logic of Parliament overlooked the fact
that by keeping the working classes in such poverty that they
could not be buyers, the home market was being ruined.

The bitterness between the Tories and the Whigs also made
factory legislation difficult. The reform movement led by Lord
Ashley, a Tory, was stigmatized by the Whigs as only an
excuse to attack the Whig manufacturers. Whigs who might
have voted for factory bills sponsored by a member of their
own party, were cold toward Lord Ashley's bill. The antagonism of the Anti-Corn Law League was also unfortunate.
The conservatism of the Government and its fear of the
experiment of shortening hours of work made reform slow.

When to all these hostile agencies was added the optimism
expressed in writers like Dr. Ure and Nassau Senior, the
problem was further complicated. The extravagance of some
of the reformers also weakened their cause. Both Lord Ashley
and Mrs. Tonna, who reflected his views, by the unrelieved
gloom of their descriptions of the factories justified the
charge that they were arguing for the total exclusion of women
from the factories.[200] Even a ten-hour day would have been
of little account in bettering a situation so full of hardship
as they saw it.

But the friends of reform for factory women were gathering
strength for their cause. As early as 1832, the Sadler commission realized that the protection of women by legislation
was necessary.[201] After the application of the Factory Laws of

1833 and 1844, many of the mill-owners themselves realized that uniform factory laws for women would benefit their employers. In 1842 Leonard Horner, in his factory report, registered the complaints of mill proprietors against the unscrupulous methods of competitors who worked a longer time than the law allowed.[202] What they actually complained against, however, was that some employers held their operatives to 74 hours a week instead of the 69 prescribed for all workers under 18.[203] In this they were legally justified, if the young workers were turned away. What was objected to, then, was this legalized overwork. The more humane employers, in opposing the practice of requiring more than twelve hours of labour from the operatives, were placed in unequal competition with other men. In the same year Horner printed several requests from manufacturers[204] and mill superintendents for the legalizing of a twelve-hour day for workers, even adults. In 1844 Sir James Graham, the Home Secretary, received a delegation of mill-owners with a similar request.[205] Lord Ashley in Parliament mentioned a petition signed by three hundred employers of the West Riding of Yorkshire for a ten-hour bill.[206] After the passage of the Factory Bill of 1844, which limited the labour of adult women to twelve hours daily, manufacturers asked for the legalization of a ten-hour day, and further petitions for such a law were made.[207]

The workers were also behind the ten-hour movement. The men, by means of the short-time committees, had persistently agitated the question. In the earlier years there is no direct evidence that the women were eager for the safeguarding of their interests by law. The indirectness shown in the inspector's report of 1841 is probably characteristic of their general timidity:

"Two females, who were eventually proved to be above 18, volunteered the statement that they themselves and very many of their companions regretted that I was unable to protect them, as they felt the work was much more than they were equal to, but that if they had not consented to conform to the hours required of them they would have been discharged, and thus thrown out of work at a time when regular employment was very valuable."[208]

In 1845 Horner wrote in his report: "No instances have come to my knowledge of adult women having expressed any regret at their *rights* being thus interfered with."[209] The most interesting revelation of women's interest in a short-time bill was shown in the request of the women of Rochdale in 1847, that they be given part of the hall for a meeting on the ten-hour bill.[210]

The immediate effect of the Factory Bill of 1833* was to write the problem of mill women in capital letters, because of the large increase in the number of women who replaced the children affected by the law.[211] Furthermore, the preference employers had for the cheaper labour of women and the consequent unemployment of men were facts given publicity by the factory reports, as well as by Lord Ashley. These facts upset Victorian ideas of propriety and natural order. It was urged that if women were limited in labour, such a law would give more work to men.[212] A second argument for the necessity of legislation was the cruel overwork to which women were driven. Even the factory inspectors with *laissez-faire* theories felt justified in advising special legislation for women.[213] The definite cases of excessive labour presented by the inspectors were used effectively by Sir James Graham and by Lord Ashley in their speeches in Parliament. The serious accidents to which women were in special danger from unboxed machinery also demonstrated their need of legal protection. Fortunately, the testimony of both doctors and clergymen could be used to show that the health and the morals of women were being undermined by immoderate labour. Both professions in Manchester supported the ten-hour bill.[214] The moral dangers had great influence upon

* The Law of 1833 forbade the employment of children under 9 except in the silk mills, and restricted the hours of children under 13 to 8 hours daily and those from 13 to 18 to 12 hours.

the pietistic temper of the time. Horner excused Government control on moral grounds almost entirely. Peel said that if he were sure a ten-hour law would elevate the character of the workers, he would support it,[215] and many speeches in Parliament for the bill made the moral arguments the most conspicuous.

Other agencies contributed to the growing sentiment for a shorter day. Numerous experiments were being made by some manufacturers which convinced them that fewer hours of work meant increased efficiency. In 1844 a factory in Preston began to make a trial of an eleven-hour day, and after a year pronounced the results satisfactory.[216] Both the day hands and the piece workers earned the same in eleven hours as in twelve, with improved vigilance as well. Increased attendance at the night schools also followed. Other mill-owners in Preston imitated their example. To counteract Senior's theory of the profit of the last hour, statements were given concerning the spoiled work of the last hour.[217]

The theory of *laissez-faire*, upon which many enemies to a shorter working day leaned heavily, also suffered repeated shocks. Clear-minded thinkers in Parliament exposed the ridiculousness of clinging to this theory when the Government had already pledged itself to interference. The Act of 1833, in spite of its omission of provisions for women, clearly recognized the right of the State to interfere with the abuses of a private industry. But the extension of protection to women, who were adults and should be free agents, was all the more strongly fought by the *laissez-faire* school after they had been defeated in the matter of child legislation.

The Bill of 1842 relating to mines was, finally, the death-knell to the doctrine of *laissez-faire*, and the influence of this legislation upon what followed is of inestimable importance. In 1840 Lord Ashley had moved in Parliament that an inquiry into the condition of children outside the textile industries be made. The Children's Employment Commission, appointed as a result, investigated the conditions in mines, concerning

which their first report, published in 1842, surpassed in horror
any of the earlier records.[218]

Considerable space was devoted to the woman worker. In
the West Riding of Yorkshire, in the Halifax, Bradford, and
Leeds districts, in Lancashire and Cheshire, in Eastern Scotland,
and in Southern Wales, women were hired as commonly as
men to work in the pits. As "hurriers" they loaded small
wagons with coal, as "drawers" dragged the wagon behind
them in places too low for horses to be used, or carried loads
of coal on their backs from half a hundredweight to a hundredweight and a half for twelve, fourteen, sixteen hours daily,
sometimes, in extreme instances, for thirty-six hours.

The testimony of many of the women is more powerful
than any comment. Betty Harris, aged thirty-seven, a drawer
in a coal-pit, Little Bolton, described her work thus:[219]

"I have a belt round my waist and a chain passing between my
legs, and I go on my hands and feet. The road is very steep, and we
have to hold by a rope, and when there is no rope, by anything we
can catch hold of. There are six women and about six boys in the
pit I work in: it is very hard work for a woman. The pit is very
wet where I work, and the water comes over our clogs always,
and I have seen it up to my thighs: it rains in at the roof terribly;
my clothes are wet through almost all day long. I never was ill in
my life but when I was lying-in. My cousin looks after my children
in the daytime. I am very tired when I get home at night; I fall
asleep sometimes before I get washed. I am not so strong as I was,
and cannot stand my work so well as I used to do. I have drawn till
I have had the skin off me; the belt and chain is worse when we are
in the family way. My feller (husband) has beaten me many a time
for not being ready. I were not used to it at first, and he had little
patience. I have known many a man beat his drawer."

Other women told how they worked in the coal-pits until
the day their children were born and then returned a week
later. Miscarriages were frequent. One mother reported that
four of her children had been stillborn. Many children died
in infancy. The testimony of these subjects of Queen Victoria
would seem beyond belief if there were less corroborative

evidence. The ultimate tragedy was their belief that the men could prevent the women's work in the mines if they themselves would work more steadily.

A girl of twenty worked for 2s. a day or less, while a man the same age asked 3s. 6d.[220] A woman was popular as a mine worker because she did not aspire to be a "coal-getter", to dig out the coal, the work most highly paid, and as a drawer she was more steady than a boy and easier to manage, one of the miners reported.

Lord Ashley delivered a speech before Parliament, June 7, 1842, presenting the evils suffered by women and children in the mines. "For two hours", he wrote in his diary, "the House listened so attentively that you might have heard a pin drop, broken only by loud and repeated marks of approbation."[221] Many men wept. Richard Cobden, whose theories of political economy had formerly kept him hostile to the work of Lord Ashley, now went over to his side. The Prince Consort read the speech aloud to the Queen, who was greatly moved.

A reading of the speech leaves an impression second only to that of the direct words of the miners quoted in the report of the Commission. But in spite of his powerful presentation of the physical hardships the women suffered, which made them old at forty, and of their constant danger from firedamp and accidents, it was the part of his speech dealing with moral dangers which secured him an immediate hearing. Young girls "hurrying" for men, working beside them in scanty garments, alone with them for hours of the day in an isolated part of the mine, were at their mercy. Covered with black, too weary to bathe at night, removed from all the decencies of life, they swore and used vile language. They were, too often, utterly demoralized from childhood.

A law was passed without delay which removed children under ten from the mines and provided that no woman should hereafter be employed underground. So immediate was the relief of this evil that the woman miner made almost no appearance in the writing of the day. In *Sybil* (1845) there is recorded the heroic action of a man who lived on bread and water to keep his daughters out of the pit.[222] Disraeli also described women at work in the mines, their rough language, their terrible labour. Mrs. Tonna in *The Forsaken Home* (1844) included the story of a young woman who worked in the mines until a few days before her son was born, and the utter demoralization and cruelty of the child in manhood from his early toil in the coal-mines. But this is all.

After 1842 Members of Parliament continued to declaim for hours about the sacredness and inviolability of private industry, but their cause was doomed to defeat. The truth was emphasized that in spite of the fact that women were adults, they were not free to decide and judge for themselves— at least, married women were not;[223] they were physically inferior to men, and they lacked the assistance of trade unions which the men had. In 1844 factory women were included in the law passed, which prescribed a maximum of twelve hours' labour between 5.30 a.m. and 8.30 p.m. for women and young persons above thirteen in the textile trades. It provided safeguards against the evasions of the law practised by unscrupulous employers in the increased power given to the inspectors, in the exclusion of protected persons from the workroom during meal-time, in the appointment of fixed periods for meals, and in the regulation of the hours of work and meals by a public clock approved by the inspectors. The fencing of machinery was also a special gain for women.

After 1844 further legislation was less difficult to accomplish. The Law of 1844 had none of the disastrous results which its enemies had prophesied. The industrial supremacy of England was not immediately destroyed. Irate manufacturers did not remove their mills to other countries.[224] Wages rose.[225] Production was not decreased.[226] Then the repeal of the Corn Laws in 1846 removed a bone of contention, for the manufacturers could no longer taunt Tory land-holders with a desire to improve the life of the factory worker while they kept the price of grain so high that the poor could not have enough bread. Lord Ashley's surrender of his seat because he had come to believe in the repeal of the Corn Laws for the relief of the poor raised him above any further attacks on the grounds of inconsistency. Party lines became broken up on the subject of a ten-hour bill.

In 1847 the final victory for factory women was secured by a bill which limited the hours of labour to 58 per week for women and young persons above thirteen. Immediately there was rejoicing all over the manufacturing districts of England. In almost every town in Lancashire and Yorkshire, special meetings of thankfulness were held.[227] The bill was passed with little opposition in a year when bad trade made it impossible to keep the mills running for even ten hours.[228]

The rejoicing, unfortunately, was premature. The Law of 1847 had failed to fix the time when the ten hours was to be worked, and immediately, in spite of the great depression of trade, the relay system was used, and female labour, because it was cheap, was worked double shifts. In 1849 a period of good trade so exaggerated this evil that Lord Ashley, who during the passage of the 1847 Bill had been absent from Parliament, but had now returned, renewed his struggle for an effective ten-hour bill.[229] In 1850 the Government proposed a measure fixing the hours of protected persons within the limits of 6 a.m. and 6 p.m., or 7 a.m. and 7 p.m., allowing an hour and a half for meals, with work ending at 2 p.m. on Saturday. Although this added two hours to the total for the week, Lord Ashley supported this proposal, and it became a law.

The testimony of factory inspectors, and of the manufacturers themselves, had shown the impossibility of enforcing factory laws if the relay system were allowed.[230] The Law of 1850, therefore, is regarded by authorities on factory legislation as "an important turning point in the history of English factory legislation".[231] It established a normal working day for women and young persons for the first time, and "by its clear and distinct provisions put a speedy and lasting end to the uncertainties that existed in the manufacturing districts".[232]

5. THE RESULTS OF LEGAL RESTRICTION UPON THE LABOUR OF FACTORY WOMEN

Toward the new ten-hour day the general feeling among the work-people was one of satisfaction.[233] Only one petition complaining of the Act was recorded by the factory inspectors.[234] In 1849 an investigation was made to discover the actual percentage who favoured the shorter time. Of the men questioned nearly 70 per cent. preferred ten hours; of the women nearly 55 per cent.; 76 per cent. of the masters were convinced that the majority of their employees would be opposed to going back to twelve hours.[235] In all the estimates made the majority of women preferred the ten-hour day.[236] In only one district was there decided dissatisfaction among the women. After 1850, when an effective ten-hour bill was passed, there are no figures. The subject of whether the regulation was pleasing to the operatives had ceased to interest the inspectors. The inference is that there was no opposition. Then, too, the period of prosperity which had begun by 1848, in 1853 was at its height, and there was enough work for everyone.

The effect of the new law upon earnings is interesting. At the same time that the Law of 1847 came into operation there was a 10 per cent. reduction on the rate of piece work and on fixed wages, as well as the one-sixth reduction for shortened time, so that workers suffered altogether a 25 per cent. reduction. With this in mind, as well as the fact that they had come through two years of great suffering on account of depressed trade, the approval of the law is the more remarkable.[237] George Henry Wood, in his detailed study of the cotton industry, shows that although there was a temporary loss of wages following the reduced hours, this was soon made up.[238]

Eventually more was earned in ten hours than had been earned in twelve.[239] It is his belief that reduction of hours has been followed in a few years by higher earnings for fewer hours.

The question of efficiency is another important problem. The operatives on piece work had hoped to earn as much in ten hours as twelve by extra exertion. By 1851 the piece work for ten and a half hours was little short of the amount for twelve hours.[240]

One object of the bill had been to give work to men by limiting that of women. In some mills the men worked twelve, thirteen, and fourteen hours, continuing after the women and girls left. In several cases boys and women were discharged for men who could work more than ten hours. In a few districts there was great distress for the time because of the unemployment of women. In most instances, however, the men worked the same time as the women.[241]

Although the manufacturers as a class opposed the ten-hour day, some could see the improvement in the condition of their employees. In 1844 they had reported that the law passed distributed orders more equally when large mill-owners could no longer monopolize big orders and fill them by overtime.[242] The great losses Horner had prophesied in 1841 would follow a ten-hour bill, he admitted in 1848 he had overrated.[243] In 1850 trade was so good that new mills were started.[244] In spite of the fact that the reports gave little information about the opinions of mill-owners on the new bill, there seemed no violent opposition after it was passed.

The improved condition of factory homes was emphasized by the reports. Some of the reform the Commissioners chronicle with so much satisfaction, however, indicates that mill women had relapsed into the conventional mode of housekeeping approved by their era. One worker testified that, after the passing of the 1850 Bill, she could do her washing and cleaning herself instead of hiring it, as she had formerly. A woman piecer stated that she "had done more with her needle since the ten hours began than she had done all her life before". The mother of daughters employed in the factories boasted of their accomplishments in housework, sewing, and knitting, since the new bill had given them a little leisure.

Night schools became much more successful with the shorter working day. Although it is a little discouraging to note the greater frequency with which men workers mentioned opportunities for evening study, women also were grateful for the chance for self-improvement.[245] A woman abandoned by her husband and with a child to support made the effort to attend night classes.[246] In one district, out of a class of 400, 118 were women and young girls learning reading, writing, arithmetic, and plain sewing, two nights a week from seven to nine. None of these had been members of the class before the passing of the ten-hour Act.[247]

The importance of educating working women attracted considerable attention. Sarah Martin, better known for her prison visiting at Yarmouth, but also interested in teaching factory girls, held a class two nights a week in the chancel of the church of Saint Nicholas in Yarmouth. An article in *Household Words* in 1852 entitled "The New School for Wives", describes the opening of the first evening school for women in Birmingham, September 1847, where reading, writing, arithmetic, sewing, including mending, and the Bible were taught.[248] By 1852 the school had a paid superintendent and a paid teacher, and of the one hundred pupils registered in the books, fifty attended regularly. A knowledge of arithmetic was found to help housewives to check up the charges of hucksters. Factory women favoured such a utilitarian aspect of being educated. The charge of 13d. a quarter put the classes within the reach of most working women. *The Voice of the People* in 1848 recorded the foundation in 1845 of *The People's Instruction Society*, with night classes for women in addition to those for men.

The interest taken by employers in the intellectual and physical welfare of their "hands" was a prominent feature of

the years following the shortening of the working day, and
their social experiments Carlyle placed above everything
else, as a force to avert "Trades' strikes, Trades' Unions,
Chartisms".[249] Although, in isolated instances, far-seeing
mill-owners like W. R. Greg had early seen the folly of an
industrial system built upon ignorance and a violation of
the laws of health,[250] plans made for the improvement of
workers could not be a complete success so long as their unscrupulous competitors evaded ineffective laws. The enforcement of a ten-hour day, then, resulted in increased interest
in night schools and libraries already in existence as well
as in the establishment of many new ones. Workers who
had formerly been too tired to consider improving their minds
now joined night classes.[251] All the power-loom weavers
enrolled in a certain night school in 1850 had entered since
the inauguration of the ten-hour day. The years of agitation
for factory reform helped to popularize all movements for the
physical improvement of mill people. Employers, roused by
public opinion, began to take an interest in making their mills
sanitary and comfortable.

After 1847 the reports of factory inspectors devoted much
space to the encouragement given by employers to education
and to social improvement, which amounted in many cases
to starting and financing such movements. In a Liverpool
mill employing 854 workers, a medical attendant paid by the
contributions of the workers at one penny weekly, and by the
proprietors, a schoolroom in the mill for the mill children
and the children of employees, a night school for adults, a
lending library, a savings bank, a sick relief fund, partly
accumulated by fines, and a yearly excursion every July for
the well-behaved workers, with a brass band for entertainment, were features that Leonard Horner described at length
in his report.[252]

Among the books in the mill libraries was a volume published by the Religious Tract Society, entitled *Young Women
of the Factory* (1845).[253] It was written with the unconcealed

purpose of uplifting the mill girl, and contained all the advice
that could be given her. Mrs. Tonna from her editorial sanctum
gave it her blessing. She wrote :

"The increased advantages of education that, by the Divine
blessing on Lord Ashley's persevering efforts are now likely to be
placed within the reach of these classes, render it necessary to
provide a supply of such instructive reading as shall help to bar the
entrance against what is pernicious and destructive."[254]

The book is divided into such chapters as : duty to parents ;
formation of habits (a number of chapters are necessary for
dealing with this important subject), with habits of industry,
perseverance, cleanliness, propriety of language, all thoroughly
presented ; the choice of companions ; discretion and modesty ;
forethought ; provident savings ; early marriages ; family
affection. Under the 'chapter Domestic Habits, needlework
is considered. Health and dress take one chapter ; the employment of leisure another. The whole is written in a pious tone,
with the use of many illustrations from the Bible, and in
simple language within the grasp of a girl with little education.
The factory worker is enjoined not to waste her master's time.
She is advised to rise an hour before going to the factory,
to pray, and to leave all around her in order. When she comes
home she'is to bustle about the house helping her mother.
Illustrations of the virtues upheld for emulation are frequently
given. There is the story of the girl who bought wool for a
coat from the prize money given her for being early to work.
The factory girl is advised to belong to a sick benefit club.
She is warned against the folly of hiring her caps washed
at three or four pence apiece or of not making her own clothes.
There is advice about health. The necessity of fresh air and
exercise is preached. Exercise, however, derived from making
beds and scrubbing floors, was especially commended by a
writer who evidently did not associate physical exertion with
factory employment. One wonders in turning the pages of
this earnest book how many tired mill girls tried to follow its

stern teaching. Luckily, human nature, wayward and prone to fall, may have saved them from too much valiant effort.[254]

The most complete record of definite social work done in this early period under the direction of the employers is a pamphlet written by Mary Merryweather, describing the fourteen years she spent at a silk mill in Essex.[255] After the passing of the ten-hour law, the wife of the senior partner of the mill decided that the girls had leisure for reading. She had previously invited Miss Merryweather to read and lecture to them. Then, after a six-weeks' training in a normal school to learn something about the organization of schools, Miss Merryweather began her work. She established a night school for the girls and for adults, a factory kitchen where a cheap luncheon was provided, a hostel for working girls, a nursery for the care of babies while their mothers were at work, an amusement society, and a sick fund. The description of the enterprise is in part a record of failure; for the hostel, the nursery, and the amusement society were given up for lack of interest. The girls resented the restraint of the hostel, and the mothers preferred to leave their babies with an incompetent old woman. Miss Merryweather partially accounted for her lack of success in gaining the sympathy and the co-operation of her charges by explaining that the object of her pamphlet was to show that factory women needed gentlewomen working in their midst. She was evidently too perfect a lady, or possibly lacking in delicate tact. Her general plans, however, were most praiseworthy, as modern developments of her schemes eloquently testify. Mrs. Tonna in *The Wrongs of Women* (1844) had earlier pointed out the need of better care for the children of working mothers.

" 'I only wish,' says Alice (to Nell Carter, a kind old woman with no family ties), 'you'd leave this business, and set up to take care of the infants of poor women like me. You might get on well enough, and many a mother would go to work with a lighter heart to think her little one was in such hands.' "[256]

But the time for day nurseries had not yet come.[257]

The literary treatment of this new sense of social responsibility, felt more and more by employers, shows how widely
the changed industrial philosophy had circulated. Geraldine
Jewsbury's novel, *Marian Withers* (1851), describes a mill
containing a room fitted up for the women, with hooks for
their clothes, a supply of water, towels, and soap. Their
employer had discovered that women worked better if they
had respect for themselves. *North and South* (1855) outlines
the plan of a mill-owner for giving his hands a cheap and
nourishing midday meal. Having observed the miserable
dinner prepared in one of the factory homes, he conceived
the idea of purchasing provisions wholesale and hiring a
matron to cook the dinner in the mill. Carlyle wrote in *Past
and Present* (1843) of a practical Quaker manufacturer: "(He)
has provided conversational soirees; play-grounds, bands of
music for the young ones; went even 'the length of buying
them a drum'; all which has turned out to be an excellent
investment."

The most encouraging element in these reforms was the
active co-operation of the workers themselves. Mrs. Gaskell
was one of the most intelligent writers on industrial subjects
to see the necessity of leaving social measures to their direction
at a time when the virtues of the employer who was like a
father to his employees were generally extolled. Mr. Thornton,
the manufacturer in *North and South*, gave expression to her
theory in presenting his plans for the mill dinner.[258]

" 'I was very scrupulous, at first, in confining myself to the mere
purchasing part, and even in that I rather obeyed the men's orders,
conveyed through the housekeeper, than went by my own judgment. . . . I think they saw how careful I was to leave them free,
and not to intrude my own ideas upon them; so, one day, two or
three of the men—my friend Higgins among them—asked me if
I would not come in and take a snack. It was a very busy day, but
I saw that the men would be hurt if, after making the advance, I
didn't meet them half-way, so I went in, and I never made a better
dinner in my life. I told them (my next neighbours I mean, for I'm
no speech-maker) how much I'd enjoyed it; and for some time,

whenever that especial dinner recurred in their dietary, I was sure to be met by these men with a "Master, there's hot-pot for dinner to-day, win yo' come in?" If they had not asked me, I would no more have intruded on them than I'd have gone to the mess at the barracks without invitation.' "

And again, in refusing a contribution to be used to "give the poor fellows a feast", Thornton said:

" 'Thank you, but I'd rather not. They pay me rent for the oven and cooking-places at the back of the mill, and will have to pay more for the new dining-room. I don't want it to fall into a charity. I don't want donations. Once let in the principle, and I should have people going and talking, and spoiling the simplicity of the whole thing.' "

Mrs. Gaskell reaches the heights of her whole conception when she represents Thornton as having accepted the whole plan of the mill dining-room from a delegation of the workers who had previously rejected the identical scheme when he proposed it. A writer who so early understood that the mill hand's independence is his only capital had not only great wisdom, but the humour which accompanies it. The workers' active part in various social enterprises was observed and recorded by Government officials, who saw in it a strong proof of progress. In many cases the libraries, schools, and sick benefit clubs were financed by both the workers and their employers. But the former took over the actual management and support of these institutions in a number of instances.[259]

After 1850 a new chapter in the life of English women textile workers was begun. Their moral character was raised as they became less overworked and also less ignorant through the steady improvement of education during the years of factory legislation. A better class of young women worked in the mills. The employers who had objected to the principle of Government regulation of factories, but had listened to the arguments for the moral benefits of a shorter working day, tended to accept greater responsibility in enforcing good conduct. One manufacturer discharged girls who had illegitimate children and also the fathers, unless they married.[260] The wisdom of such a practice will, however, always be a matter for argument. That, at the present time, of two mills separated by only a few miles and subject to the same local conditions, one owned by succeeding generations of men who have always taken a deep interest in their workers and have refused to employ any but men and women of good character, should have a record of three illegitimate children born to the operatives in a long period, while the other, managed by a limited company owning many mills and permitting unmarried mothers to return to work as soon as they are able, should have had a considerable number of illegitimate children born to its employees, leads to the obvious conclusion that the personal relation of an employer to the worker plays considerable part in raising moral standards. But such paternalism, even though it has almost disappeared with the increasing size and complexity of production, has been replaced by social agencies, which are continuing the sense of responsibility first roused in many employers during this early period of legislative agitation.

The results of parliamentary restriction upon the labour of factory women were admitted at the time and have since proved to be, in general, beneficial, not only to the individual, but to the textile industries as well. Earnings were not decreased. Efficiency became greater. Trade did not suffer. Women and girls in the mills, when they were no longer physically exhausted, had ambition to look after their homes and to improve their minds. Employers lent generous assistance to measures for the betterment of their workers. What was accomplished in other kinds of women's labour only after years of delay in legislation or by the slower force of public opinion was quickly brought about for factory women by the Law of 1850. They were the favoured class of women workers by the middle of the century, protected by law, and earning the same wages as men, where their work was equal in quantity and quality. Although in small part they shared the benefits of various philanthropic measures designed to assist working women, they were in less need and consequently made little use of such relief.

6. THE LITERARY TREATMENT OF THE TEXTILE WORKER

That the factory girl never attained the popularity of other wage-earning women as a heroine in fiction is easily seen by the preponderance of non-literary material in this chapter dealing with the textile industries. The primary reason is, of course, that Parliament attended so steadily to the factory question between 1832 and 1850 that novelists burning with a zeal for reform left her to powers stronger than theirs. It is in the records of parliamentary debates and in the factory reports that she is an important figure. Furthermore, the factory girl was of all working women the most remote from the experience of both authors and reading public. The mill was a world in itself, and so it has remained. To understand it, one must learn its mysteries in childhood. When Dickens tried to write of Manchester in *Hard Times*, he made a dismal failure. Then, too, the life of the mill girl lacked almost all of the romantic elements beloved by novelists. She was not beautiful. Her hard labour from childhood had marred any natural endowments of grace and feminine charm. She was surrounded by noise and dirt, and could not escape being dirty herself. It was hard to make the courtship of a mill boy and girl idyllic. Mill girls didn't often marry their employers' sons, and such intrigues as they had with them would have sullied the pages of a lady novelist. She found it difficult to penetrate the inner life of a character so unlike herself. The mill girl smoked, drank, swore, had the adventures in sex the Victorians reserved for men, and cheerfully slaved to support the almost inevitable babies. Other kinds of working girls, as we shall later show, those with cleaner jobs, not so difficult to comprehend, were more attractive. One notes that Disraeli does not make Sybil a worker in Trafford's mill, where in real life she would have been, and Mrs. Gaskell keeps Mary Barton from following the trade of her father, her mother, and aunt. The factory girl lacked all the qualifications for the ideal Victorian heroine.

In examining the literature, one discovers no mill girl turned author. There were no feminine counterparts of Samuel Bamford, Thomas Cooper, and William Lovett, humble workers who recorded their struggles, nor of Gerald Massey, a factory boy who became a poet. No woman close to the working life of the mills wrote about it. Authors desirous of keeping up with the times made a subordinate character a worker, without being too specific about the kind of labour performed. Mrs. Tonna alone described the processes of manufacture and concerned herself with the economic aspects of mill life. The majority centred their interest upon social conditions, the home as it was affected by the employment of mothers in factories, the resulting bad housekeeping, poor food, neglected babies, the daughters brought up in ignorance of household management. Moral and religious questions loomed large. In suggesting the reform of conditions, writers like Mrs. Tonna and Mrs. Gaskell urged that married women be kept out of the factories instead of studying why they were there. In this they were not so much limited by their sex as by their Victorian prejudices. Lord Ashley shared these, but not Harriet Martineau. Disraeli was equally blind to the reality of the situation and ran off into the most ridiculous panaceas in *Sybil*. Mrs. Tonna, in spite of her hostility to factories, allied herself with the cause of factory reform, and in *Helen Fleetwood*, begun as a serial in the *Christian Lady's Magazine* in 1840, prepared the way for the Bill of 1844 by exposing the weakness of the legislation of 1833. Whether her faithful reading of Lord Ashley's speeches and Government documents were supplemented by actual visits to factories, her autobiography does not make clear. If not, her remarkable accuracy and the wisdom of her comments are the more remarkable.

But what literature there was gave great service to the mill girl. Without it, the facts which Government reports had given the public would have lacked the necessary dramatic presentation and interpretation. Mrs. Gaskell, in her sympathetic and humorous pictures of the lives of the industrial poor, was the greatest force of her day. She made the homes real and the people in them. She educated her readers in matters new and strange. She explained what caused strikes, what Chartism meant, what misery entered the homes during periods of trade depression and disturbance. Her novels made clear the relation between such questions and the lives of working women. *North and South* is easily the greatest novel of industrial life in English. Mrs. Tonna, by giving the Government investigations a fictional framework, brought to the lay reader a rudimentary knowledge of the factory. *Helen Fleetwood* is the most effective single literary agency in getting technical information before the general public. Only a writer who had a greater regard for truth than for art, who sacrificed the interest of her tale for what it taught, could be so wilfully dull and, at the same time, so important. Together these novelists give a picture of the textile worker at home and in the mill which complements the Government Blue books by clarification and emotional understanding.

CHAPTER III

THE NON-TEXTILE WORKER

1. Her Economic Life

JOHN BRIGHT, a consistently violent opponent of all parliamentary factory reform, on March 15, 1844, was forced to listen to Lord Ashley's long speech urging a ten-hour factory law. Rising from his seat, he began a harangue full of personal abuse of the preceding speaker, and proceeded to prove that the persecution of cotton manufacturers was unfair, since workers in other industries were in a much worse condition.[1] Three days later Sir Robert Peel indulged in the same kind of shaky logic.[2] He then described the excessive hours of work and the intolerable conditions suffered by women and children in the making of earthenware, block-printing, the metal trades, and finally in agriculture. When he concluded: "Is it right, then, to deal only with this one branch of industry, and leave others altogether untouched, in which it appears that female children work fourteen, fifteen, sixteen, or even as much as eighteen hours a day?" and added: "If you are prepared to legislate for them", his too dramatic presentation was greeted with "Hear!" instead of by the jeers he anticipated for a proposal to him so clearly ridiculous and impossible. His anger at this unexpected use of his eloquence was not concealed.

The bulky reports of the Children's Commission of 1842–43, upon which Peel had based the facts of his speech, were quickened with a spark of life at this touch of notoriety. For the first time the non-textiles shared with the textile industries some of the public attention. The Commissioners, in spite of their special concern for the child labourer, had been intelligent investigators of women's employments. They had worked out the proportion of men and women in a great variety of industries, compared the work open to men and to women, examined the shops where only women were found, and studied the conditions which especially affected them. The omission of comparisons of the wages of men and women, included in the factory reports, is due to the fact that, since women monopolized some trades or performed unskilled work not parallel with that of the men, nothing would have been gained by such figures. Their observations revealed the sufferings of women in a variety of occupations covering practically the whole field of industrial life. But for the purposes of this chapter we shall use the term "non-textile" to include only that part of their inquiries relating to all kinds of manufacturing except the making of cloth, on both a large and small scale, with the exception of certain scattered references to activities still carried on as a domestic enterprise. The evils of dress-making and millinery, exposed in the same report, will be reserved for a later chapter.

But before this chronicle of female toil is examined in detail, the most cursory glance at its pages discloses a problem beyond that presented to factory reformers. The irregularity of certain trades, the impossibility of restricting the work done in the homes, and the superhuman task of reaching thousands of small shops hiring only a few workers, explain immediately why the efforts of the Commission counted for almost nothing. Because of the lack of information regarding many kinds of labour and the failure of any effective legislation before 1850, this part of the study would be omitted altogether if it did not afford a powerful contrast to the regularized employments in textile mills. Here, in a class of labour little affected, in many cases, by the Industrial Revolution, one has an extensive view of what working conditions were for all women before machinery changed the making of cloth into a factory enterprise. Fortunately, the Government reports are supplemented by Charlotte Elizabeth Tonna's *The Wrongs of Women*, published in instalments in the *Christian Lady's Magazine*, during 1843 and 1844, by a series of articles in *Household Words*, and other magazine material.

The Commissioners in their inquiries discovered that

women in great numbers were massed in the occupations of frame-work knitting and lace-finishing, both in part cottage industries, suffering the same evils and following a somewhat similar history.

The frame-work knitters belonged to an old trade, dating back to 1589.[3] The eighteenth-century fashion of leg decoration with its demand for fancy hosiery had made them prosperous, but with the soberer tastes of the nineteenth century, which demanded the unprofitable plain stockings, their good days were over. By 1810 the period of the Luddite Riots had begun. Frames were smashed as a protest against reduction in wages; 1816 and 1817 were years of great misery. Sixteen and eighteen hours of toil daily brought only 4s. to 7s. a week. In 1821, 2,000 out of 8,000 frame-work knitters were unemployed.[4] Many went into lace-making. In 1833 a petition was sent to Parliament for the fixing of a minimum wage, but nothing was done. Thomas Cooper, the Chartist, in his autobiography, has described the uncertainty and misery of the hosiery workers in Leicestershire when he lived there, 1841–43. In 1843 a second petition signed by 25,000 frame-work knitters of Nottingham, Leicester, and Derby was presented to Parliament. Their complaints included not only low wages, but certain practices connected with their trade. The owners of the frames demanded a weekly rent of from 3d. to 8d., which was 30 to 60 per cent. interest on the cost of the frame, to be paid whether the knitters worked or not. They requested Government supervision of the bargaining between employer and employed in an industry where they were at so grievous a disadvantage with those above them.[5] The full extent of their sufferings was not generally known until the report from the Commission on Frame-Work Knitters was published in 1845.[6] In this document of 1,053 pages the trade is exhaustively described.

Mrs. Tonna in *The Wrongs of Women*, presented the hardships of the hosiery workers at the time the Children's Commission made its report. Kate Clarke, a young lace-finisher, had gone to visit a stocking worker, whose labours she considered less irksome than hers.

"There amidst much dirt and misery she finds the stockener, a very pale-faced young woman, with exceedingly weak eyes, stretched out on a low bed. Kate inquires whether she is ill: 'No,' answers the other, 'not more ill than any other day; but after sitting all the week one's glad of a stretch. . . . I work at a neighbour's six doors off: he has four frames, one to himself, one for his wife, one for their daughter Betty, and t'other for me. We carry on the whole business in that house, as much as in the biggest shop or factory; for the family is large enough.' "

When Kate abuses her own trade the girl interrupts her.

" 'Don't be so foolish as to change to stockening at any rate. . . . You don't know what 'tis to sit tied by the legs, as it were, all day long, close beside men that have no manners nor decency, talking bad language, drinking and swearing, and maybe beating wife and child, with a stray stick for the 'prentice. . . . Why, Brown, and his wife, and Betty and I have frames, each one, and the stocking is wove upon it; the two smallest children wind the cotton, the two next to them sew the seams, and another one stretches them on the board, to put them into shape. The chevening is every bit the same, in its way, as your lace-running, only it blinds the eyes faster. We want a power of light, and it soon takes the sight away.'

" 'But there is more change, like,' persists Kate, 'more different things going on.'

" 'That doesn't make a difference to them concerned: it only crowds us more, and cramps us up. Every one must sit down in their own place, and no room to move from it. Talking don't answer: at least the man and woman that gets all the profit don't choose their workers to talk. Brown, like many more, takes holiday Mondays, and often Tuesdays, and drinks away a week's earnings; and we are made to work it out at the week's end.' "[7]

From such a passage one gets the essential conditions of the trade. Home workers, known as "bag hosiers," used frames worked by hand. Steam-worked frames were not introduced until 1846.[8] In 1845 the Commissioners found that women were employed at rotatory frames.[9] In one parish over one-third of the 200 frames were worked by women. Formerly few women had been employed in the frames. They had done spinning and hand-knitting. Women not strong enough to take a frame did seaming. The miner's wife in the story "The Miner's Daughters", in *Household Words*,[10] seamed stockings for a frame-work knitter. In 1844, when a census was taken showing the number of women in various industries, 10,140 women over 20 in Great Britain, 2,940 girls under 20 were employed in the hosiery trade, as compared with 32,870 men over 20 and 5,005 boys.[11] Men and women received the same rate of pay.[12] In 1833 wages for making cotton hose on single frames for a fifteen-hour working day (except Monday and Saturday) were 6s.; on the wide frames from 9s. to 13s. For making silk hose wages ranged from 9s. to 13s.[13] The figures given the next year are practically the same.[14] By 1845 they had sunk to 3s. or 4s. for half-hose knitting,[15] and even as low as 1s. 6d. and 1s. 2d. Footing was done chiefly by women and young persons. In the more difficult work, for the making of drawers and shirts, a mother and her children together made 10s. weekly, an unmarried woman 6s. 3d.[16] The falling off in piece-rates was assigned by the Commission to the fact that women received the same terms as men, and excessive competition had cut the pay. More women were then compelled to take frames because the wages of the husband were insufficient to support the family. After the introduction of steam-worked frames the old hand frames were used almost exclusively by women and children, who between 1846 and 1867 suffered hardships not surpassed in any other of the industries investigated by the Commission of 1862.[17]

Glove-making was closely associated with the hosiery trade, since gloves were made on similar frames.[18] Women called "cheveners" embroidered gloves and hose, work commonly bringing in 6s. weekly. The same unfair system of renting out frames existed in glove-making as in the hosiery.

In the lace trade, a factory industry by 1810, so far as the actual making of the lace was concerned,[19] Luddite riots had broken out in 1816.[20] In 1811 the lace-runners, who

embroidered the designs on the net, had combined for the purpose of raising wages, which then ranged from the average of
7s. to 12s. for ordinary work to 15s. and 21s. for expert. Their
organization has already been referred to under the discussion
of women's unions. In 1817-18 the poet Shelley, living at
Great Marlow, Buckinghamshire, learned of the misery of
the poor lace women. In moments stolen from his work on
The Revolt of Islam, he visited their damp, unhealthy cottages,
to the danger of his own health, his wife recorded, offered
what relief he could, and, with the canny sense with which
he is too seldom credited, distributed soldiers' blankets,
carefully stamped with his name to keep them from the pawn-
brokers. By 1843 much information was available about
women in this industry. Three closely printed columns in
Mrs. Tonna's *The Wrongs of Women*, under the division *The
Lace-Runners*, are devoted to a description of the factory and
the home division of this trade. The details agree in every
particular with the Government report of 1843,[21] and are
clearly presented. She wrote:

"The manufacture of the main fabric is carried on by machinery,
varying in some points. The machines that are worked by hand
are sometimes used singly, in separate houses; but more frequently
a small number are worked together in a house; while, in a few
cases, they are placed together in factories, to the number even of
fifty. . . . The work is carried on, very frequently, twenty out of
the twenty-four hours; and the labourers of all ages are consequently liable to be called for at all times of the day and night. It is
usual, towards the end of the week, to keep it on during the whole
night, to make up for time lost in the early part by idleness and
debauchery. . . .

"The machines propelled by steam-power cannot be thus worked
with, but must be attended to incessantly, while the engines are
going. But this usually commences at four in the morning, and
continues till twelve at night, making twenty hours of regular
work. . . . It is not uncommon in some factories to go on throughout the whole twenty-four hours, allowing one hour for cleansing
the engine and machinery. Two sets of men or lads are employed in
such cases, each party taking five or six hours at once, called a

'shift'; and thus every one has ten or twelve hours' work per diem."
She then went on to describe, taking great care to make all technical
expressions intelligible to women readers, the operations, such as the
winding of the bobbins and the process called "threading", which
were performed by women and children in the factories. The
bobbins "when wound, were placed in the 'carriages' which kept
them in place on the machines, and when so placed, the end of the
thread was passed through an eye in the carriage, which was thus
threaded."

This much quotation serves to indicate her method. She then
went on to show that after the bobbins were wound, many
of the women and child winders had to wait until the bobbins
were exhausted, and then take them out, refill them, and replace
them in the machines. Their employment was, accordingly,
irregular and spread over a long stretch of hours. Then in the
dressing and the finishing of the lace, which included examining
and mending the manufactured product, drawing out threads,
clipping, folding, winding, and carding, operations employing
a large number of women in the warehouses or their homes,
long hours were worked. Lace-running was done either in
the homes of the "mistresses" who employed girls to work
for them, or in the workers' own homes.[22] Kate Clarke,
the heroine of *The Lace-Runners*, was a cottage worker, a
stalwart young country girl, devoted to children and kind
to her mistress in her time of trouble. Her touching history
is a record of declining health, rebellion against ceaseless
toil with no exercise, her attempt to better her condition,
and her final ruin. The young "winder" who lodges in the
same house takes to drink. Mrs. Tonna, with her inevitable
gloom about industry, has to make her usual decision to
consign her pious workers to tuberculosis and an early grave,
and the more spirited ones to the public-house and the steep
paths of sin. There is no other course open to them.

According to the census report of 1844, in all the branches
of the lace industry in Great Britain there were 15,876 women
over 20 and 6,040 girls under 20, to compare with 5,373

men and 1,082 boys.[23] Early statistics for women's wages are incomplete.[24] In 1834 the average pay was from 5s. 1d. to 12s.[25] In 1843 lace-runners, by working 11 hours, earned 3s. 6d. weekly.[26] Some reported beginning their work at 4 a.m. or 6 a.m. and continuing it until 8 or 12 at night.

The most common complaints concerned the practice of the factories of delivering out work to lace mistresses, or distributing agents, often two or three gradations of them, who naturally got some of the profits that by a different system would have gone directly to the workers.[27] Wages had thus been much reduced and hours consequently lengthened. In Nottingham a petition was sent to the manufacturers protesting against the agent system, but nothing came of it.[28] Agents offered different prices for the same quality of work, Mrs. Tonna stated.[29] The "runners" were sometimes paid with poor bread and candles, the last a large item of expense, because of the long hours of nightwork.

For the relief of women and children who were virtually slaves in the lace districts, the passing of the Factory Act of 1861 regulated the trade so far as it was done by machinery. The cottage work was not included until the passing of the Workshops Act in 1867.

The similar conditions of work in frame-knitting and lace-finishing, irregular hours at the whim of those who hired the labour, the cramped position, the congestion of people in cottages without good light and often working late at night, resulted in indigestion, general debility, consumption, short sight, and blindness. Kate Clarke was changed, after a few months, from an active country girl into a broken-down wreck, misshaped and weak-eyed, unequal to a brisk walk.[30] Many a brief sentence in the reports chronicles blindness as the tragic end to a life of steady and honest toil.[31] The trades were overcrowded. Frauds in wages and the profits of the middleman kept the workers in the depths of poverty.

Pin-making, screw, steel and brass nail making,[32] chain-making, the manufacture of steel pens,[33] and of hooks and eyes all employed women, although the proportion of women and girls was small in most of these industries. In pin-making,[34] although the Government reports gave no uniform testimony about hours or pay,[35] a labouring day of from 12 to 14 hours brought wages averaging 6s. weekly for energetic young women. Pin-heading was a continuous occupation generally, one girl of 20 having headed pins for 13 years. Overlookers, with large numbers of children under them, were generally women, and complaints of their cruel treatment were frequent. In the chapter "The Little Pin-headers", in Mrs. Tonna's *The Wrongs of Women*, the employer of the Smith children is a female monster of gigantic proportions.

Mrs. Tonna represents conditions in the screw factories which are not borne out by the Government reports,[36] at least so far as the prevalence of female labour is concerned. She introduces into *The Wrongs of Women* a country labourer forced into the town to look for work and trying to get a place in a screw factory.

"Not above one in ten of the artisans is a man; women of all ages are stationed among the machinery pursuing their avocation, and in the midst of what Smith regarded as frightful dangers; for the straps crossing in every direction close over his head, and moving swift as lightning in all parts of the room, with wheels whirring, shafts revolving, and horizontal stones flying round at a terrific rate, while the clang of a hundred hammers going at once salutes his ear; these things almost paralyse the astonished rustic, who has never before witnessed such a complication of machinery, never heard such a terrible discord of noises, nor even imagined their possible existence."

The husband was told that there was no work for him, but that his wife could easily find employment.

" 'Why should not your wife do the same as other women?' the foreman asked him. . . . 'Why, here are mothers of six or eight children working all day, as merry as larks, and none the worse for their industry. I say, Betty,' tapping a woman near him on the shoulder, 'do you find yourself the worse in health for your work here?'

" 'No, sir, I don't; I'm very well off, and makes no complaints.'

" While she spoke, Smith, noticing some dirty rags wrapped round her fingers, observes she seems to have got a hurt.

" 'No, I ain't; these bits keep my knuckles from the stones: nobody need be hurt that can take care of their own fingers.' "

Alice Smith was finally hired to "worm" screws. "Her business was to apply each screw, already fashioned out, to a machine which, with a very rapid motion, cuts the worm round it. This requires great care, as nothing can stop the revolutions of the engine, and a slight degree even of tremor will bring the fingers into contact with the whirling steel, cutting, bruising, and perhaps crushing the hand."[37]

Articles in *Household Words*, with the same excellence of exposition as Mrs. Tonna shows in the above passage, have a similar tendency to exaggerate the importance of women in certain industries. Harriet Martineau in *The Wonders of Nails and Screws* described a visit to a factory. She was informed that women were preferred to boys for snipping off the screws at the proper length, because they were more steady and careful. They polished and "nicked" the heads of the screws and also "wormed" and packed screws. Their pay ranged from 5s. to 12s. weekly. They appeared healthy and were neatly dressed. The article closed with Miss Martineau's characteristic sermonistic note, a warning to the workers to have "no screw loose in their household ways".[38]

Another article in *Household Words*[39] described the work of women in the foundries.[40] Many passed their lives in sorting patterns as they came in from the casting. Burnishing, where there was a somewhat larger proportion of women, according to the statistics,[41] was also done by women, but this the writer considered too hard for them. In the lacquering department, although they worked in a noisome atmosphere and in terrific heat, women earned good wages. "The demand for female handiwork," added the author, "in Birmingham has so increased, that women's wages have risen lately about 20 per cent." Some women were earning 11s. per week. In another Birmingham sketch in the same magazine,[42] "An Account of Some Treatment of Gold and Gems", the employment of women at cutting, piercing, and snipping machines, seated in a quiet warm workroom, was represented as one of the better classes of labour.

Match-making, earlier investigated by the Children's Commission,[43] was described in *Household Words* as easily the worst labour for women.[44] A girl of 20, employed in a match factory from the age of 9, worked in a small establishment of two rooms with poor ventilation. After four years she began suffering with toothache. Her clothes, full of phosphorus, glowed on her chair when she took them off at night. Her hands and arms glowed. Her lower jaw had been eaten away, and there were two or three holes in the side of her mouth. Another girl of 23 had formerly sorted matches after they were dipped and dried. She had had five operations, and her under jaw was nearly gone. The shape of her face was destroyed, and she had to live on soft food. At the time her case was reported she was making boxes to be away from the fumes. The Government reports contain the same almost unbelievable facts about match factories in this earlier period. A good system of ventilation and education in the precautions of washing would have removed some of the danger.

In a great variety of occupations employing women the Government investigations are chiefly valuable as a revelation of their scattered activities.

Fustian cutting, the cutting of cotton-velvets, velveteens, or corduroy, was a trade followed at irregular hours from 3 a.m. or 4 a.m. until 9 p.m. or 10 p.m., sometimes with periods of idleness following.[45] Mary Higgins in *North and South*, whom her sister Bessy had tried to save from a cotton factory, was a fustian cutter. In the glass and the lead works unskilled work was done by women. Washing and polishing glass from 6 a.m. to 6 p.m. brought from 14s. to 20s. a week,[46] an unusually large wage in comparison with the lace and the hosiery trades. The rooms in which the polishing was done were without fresh air, because dust was injurious to the polishing process. In a plate-glass works in Newcastle the employer reported the women "bad to manage". Whether the absence of fresh air or the relatively good wages contributed to this unregeneracy one cannot decide. Glass-polishing may have attracted the Amazon worker who did not lack man's physical advantages to defend her rights. Since none of the women in any of the glass works were called as witnesses, their complaints were unregistered.[47] *Household Words* in "Plate Glass"[48] gave an account of a visit to a glass works. In the "smoothing" of the glass done by women emery was used, but the slippery surfaces were also rubbed over each other. At this period polishing was done by machinery instead of by hand. In the lead works[50] women carried loads of 56 pounds. They worked from 6 a.m. to 6 p.m., with $1\frac{1}{2}$ hours for meals, in an atmosphere choked with the dust of dry white lead, and earned as much as 10s. weekly. In the button factories in Birmingham, with hours similar to those in the glass and lead plants, women could earn 6s. weekly.[51] The drilling of the pearl buttons was especially complained of because of the dust. *Household Words* has a very interesting description of button-making in "What There is In a Button".[52] Hundreds of women worked at machines for punching, drilling, stamping, and polishing the buttons. Rows of them sat at their machines, the head of the machine in the right hand, a sheet of iron, brass, or copper in the other, and punched out the circles. The piercing of the button with four holes was performed by a woman operator at the rate of 15 gross per hour. In the making of silk-covered buttons the chalking of the circles was done by machines operated by women; a second machine stamped out the chalked bit. A woman could cover dozens of buttons in a minute. In one plant employing three or four hundred people nearly all were women and children. Few men were employed, except in the silvering and burnishing departments. A woman in her own home, assisted by children, tacked the buttons on stiff paper at the rate of 40 gross per day.[53]

The information collected by the Commissioners concerning the girls and women employed in rope-making, earthenware manufacture, willow-weaving, the cleaning of files, the making of tin toys, japanning, bridle-stitching, lint-scraping, tambouring (the making of flowers on lace for women's veils), is too unsatisfactory to be of much value. Miss Flite, the unfortunate victim of Chancery in *Bleak House* (1852–53), had done tambour work,[54] and Judy Smallweed, in the same novel, the disagreeable granddaughter of a disagreeable grandfather, was "apprenticed to the art and mystery of flower-making".[55] *Household Words*, however, contains descriptions of these complicated trades written by eyewitnesses. In "Birmingham Glass Works",[56] girls as assistants to potmakers were watched by the writer as they moulded masses of clay into sausage-like rolls. They also assisted the potter at his wheel and dropped colour on the patterns.[57] In boxmaking they were gluers and also operated machinery.[58] In pottery, women were unimportant until the introduction of machinery after 1845.[59] Before that date they were merely helpers, receiving no share of the funds distributed by the unions in the great strike of 1836.[60] By 1845 the potters' unions were expostulating with the women employed for the first time on the new flat-press machinery, and warning them that machinery was their deadliest enemy.[61] With the widespread use of machines the percentage of women rose to nearly half,[62] and the character of their occupation became rougher and rougher, with consequent moral and physical deterioration. But this part of the history of pottery belongs to the years after 1850, with the 'seventies and 'nineties witnessing the darkest developments.[63]

In all of the employments open to women connected with the book trade, the labour in the paper mills was the lowest.[64] In the rag-rooms, where the dust and the foul atmosphere were especially annoying, and in the glazing and the sorting departments, women earned from 2s. to 4s. weekly for a working day from 6 to 6 either day or night.[65] Harriet Martineau's article in *Household Words* was more cheerful than the Government report.[66] She stated that the paper-mill workers were thriving, and the women seated at tables shredding rags with knives and working in the boiling-room and the cutting-room were not represented as objects for pity. Dickens in *Our Mutual Friend* (1864–65) described Lizzie Hexam as happy and satisfied while she was employed in a paper mill, and he gave an idyllic picture of the mill and the released workers.[67]

"The Paper Mill had stopped work for the night, and the paths and roads in its neighbourhood were sprinkled with clusters of people going home from their day's labour in it. There were men, women, and children in the groups, and there was no want of lively colour to flutter in the gentle evening wind. The mingling of various voices and the sound of laughter made a cheerful impression upon the ear, analogous to that of the fluttering colours upon the eye."

Lizzie says of her work: "I live here peacefully and respected, and I am well employed here." Dickens emphasized the social stigma cast upon her as a working girl, however, although the surprising circumstance that a paper mill had a somewhat higher status than a cotton factory, perhaps on account of its comparative escape from publicity, could be read into Lightwood's quick answer to Podsnap, who had asked him if Lizzie Hexam were not a factory girl. "Never", was the answer. "But she had some employment in a paper mill, I believe." *Bradshaw's Manchester Journal* repeated Miss Martineau's picture.[68] The women sorting cotton-waste were represented as dirty, but not unhealthy. An illustration showing the dusting machine with two women at work on either side was reproduced in the journal. Women were also reported to be employed examining the paper sent in from the cutting machine. Nothing about hours or the variety of work open to women was given by the writer.

In the book-binding trade—the aristocracy of labour for women—girls, generally apprenticed between the ages of 15 and 18 for a period of 9 months, were taught stitching, sewing, and folding.[69] In many establishments the girl apprentices paid a premium for instruction, but in others they

earned a small sum, about 1s. 6d. weekly. Journeywomen
earned from 10s. to 15s. weekly, and at the end of the apprenticeship, 20s. Although in the best shops the apprentices were
well instructed, and did not work more than from 9 a.m. to
8 p.m., in others the women interviewed by the Commissioners
complained that in busy times girl apprentices worked until
10 and 12 every night, and even up to 3 and 4 in the morning.
Their more common grievance was that they were taught
only part of the trade, so that when they left the shop where
they had been apprenticed, they often had to learn the business
afterward in another place, if they wanted employment.[70] In
the first union of book-binders, founded in 1779–80, and known
as "The Friends", women were not members, although they
were employed as folders and sewers.[71] In a strike in 1786
the women continued at work. Before 1806, although the
afternoon tea half-hour was the exclusive privilege of the
women, the men were generally presented with a surrep-
titious cup. In 1806, encouraged by the women, they demanded
a similar right, which was eventually secured. In a dispute
in 1834 a charge was brought against the British and Foreign
Bible Society, which had caused a drop in wages by bringing
down its prices. A similar charge had been brought against
the Society for Promoting Christian Knowledge in 1825. In the
strike which resulted, the sufferings of the women were particularly emphasized by the men's union. Two hundred women
employed in binding books for the Society were represented
as paid wages so reduced that they could no longer earn an
honest living. In 1845 the struggle was renewed, and on the
advice of the men's union the women left work. The strike,
although it eventually failed, showed the friendly co-operation
of the men, whom the strike cost £146; and the women's
leader, Mary Zugg, was one of the first women to show an
understanding of the necessity for organized effort among
women workers. The women did not form a union of their
own, however, nor did they become members of the men's
organization. In 1874, under Mrs. Emma Patterson, women

book-binders formed their own society, but it has never been a force in trade disputes.

In printing, women were employed as early as the end of the fifteenth century as compositors.[72] In the United States a woman, Mary Catherine Goddard, printed the first issue of the Declaration of Independence. In England Thomas Beddoes gave his *Alexander's Expedition* to a woman of his village, Madely, to set up. In the advertisement of the book he wrote: "I know not if women be commonly engaged in printing, but their nimble and delicate fingers seem extremely well adapted to the office of compositor, and it will be readily granted that employment for females is amongst the greatest desiderata of society." During the period of investigation, unfortunately, no advance was made by women in the printing trade. Miss Emily Faithfull's Victoria Press, in which women only were employed, was not founded until 1860.

In all of this confusing array of occupations, one gets an overwhelming impression of the bulk of unskilled, poorly paid labour which fell to the share of women. The information collected by the Commissioners[73] is a detailed record of unsanitary working conditions, dark workshops, bad air, and the lack of safety devices. But by this time they, unlike the factory investigators of the early commissions, recognized the woman worker as a special problem. They found that the darkest and the most badly ventilated shops were assigned to women, and that long hours and poor pay were their portion in practically every trade.

2. HER SOCIAL LIFE

Not only was the economic condition of the non-textile workers far below that of the factory hands. Housing conditions, bad housekeeping and extravagance, the neglect of children, and the heavy death-rate repeat information given in an earlier chapter. Because wages were lower, social evils were far worse than among the textile workers.

To the exposure of moral conditions the Government investigators gave much anxious thought. The prostitution of young girls, the general immorality, the drunkenness, and the use of laudanum among women were described by a variety of witnesses. A chemist testified that some of his customers used an ounce of laudanum daily.[74] The Superintendent of Police in Birmingham ranked the girls in the button factories with those in the screw and pen factories as notorious thieves,[75] and he stated that girl prostitutes of 13, 14, and 15, encouraged by the awful conditions in the lodging-houses, were recruited from these young workers. In a Birmingham lodging-house an inspector reported that in the same room two men slept in one bed, two young women in the second, a man and a woman in the third, and two or three children in the fourth. An article in the *Westminster Review*[76] gives a mass of sickening detail which proves conclusively that Victorian respectability had its moments of dark revelation; at least, the section of it subscribing to the radical journals. In the homes of the workers a whole family slept in a single bedroom.[77] A pen manufacturer, advised to place a respectable older woman in charge of the morals of the girls in his employ, retorted that he would be willing, if he could find such a woman among his work-people.[78] The testimony of an Independent minister in Birmingham was that early marriages were common. Equally common was the practice of young men under 21 keeping girls with whom they lived in irregular unions, the association formed often, according to the witness, in the first place in the workshop.[79] In a district where the girls were employed in the manufacture of gun-locks, hinges, stirrups, files, buttons, and screws, some of them worked to support three and four illegitimate children.[80] They drank and smoked, but life was harder for them than for the men they tried to imitate. Of this class of workers, Disraeli wrote in *Sybil*:

"There are great bodies of the working classes of this country nearer the condition of brutes than they have been at any time since the Conquest. Indeed, I see nothing to distinguish them from brutes, except that their morals are inferior. Incest and infanticide are as common among them as among the lower animals. The domestic principle wanes weaker and weaker every year in England."[81]

Other evidence, notably that of R. H. Horner, the inspector, told a somewhat different story. In describing the Wolver-hampton ironworks, he testified that although young men and girls walked about the streets together and entered the public-houses, very few of the girls became the victims of the streets and the number of illegitimate children was small. His explanation for this latter condition was not, however, the usual one. The confinement and the nature of the employ-ment retarded puberty, so that boys and girls of 14 and 15 looked like children of 11, 12, and 13.[82] His final conclusion is worth quoting:

"I do not consider them to possess any moral restraints; but that poorness of diet, poverty of blood, and constant exhaustion, or at least fatigue from constant work, leaves them neither time, nor inclination, nor stamina, for the excitement of the imagination and the senses. There is a balance maintained by nature even where all seems evil. They are protected by their injuries."

A clergyman told the inspectors:

"You will find poor girls who have never sung or danced; never seen a dance; never seen a violet, or a primrose, and other flowers; and others whose only idea of a green field was derived from having been stung by a nettle."[83]

In the midst of this degradation a primitive Methodism was found to flourish; the Ranters, fanatical and noisy, with preachers recruited from the ranks of miners, endowed with a picturesque gift for conjuring up terrible visions of Hell.[84] In one of the meeting-houses a kind of morality play was given, in which a boy represented Justice, a girl Mercy, and a boy the victim brought for trial. Religious drama could

easily have been used more extensively with powerful effect
among people of such universal ignorance. The chapels were
often densely crowded. Many new churches were beginning
to be built to offset the influence of the gin-palaces.[85]

In the various attempts made to explain the widespread
degradation, resulting in conclusions repeating those made for
textile workers, the menace of ignorance, worse among girls
even than boys, was powerfully presented.[86] Sue, the file
worker in *Sybil*, with a back like a grasshopper from her
cramped occupation, married without a religious ceremony
to an apprentice-boy who did not know his own name,
boasted of her young husband, who believed "in our Lord
and Saviour Pontius Pilate, who was crucified to save our
sins; and in Moses, Goliath, and the rest of the Apostles".[87]
Such a passage is proof enough that Disraeli read the Government Blue books, which were full of similar proofs of
ignorance. In trades where wages were far lower than in
textiles the temptation to thievery and prostitution was
correspondingly stronger. Hard work which brought as its
reward 3s. or 4s. weekly was not encouraging to virtue. The
conditions under which girls toiled often invited evil. Girl
nail workers, the *Edinburgh Review*[88] pointed out, laboured in
scanty clothing in crowded shops. Women metal workers
in Birmingham were herded together in dilapidated buildings,
with dark narrow windows. In the screw factories the tool-
setters could keep women at piece work waiting for their
tools, and workmen of bad character had used this circumstance
to victimize the women.[89]

Mrs. Tonna, writing of the screw worker in *The Forsaken
Home*, devoted much of the story to the tragedy of a home in
which the mother had to support her husband and her children.[90]
Alice Smith, an unusually high type of woman, was a faithful
wife and mother before she became worsted in a struggle to
take care of her home in addition to the burden of supporting
both her husband and her children. Her husband changed
rapidly from a decent and industrious farm labourer to a town

idler, took to drink, her children ran wild, and out of her pay of 9s. a week she failed to keep her household going. Involved in debt, hampered in her efficiency by a tool-setter, who afterward misrepresented her uprightness, watching her baby die because she could not take care of him, she sank first into degradation and then into her grave. Of such a tragedy the author concluded:

"Now, where is the English lady who, on reading these simple statements, will rest satisfied with merely expressing her grief and abhorrence at such inhuman wrong inflicted on her poverty-stricken countrywomen, and make no effort towards removing the burden of cruelty and crime? . . . There can be no compromise of our duty, no loophole of escape from the condemnation that overhangs us if we rouse not ourselves without delay. We may prepare and dispatch missionaries to every corner of the world; we may shower Bibles like hail over earth's wide surface; we may exhibit in our own conduct and conversation a very model of all that Christian women ought to be; but this one thing God requires of us, and will not acquit us if we refuse to do it, whatever worthy deeds we may choose to do, that we enter our strong, urgent, unanimous protest against the frightful degradation of our sisters, and demand from those who have the power to accord it the boon of their emancipation."[91]

Mrs. Tonna looked to the Queen to take the lead in putting an end to the unrestricted toil of women.

"How sweetly will it become a youthful Queen of England to say, with the confidence of one who knows she may be absolute where God's word is unquestionably confirming the decree, 'Throughout my realm female slavery shall cease'."

But neither the Queen nor the ladies of England did anything. In Victoria's reign manufacturers no longer bowed before the throne as in a fairy-tale. Nor did the husbands of tender-hearted wives reading Mrs. Tonna's stirring words bow before ladies, where business was concerned. Even if both queens and ladies had possessed the magical powers which the earnest editress of the *Christian Lady's Magazine* attributed to them, they might have been bewildered as to what they were to do. The wisest men in England could not agree on any definite action.

3. Attempts at Reform

In all debates upon the "sufferings of women crowded into the rough labour investigated by the Commissioners, troubled reformers were invariably convinced that woman's place was in the home. They were unable to approach the subject without sentiment. Harriet Martineau was one of the few writers, the only woman writer in fact, who viewed the question of women's employment with the necessary scientific detachment. In visiting the various industrial plants she looked for the violation of principles of political economy as a partial explanation for the difficulties of women as workers. In the ribbon factories, an industry Thackeray. introduced into the pages of *Pendennis* to reveal the social complexity of Pendennis's native Clavering and the rude provincialism of the factory workers,[92] Miss Martineau saw whole families overcrowding ribbon-weaving, to the detriment of the scale of wages. She prophesied that what had already happened to ruin the lace workers in Nottingham and the hosiery slaves in Leicester would be repeated here.[93] She also observed the discrimination the men used against the women in the ribbon factories. They were not allowed in the dye-house nor could they make pattern-cards and -books, in which the delicate matching of colour would be an operation peculiarly suited to the capability of women. Similarly,[94] the watch-makers in Coventry would not permit the employment of their wives and daughters in their trade, although they had no objection to their working in the factories. One woman, the object of Miss Martineau's unstinted praise, insisted upon engraving the interior of watches at home, and she taught her daughters engraving. But in all this it would seem that Miss Martineau was blaming workers for the wisdom the ribbon-weavers lacked. The exact adjustment she preached is more difficult than her sure-footed opinions would lead one to suspect.

In the establishment of the Government School of Design the author of the political economy tales also observed an opportunity for women. In 1837 the school was opened in Somerset House, London, as a national institution. With the development of industry the Government, long aware that artists from France and other countries were imported to sketch designs and make patterns for printed cloth, wall-paper, pottery, at last had the wisdom to train English workers. The provision in the original plan was that applicants fifteen years of age or more should receive instruction in morning and evening classes with the nominal fee of 2s. a month.[95] Many of the students were employed in factories during the day. By 1850 there were eighteen branch schools in England, Scotland, and Ireland.

In London the school for women was moved from Somerset House to quarters across the street in the Strand. Miss Martineau discovered the place over a sponge and soap shop, which, as she described it, lacked all the facilities for efficient work.[96] The rooms were hot, close, and badly lighted, the windows dusty, and the students so crowded together that their shoulders were touching. Some of the girls worked in an attic above the regular room. In spite of the discomfort, which resulted in headaches and aching eyes, good work had been done. Seventy students were enrolled here in 1851, the year Miss Martineau visited the institution. Government reports verify her description.[97] Medical advisers had condemned the rooms. An equally serious disadvantage was the insufficient number of teachers.

The opening of the school to women had promised a new field of work for their restricted energies. The Commissioners in their report wrote:

"It is to be hoped that the opportunity of obtaining an education in industrial art will widen the limits of female occupation, the restriction of which, compared with the various employments exercised by females in France in connection with ornamental manufacture, is a reproach to the country."[98]

This praiseworthy missionary programme was too visionary for the middle of the nineteenth century. The women had no chance against the men.[99] In Sheffield no female class and no prospect of any was reported.[100] There was general difficulty in establishing such classes, probably with good reason, since women soon discovered that restrictions were placed on the employment of women designers in various industrial plants. In the London school numerous prizes were given to men entering the competitions. Only one prize was open to women competitors. The jealousy of the men was a serious obstacle. In the pottery schools at Stoke and Hanley, where 170 men and 35 women attended classes, the regulations against the employment of women in the manufacture of pottery discouraged them in learning designing. The Government official studying the whole question could see no hope of better employment for women in the potteries until "the young men now receiving their education in the school have displaced the existing generation of operatives, and with them some of their habits and prejudices".[101] In Birmingham,[102] where the pupils were entered in the school by a system of nomination by the Society of Arts, most of the nominations were in favour of the men. Women in the plants did nothing but burnishing. For the better class of factory women for whom such classes would offer a chance of rising to a skilled occupation, there was no evening class. "It is to be wished", wrote the inspector, "that the school might have the effect of extending in favour of females the employments in which their taste and skill might be advantageously brought into action."

Encouragement, in some few cases, was given to women. "A noble visitor" to the London school presented the sum of ten guineas to be distributed in prizes to the female classes on the prize day.[103] A prominent manufacturer was quoted as favouring the lifting of all discriminations against women in work for which taste and skill fitted them. The Government officers expressed themselves strongly on the subject of opening more occupations to women. In some of the schools favourable signs were recorded. In York the female class increased from 26 to 31; in the same year the male class fell from 73 to 51.[104] One of the women, who became a teacher in Leeds after she finished her course, had published a botanical work with coloured lithographic engravings.[105]

For their lack of improvement the women were themselves sometimes to blame. A teacher in the York school complained of the difficulty of keeping the girls to elementary study. Their ambition was to draw the figure, although few proceeded beyond the heads. Not many pupils attended to ornament.[104] It was equally true that the men suffered some of the same handicaps. A scheme started so that pupils in Government schools should be taken on as pupils to designers in the factories had not materialized.[106] In Manchester the manufacturers had been slow in co-operating, although skilled native designers would have been a distinct advantage to them. With all its shortcomings, the beginning made by the School of Design in opening a new profession to women held out some future for the working woman.

An article in *Household Words*, "More Work for the Ladies",[107] indicated other possibilities of employment. In France women sold tickets at the railroad stations and were telegraphers. The widows of sailors and fishermen inspected baggage at the ports. Women were auctioneers, acted as box-openers and attendants at the opera and the theatres. They sold milk and general produce. All of this varied activity was healthier and more suitable for females than the degrading labour in the workshops of industrial England.

For relief in the great mass of toil reviewed in this chapter, neither the findings of the Commission nor the force of public opinion compelled Parliament to pass corrective legislation. In small works the difficulty of enforcing laws made hope of reform by such means more remote than in the cotton mills. Happily many of the employers in plants where the workers were dependent upon their good will, rather than upon new laws, were keenly interested in the welfare of their "hands", and made provision for the safeguarding of women and girls. Men and women were assigned to different shops. Only married men of good character were given places as tool-setters. One screw manufacturer, employing 60 men and 300 women, reported to be a good master by his workers, showed a creditable care for the women he employed, encouraging neatness of dress and regarding their general welfare.[108]

Price's Patent Candle Company in London set aside the sum of £900 per annum to maintain an educational system in connection with the factory. A chapel for the workers was attended by three or four hundred every Sunday. The rooms in which the girls worked were cheerful and pleasant. At a meeting of the proprietors at London Tavern, Bishopsgate, March 24, 1852, the following resolution was passed:

"It is said—you must all have frequently heard it—that Joint Stock companies have no consciences. Let this Company prove itself an exception to any such rule by acting towards its factory 'hands' as not forgetting that those 'hands' have human hearts and immortal souls."[109]

The employers, widely criticized because of their lack of a feeling of responsibility toward their work-people, seem to have roused themselves, as the period advanced beyond 1850, to remarkable effort, not only in the textile mills, but in all classes of manufacturing.

Religious agencies also began to do more effective work in raising mental and moral standards.[110] The Anglican clergy, the Dissenting ministers, and Catholic priests saw the necessity for educating the youth in their congregations, but even when they could get the children into Sunday schools they were unable to accomplish much. After an attendance of three or four years many could not read or write. The teachers in the Church and the Roman Catholic schools were educated and generally superior to those in the Dissenters' Sunday schools, where uneducated working men too often took charge of the instruction. The National and the British schools, where free education was provided, were ineffective, not only because the teachers were poor, but because the children were removed before they had received any benefit from the instruction offered.

Relief for these workers by legislation was still hoped for. The Commission of 1862, appointed at the recommendation of Lord Shaftesbury, sat for about five years and issued reports dealing with a large number of industries. The Act of 1864 and the Workshops Act of 1867, which went farther in their power over small industries and homework, corrected some of the most glaring abuses endured by women. In much of this labour, however, although legislation could shorten hours and provide some health protection, in the lead, the china, and the pottery works, in the manufacture of phosphorus matches, the deadly nature of such employment has prevented reform. Mrs. C. Mallet in *Dangerous Trades for Women* (1893) described the common tragedies of many trades. Mrs. Annie Besant had been a pioneer in organizing girls in the match factories, in getting shorter hours for them, and more sanitary working conditions. The difficulty of enforcing laws in small works continued. It was only in 1909 that the establishment of Trade Boards fixing a minimum wage for workers in badly paid industries such as chain-making, lace-making, box-making, and similar labour, secured effective legislation for women. The real history of women in non-textile industries, then, belongs in small part only to this study. A certain publicity was accomplished, but no victories, like those for textile workers, can be chronicled.

4. LITERARY TREATMENT OF THE NON-TEXTILE WORKER

From the combined material dealing with textile and non-textile employments for women one gets a wide view of the new life which followed the Industrial Revolution and also

the manifold activities of women. But non-textile workers
are even more scantily represented in literature than those
in the textile trades, and largely for the same reasons. They
offered more difficult technical problems to the author, their
lives were equally barren of romantic interest, and were more
completely hidden from public scrutiny. They were in greater
need of literary defenders, however, for Parliament was unable
to assist them. The same up-to-date writers who made general
reference to the factories introduced into their stories characters who toiled in the paper mills and screw factories, who
were fustian cutters, makers of artificial flowers, and tambour
workers; but almost none went farther. Journalists who wrote
technical articles for *Household Words* made extensive expedi-
tions to industrial plants to collect facts and to study manufacturing processes, but the novelists made almost no use
of such material. Disraeli contributed the excellent realistic
study of Sue, the file worker in *Sybil*, but unfortunately
subordinated it to much less worthy matter. Here again
Charlotte Elizabeth Tonna, by her persistent reading of
Government reports, laboured to penetrate the underground
life of thousands of women hidden away in small and dirty
shops. Her exhaustive treatment of so large a body of employment, unknown perhaps to all contemporary women but
Harriet Martineau, demonstrates both industry and comprehension. That she was unable to make artistic use of so bulky
a mass of fact is less to be noted than that she could use it at
all. Other novelists were either ignorant of this industrial
chaos or were unequal to the task of handling it in fiction.
In *The Wrongs of Women*, dealing with the non-textile trades,
she is the historian of the new working woman who emerged
after the Industrial Revolution. Her limitations in interpretation and reform mean little to the student who is primarily
concerned with her reliability as to fact and her sympathy.
She gave life to the dead pages of Government documents
and forced her contemporaries to a consciousness of a largely
unknown class of women workers.

CHAPTER IV

THE DRESSMAKER

1. Her Introduction to the Victorian Public

The needle is an even more primitive instrument of women's toil than the spinning-wheel. Yet between the days when fish-bone, bone, or ivory was used to fashion the skins of animals or rude fabrics into clothing, and the age when the domestic manufacture of steel needles planted in Worcestershire and Warwickshire towns by the Germans was developed into one of the great machine industries, stretched a period of obscurity for the English women who wielded the needle. As civilization increased its importance, sewing-women were more fre-quently mentioned in literary annals. In *Piers Plowman* they appeared as fine ladies using the needle for charity.

> "And ye, lovely ladies with your long fingers
> That have silk and sendel, sew when you have time
> Chasubles for chaplains and churches to honour"
>
> (p. 194).

But humble seamstresses toiled hard to support themselves. Tibet in *Ralph Roister Doister* (ea. 1553) plied her needle busily. Jane in Dekker's *Shoemaker's Holiday* (1600) worked in a seamster's shop making "fine cambricke shirts and bands". Little is known of the conditions of life endured by these workers. In the middle of the seventeenth century sewing-girls were bound as apprentices for a term of seven years, but the exact terms of their hire have not been ascertained.[1] There was no trace of organizations existing in any of the skilled trades followed by women, such as upholstery, millinery, mantua-making, in these early years.

But by 1833 dressmakers, like other working women, began to excite public notice. In the midst of the discussion over factory legislation came discontented grumblings that workers in cotton mills were no worse off than those in other branches

of industry.[2] They were found to be healthier than milliners
and other labourers.[3] Milliners and dressmakers, investigation
showed, worked from 4 a.m. to 10 p.m.; in some cases until
midnight.[4] Finally the inquiries of the Children's Commission
in 1843 not only informed the public of the sufferings of non-
textile workers, reviewed in the preceding chapter, but also
of the hardships endured by milliners and dressmakers in the
provincial towns and in London.

In millinery and dressmaking, millinery including mantua-
making and often not clearly distinguished from dressmaking
at this time, a large number of women and young girls worked.
In both trades the census of 1841 showed that in Great Britain
there were 84,064 women over 20, and 22,174 under 20.[5]
They represented more varied social classes than factory
women. The majority were girls from the country, apprenticed to the owner of a shop, like Ann and Frances King in
Mrs. Tonna's *The Wrongs of Women*. Others, like Mary Barton,
were the daughters of mill workers who were unwilling that
their children should work in the factory. Some were of
gentle birth and well educated.[6] Lord Ashley stated that the
daughters of poor clergymen and Nonconformist ministers,
half-pay officers, or tradesmen who had suffered reverses, were
crowded into these trades. Ruth Hilton in Mrs. Gaskell's *Ruth*
was the daughter of a poor curate. Kate Nickleby was the
orphan child of a ruined father. The most casual examination
of the fiction during the period under investigation gives the
impression that many a heroine took to her needle when she
was forced to support herself. When Jane Eyre ran away
from Mr. Rochester, she tried to get work first as a dressmaker, then as a plain sewer, and finally as a servant. Maggie
Tulliver said of herself: "Plain sewing was the only thing
I could get money by."[7] Even without the evidence of Government Blue books, the frequent appearance of dressmakers in
fiction gives the suspicion that they were more numerous in
real life. Meg in *The Chimes* did embroidering. The heroine of
Mrs. Gaskell's tale, *Libbie Marsh's Three Eras*, sewed at home.

Miss Flinder in *The Newcomes* was a dressmaker; Miss Minnifer in *Pendennis* kept a millinery shop. Miss Betsy Barker and her sister, the milliners in *Cranford*, invested their savings in an exclusive shop where they sold caps and ribbons to any one with a pedigree.

2. THE WORKING LIFE OF THE DRESSMAKER'S APPRENTICE

When the Children's Commission undertook the investigation of dressmaking and millinery, it was the girl apprentices upon whom they directed most of their attention. These workers were little removed in age from the children who had roused a sentimental public to the necessity of Government interference, and they were equally in need of help, since they endured conditions in some respects even worse than those of the factory women who had already received attention from Parliament. Detailed accounts of the regulations governing the apprentice system were given in their reports and corroborated by the testimony of Members of Parliament and various novelists. Indoor apprentices bound for two or three years, boarded and lodged during the period of their apprenticeship, paid a premium of £50 to £60.[8] This premium, however, was computed with lower figures by John Bright, who in a speech in Parliament cited the case of a girl of seventeen paying a premium of £40 for a three-year apprenticeship.[9] As high as sixty guineas was paid, according to the figure of an article on "Milliners' Apprentices".[10] Ruth Hilton was bound for five years. Little Emily, apprenticed to Omer and Joram for three, had accommodating employers who were willing to cancel her articles if she wanted to marry. Outdoor apprentices, who lived at home, paid no premium and received no salary.[12] Mary Barton at sixteen, although she could not enter any of the best shops in Manchester where high premiums were charged, became an outdoor apprentice at Miss Simmonds's establishment, where she worked for two years without pay and brought her meals with her.[13] A girl of good

appearance was often employed as a show-woman in the best
shops. Mary Barton could have been employed in this way if
her father had taken her with him when he made a round of
the dressmaking establishments. Ralph Nickleby found such
occupation for his niece Kate at Madame Mantalini's, where
in spite of the fact that she had to endure the rude stares of
ill-bred customers, she met conditions far more favourable
than either the reports or other novels show.[14] Improvers,
girls who had already learned part of the business in the
country, often came to London for the last part of their
training, served a further apprenticeship of one or two years,
were lodged and boarded, and paid a premium. Ann King
was an improver, bound for three years, and paying a £30
premium.[15] If a girl were unable to serve the full period of her
apprenticeship, no part of the premium was refunded. The
poor farmer in Mrs. Tonna's book, ambitious to settle his two
daughters advantageously in a good trade, paid large premiums
out of his scanty resources. Ann broke down in health after a
year in a London millinery shop, and the younger girl, through
a quarrel with her mistress, had her indentures cancelled
within six months of their expiration, so that she could not be
taken into another shop; but the father received no refund.[16]
In addition to the apprentices and the improvers, a number of
journeywomen were engaged in the London shops for the
busy seasons. There was frequent complaint that, in spite
of the payment of a heavy premium, girls often failed to learn
the trade to which they were bound. They were kept at plain
work and taught only part of the business.[17] Frances King
spent most of her time matching silks and serving as
general errand girl, so that after two years she had learned
nothing.[18] Mary Barton and Ruth Hilton performed the same
services.

The investigations concerning hours were closely connected
with the rush of work during the two London seasons from
April to July or August 1st, and again from October to
Christmas. In the country towns local festivities, such as the

hunt ball in *Ruth*, brought about the same result. Mr. R. D. Grainger, the Government inspector, found that girl apprentices began work at five or six in the morning and continued sometimes until two or three the next morning.[19] In other cases the working day lasted from four in the morning until midnight. Some witnesses testified that for three months they had worked twenty hours out of the twenty-four. Many girls had only two hours of sleep for months together. One witness, a milliner, Miss H. Baker, worked from 4 a.m. on Thursday until ten-thirty Sunday morning because of orders for the general mourning at the death of William IV.[20] A girl of seventeen, on account of an order for general mourning, did not change her dress for nine days or nights. She rested on a mattress on the floor; her food was cut up and placed beside her so that she could sew while she ate. As a result she lost her sight.[21] In some places the apprentices worked on Sundays. In others they were kept up late Saturday night.[22] Out of season, twelve and thirteen hours, including the time for meals, was the usual working day. "No slavery is worse than that of the dressmaker's life in London", one witness told Mr. Grainger.[23] In Liverpool[24] and in Norwich [25] the same long hours were reported. In Nottingham shorter hours were worked, with overtime not later than eleven or twelve at night.[25] Mrs. Tonna, depending on Mr. Grainger's report, represented Ann King as starting work at 6 a.m. and continuing it until 2 a.m.[26] She repeated the Government statement that twenty out of the twenty-four hours were spent over the needle.[27] During Drawing-Room Week the hours were even longer.[28] To fill orders for a fashionable wedding Ann King worked almost all of Sunday.[29] The girls here, as in other establishments, received no extra pay for their long hours, and they got no relief through the help of extra hands.[30] In many places, however, journeywomen were hired for the London season.

Jenny Wren, the doll's dressmaker in *Our Mutual Friend* (1864–65), says of her profession:

" 'Poorly paid, and I'm often so pressed for time. I had a doll married, last week, and was obliged to work all night. And it's not good for me, on account of my back being so bad and my legs so queer.'

"They looked at the little creature with a wonder that did not diminish, and the schoolmaster said: 'I am sorry your fine ladies are so inconsiderate.'

" 'It's the way with them,' said the person of the house, shrugging her shoulders again. 'And they take no care of their clothes, and they never keep to the same fashions a month. I work for a doll with three daughters. Bless you, she's enough to ruin her husband! . . . I finished a large mourning order the day before yesterday. Doll I work for, lost a canary bird.' "

Never did Dickens indulge in more delicate satire than here, where Lilliputian Jenny Wren flays the world of fashion. But the late date of the novel and the author's energy in keeping up to the latest in causes are foreboding circumstances to chronicle at this stage of the history of dressmaking.

Other writers dwell upon the overwork of apprentices. Ruth had only three hours of sleep the night before the hunt ball.[32] Young Pendennis, in a philosophic mood, looked out of his room at dawn and thought of "the work-girl plying her poor needle".[33] Mary Barton began work at six in summer, in winter after breakfast, but there was no time fixed for the end of her labours. She was not represented as overworked. Kate Nickleby was the most favourably situated of any of the dressmakers or milliners in fiction. Her hours, as a show-woman, were from nine until nine, and she was paid for overtime.[35]

During the busy season there was no fixed time for meals.[36] Ten minutes were allowed for breakfast, fifteen or twenty minutes for dinner, fifteen for tea, and supper was postponed until the work was finished, at eleven, twelve, or even later. Mrs. Tonna copies these figures from the reports.[37] She represented ten minutes as the period for the supper eaten about three in the morning, and Mrs. Gaskell half an hour at two for supper and a rest afterward.[38] The kind of food offered

delicate, overworked girls attracted much deserved censure.
Mr. Grainger reported that the food provided in the majority
of establishments was coarse and unfit.[39] Cold mutton, salt
beef, hard puddings were the usual fare.[40] Ann King in the
shop of her employer, a French milliner in London, dined on
cold mutton, suet pudding, potatoes. The delicate girls in the
workroom were unable to eat such a meal. For tea, sickly slop
and slices of coarse bread with a scraping of rancid butter were
served.[41] The late supper of cheese was equally unsuited to
the apprentices.[42] Frances King told her father she had been
fed on stale bread and poor butter.[43] Ruth at two in the
morning was given bread, cheese, and beer.[44] Mary Barton,
when she had completed the first two years of her apprenticeship and had two of her meals furnished by Miss Simmonds,
was deprived of her tea when hard times forced everyone to
small economies, so that she fasted from one o'clock dinner
often until midnight.[45] Kate Nickleby at Madame Mantalini's
dined on baked leg of meat and potatoes served in the kitchen.
Sunday was an especially trying day for country girls employed
in shops away from home. Mr. Grainger discovered that in
some houses no meals except breakfast were provided on
Sunday. One friendless young woman walked the streets all
day.[47] A girl in Norwich complained that she got black looks
for dining at the house of her employer on Sunday.[48] Frances
King had nothing to eat the first Sunday she spent in London.[49]
Mrs. Gaskell described Ruth left alone on Sundays, when no
dinner was cooked for the workers and no fires were lighted.
After breakfast had been served in Mrs. Mason's parlour, the
room was closed, and Ruth, without friends in a strange town,
ate a bun or biscuit in the cold deserted workroom at dinner-
time.[50]

The rooms in which these overworked and undernourished
girls toiled were too small for the number of apprentices and,
without adequate ventilation, they were either too hot or too
cold, Mr. Grainger stated in his report.[51] Kate Nickleby, when
she was not in the showroom, worked in a close room with a

skylight. Ann King was oppressed by the bad air of a room in which thirty persons were crowded, the gas-lights adding heat and fumes to the already vitiated atmosphere.[52] Frances King complained that the workroom was not ventilated.[53] Ruth Hilton suffered in the same way from the bad air.[54] Mary Barton, in enumerating her woes, remembered the "close, monotonous workroom".[55] The sleeping-rooms to which the girls were assigned were equally dangerous to their health. Mr. Grainger described them as crowded and confined.[56] In another case the sleeping-quarters were over the stables and were damp. Eighteen girls in a third establishment slept in a room with only one window. In fiction this dangerous practice of overcrowding was made much of. Mrs. Tonna wrote that Ann slept in a bed with two other girls and was so disturbed by them after a heavy working day that she got only an hour of sleep.[57] Ruth Hilton shared a room with four other girls.[58]

3. Her Health

The long hours in a stifling atmosphere, with irregular meals of poor quality, insufficient rest, and no exercise, naturally broke down the health of even the strongest country girls. The factory report of 1834 had already given the opinion that the health of milliners was more affected by their work than that of factory girls.[59] A physician quoted by Mr. Grainger said: "No men work so continuously with so little rest."[60] An indignant article in *Fraser's* stated that seamstresses in London could hardly use their feet, and that spinal curvatures were common. One of the reasons for the stunted race of beings in London was given by the writer as the treatment of female apprentices, some day to be mothers.[61] One witness told the Government agent that her legs and feet swelled as a result of long continued labour.[62] Exhausted girls fainted. A constant supply of fresh hands from the country replaced the girls who were no longer of any use. Consumption and poor eyes, another witness stated, were the most common results of the violation of all rules of health.[63] The *Illustrated London News* quoted the *Edinburgh Review* for the statistics of the North London Ophthalmic Institution, that of 669 patients, 81 were needle-women.[64] Miss La Creevy, the painter in *Nicholas Nickleby*, disapproved of Kate's becoming a milliner because three milliners sitting to her had been pale and sickly.[65] Kate, going to her work the first day, saw girls following the trade her uncle had chosen for her who did not add to her cheerfulness about it. Dickens wrote:[66]

"At this early hour many sickly girls, whose business, like that of the poor worm, is to produce with patient toil the finery that bedecks the thoughtless and luxurious, traverse our streets, making towards the scene of their daily labour, and catching, as if by stealth, the only gasp of wholesome air and glimpse of sunlight, which cheers their monotonous existence during the long train of hours that make a working day. As she drew nigh to the more fashionable quarter of the town, Kate marked many of this class as they passed by, hurrying like herself to their painful occupation, and saw, in their unhealthy looks and feeble gait, but too clear an evidence that her misgivings were not wholly groundless."[67]

The girls among whom Ann King worked Mrs. Tonna represented as suffering from indigestion, asthma, and consumption.[68] Because they were so overworked, they often neglected personal cleanliness. Ann, when she first entered a fashionable millinery shop, a rosy country girl, envied the elegance of the other apprentices. "She imagines that universal air of languor, that absence of healthful glow, that reed-like attenuation of figure, to be the result of London polish."[69] During the second year of her apprenticeship she developed tuberculosis and was soon dead. The description of her sufferings which she gave to the dispensary doctor would be too painful to dwell upon if it were not a repetition of some of the testimony members of the Commission took from dying girls.[70]

" 'The pain, sir, in my chest is constant. I must stoop, because it seems to relieve the great pain in the shoulder-blades; but the stooping makes my breath shorter. Palpitation of the heart comes on if I only change my attitude, or speak; and a mist is over my eyes, and a choking in my throat and very great sickness. Often I feel so hungry as to reckon of dinner-time, but the sight of my food turns it all to disgust; not that I have any complaint to make of what is set before us, but my fancy will run upon things that I cannot get. Sometimes I reconcile myself, and persuade myself to eat, but the short time allowed us is gone, and we must make the best of our way back to work. Then there is such a headache! grievous racking pains in the limbs, and you may see my right shoulder-blade is growing out. At night, or rather in the morning, when I lie down to sleep, my eyes will be staring wide open, notwithstanding that they are so tired it seems a wonder to me how I can help shutting them. But it is the same with many others. Indeed, except the very new hands, hardly one of us but could say as much as I, in some particular or another, though just now I suffer most.' "

Distortion of the spine and ulcers, according to Mrs. Tonna, were a common result of excessive work.[71] Jenny, Ruth Hilton's friend, broke down in health.

"She could not sleep or rest. The tightness at her side was worse than usual. She almost thought she ought to mention it in her letters home; but then she remembered the premium her father had struggled hard to pay, and the large family, younger than herself, that had to be cared for, and she determined to bear on, and trust that, when the warm weather came, both the pain and the cough would go away."[72]

Two days later she could work no more, and she was forced to go home for a long rest. She was more fortunate than many a victim of the needle. Mrs. Tonna affirmed that almost all establishments killed a girl a year.[73] Although she can be trusted to take the gloomiest view possible on all the sufferings of working women, here she has a wealth of tragic support. From varied sources came the inevitable conclusion that the dressmaking trade was suicidal for young girls. Only needle-grinding, the Commission declared, was more destructive of health.[74]

4. THE APPRENTICE'S REPUTATION

The moral consequences of the manner of life followed by these young slaves of the needle received as much comment as their physical ruin. The Commissioners reported that immorality was proverbial among dressmakers,[75] a statement agreeing with the slurring reference in fiction. In *Vanity Fair* Dobbin assured the messroom that Osborne was "not going to run off with a duchess or ruin a milliner", but was going to marry Miss Sedley, "one of the most charming young women that ever lived".[76] In the same novel Rawdon Crawley is described as amusing himself by "courtships of milliners, opera-dancers, and the like easy triumphs".[77] Foker, when he went to visit his friend Pendennis, "flattened his little nose against Madame Fribsby's window to see if haply there was a pretty workwoman in her premises".[78]

A large part of the material dealing with the morals of dressmakers is concerned with those of the young apprentices. Mary Barton's Aunt Esther, a sick, weary woman of the streets, when she learned that her niece was learning the dressmaking trade, said: "I began to be frightened for her; for it's a bad life for a girl to be out late at night in the streets, and after many an hour of weary work, they're ready to follow after any novelty that makes a little change."[79] The writer of the article in *Fraser's*, "Milliners' Apprentices",[80] already referred to, was of the opinion that these young girls did not take to drink as factory girls did, but their fondness for clothes, encouraged by their trade, in which the attention centred around nothing else, led sometimes to prostitution.

Most of the causes of immorality have been mentioned. The monotony of the trade and the unhealthy atmosphere in which girls worked huddled together all the day and most of the night drove them to seek any excitement that gave temporary relief. Mary Barton, reviewing her folly in encouraging the attentions of the factory owner's son, looked back upon the affair beginning as "a pleasant little interlude"[81] in an existence made up "of the morrow, and morrow beyond that, to be spent in that close, monotonous workroom". "Oh, how she loathed the recollection of the hot summer evening, when, worn out by stitching and sewing, she had loitered homewards with weary languor, and first listened to the voice of the tempter." The financial dependence of the apprentices upon their employers was also a menace to strict virtue. Ann King said of her fellow-workers: "Our number is thirty, or thereabouts; and I can undertake to say that twenty of them have nothing but the charity of their friends or the public to depend on if they leave their present situation."[82] The journey-women, who were paid little and hired only for the season, too often resorted to prostitution when they could find no other way of support.[83] Their pay varied from 7s. to 9s. weekly, according to one writer on the subject.[84] Mary Barton received a little over half a crown a week. The girls met temptation daily in the streets. The outdoor workers going home late at night were often in danger.[85] Kate Nickleby's mother waited for her every night. Those who lived in lodgings were not protected as strange girls in a big city it was then thought should be. Ruth Hilton returned from an errand at two in the morning.[86] Both indoor and outdoor apprentices were constantly exposed to evil sights and wicked speech on the streets. Frances King did not want her father to know the evil she had confronted as she went back and forth matching silks.[87] One of Mary Barton's associates picked up the latest news of a sensational murder between errands.[88] Both Mary Barton and Ruth Hilton met men above them in station who endangered their safety when they were on the streets alone. Vulgar associates, crowded close to them in the workroom and at night sleeping with them, could easily initiate them in evil ways. Sally Leadbitter, a low-minded fellow-worker of Mary, acted as a go-between to assist young Carson in his lovemaking with Mary. So unhealthy was the moral atmo-sphere of Miss Simmonds's shop that this girl could say of Mary's connection with the Carson murder trial:

" 'Miss Simmonds knows you'll have to be off those two days. But, between you and me, she's a bit of a gossip, and will like hearing all how and about the trial, well enough to let you off very easy for your being absent a day or two. Besides, Betsy Morgan was saying yesterday, she shouldn't wonder but you'd prove quite an attraction to customers. Many a one would come and have their gowns made by Miss Simmonds just to catch a glimpse at you, after the trial's over. Really, Mary, you'll turn out quite a heroine.' "[89]

Kate Nickleby's associates were all cringing, mean-spirited young women. Ruth's only friend at Mrs. Mason's, the forewoman Jenny, was soon removed by illness. In *David Copperfield* both Emily and her fellow-apprentice, Martha Endell, could not resist temptation. It is significant that Dickens makes little Emily a dressmaker. The reading of these girls was in keeping with their general philosophy. In Ann King's millinery establishment late at night, to keep the sleepy girls awake, a sensational book was read which Mrs. Tonna described as "a tale, the very meaning of which she can hardly make out, but where murder, and violence, and situations of fearful peril, and bursts of unbridled passion, at the expense of filial and conjugal duty, make up the exciting compound".[90] Such books the pious authoress branded as "moral poison". This tale was followed by a play in French for the benefit of the French apprentices. For such literature no words were adequate, even for Mrs. Tonna, whose vocabulary to designate what did not harmonize with her Evangelical tenets was usually voluble enough. Mrs. Gaskell, too, mentioned "the romances which Miss Simmonds's young ladies were in the habit of recommending to each other", and the "simple, foolish, unworldly ideas" they picked up from them.[91] Their employers were interested in little but the swiftness of their apprentices' needles.[92] As Ann King confided to her physician: "Nobody that they can look up to cares for them except as working machines."[93] The treatment employers gave their workwomen on Sundays was the most powerful proof of a callous attitude. They were never asked how they spent the day so long as they had the discretion not to bother those who hired them. They often picked up acquaintances on the streets or in the park.[94] Ruth Hilton's employer spent Sundays in the country, forgetful of how a girl in a strange town would provide herself with either food or recreation. It was only when she by accident met Ruth with a lover and saw him caress her that Mrs. Mason grew concerned. As Mrs. Gaskell explained her attitude:

"Mrs. Mason was careless about the circumstances of temptation into which the girls entrusted to her as apprentices were thrown, but severely intolerant if their conduct was in any degree influenced by the force of these temptations. She called this intolerance 'keeping up the character of her establishment'. It would have been a better and a more Christian thing if she had kept up the character of her girls by tender vigilance and maternal care."[95]

Without any preliminaries she discharged her. "Don't attempt to show your face at my house after this conduct. . . . I'll have no slurs on the character of my apprentices." Ruth, thrown back upon the chivalry of her lover, went with him to London, and spent the rest of her life repenting the consequences of her action.

Dressmakers, like most other working women, neglected their spiritual development. Their weekly toil did not encourage church-going on their only rest-day. Ann King confessed with bitter regret to her physician that she had soon left off going to church.[96] Sometimes she worked most of Sunday, or on Saturday night so late that she needed Sunday morning for sleep. In the afternoon she walked in the park. Ruth started out by going to both the morning and the afternoon church services, but her lover soon persuaded her to go out into the country with him in the afternoon.[97] Most writers emphasize the need of moral and spiritual support for these overworked girls. The Church, in their opinion, would help them to endure such a life as that of the apprentice.

5. THE SEWING-WOMAN AND THE SLOP WORKER

Although most of the interest of the Government reports and the fiction of the period was primarily in the apprentice, some facts were given concerning the dressmaker who went out working by the day or did plain sewing at home.

The sewing-women were paid from 1s. to 1s. 6d. per day, according to one estimate, and received additional pay for extra time.[98] Little Dorrit went out sewing by the day. She laboured from eight to eight, and her meals were included.[99] Margaret in *Mary Barton* sewed at home until working on mourning made her blind.

Women who did plain sewing at home, the making of shirts generally, and were designated "slop workers", belonged to the most degraded class of needlewomen. They were completely at the mercy of a contractor, who paid them the lowest price possible. The poorest women, who could not pay a guarantee when work was taken out, had their earnings further decreased by a middleman lower down. The *Christian Lady's Magazine* for December 1835 stated that a woman who sewed from 7 a.m. until midnight could not earn 1s. 6d. daily.[100] Often her daily earnings were 6d. Workers for Army clothiers were paid 8d. for making jackets. A stay stitcher earned about 2s. 6d. weekly. A mantua-maker labouring from 9 a.m. to 11 p.m. earned 4s. 8d. weekly.[101]

The shirt-maker received a belated publicity from the report of the Children's Commission of 1843. Mr. R. D. Grainger collected a mass of revolting facts about slop workers. He reported 10d. per dozen as the pay for making striped cotton shirts. A better grade brought 2s. 6d. per dozen. Common white shirts were 5s. per dozen, better ones 10s. per dozen.[102] In one establishment employing from 1,200 to 1,400 women, workers earned from 1s. 6d. weekly to 9s. or 10s.; 5s. 6d. was the average amount. A witness stated that she was paid 2s. per dozen for common striped shirts and 3s. 6d. per dozen for a better grade. Another witness, with the aid of two young

children, at an average rate of from 6d. to 9d. per shirt earned
6s. or 7s. weekly, provided she sat up half the night two or
three times a week.[103] Two years earlier she had received
1od. for making a shirt. *Punch*[104] appropriately pictures a
shirt as a shroud, represented with skulls and 2½d. on it; and
Carlyle writes of "this blessed exchange of slop-shirts for the
souls of women".[105]

William Shaw, an Army clothier, wrote a report of a meeting
of slop workers held December 3, 1849, in the British School
Room, Shakespeare Walk, Shadwell, attended by from 1,000
to 1,200 slop workers.[106] Lord Ashley and Sidney Herbert
were present at the meeting. The purpose of the gathering was
to learn the sufferings of these women and to discover the
reason for the low prices of their toil. By asking the women
to hold up their hands, rough statistics were gathered about
the kind of work done. Although shirt- and trousers-
makers were represented in the largest number, the figures
showed a variety of labour with the needle. Only three or
four of the wretched throng had underclothing; 508 had
borrowed clothes to come; 151 had never had beds; 464 had
asked for parochial assistance the past week; 232 had been
forced to leave their lodgings because they couldn't pay the
rent. In the whole number only five had earned 6s. the last week.
Earnings commonly ranged from 2s. 6d. to under 1s. Among
those who came on the platform to give testimony, an orphan
who earned 4s. weekly making trousers, out of which sum
she paid 8d. for thread, had only 2s. 4d. to live on weekly
after she paid for her lodgings. Defective work had been
thrown back on her, so that she was arrested for a debt to her
employer of 15s. A letter appearing in the *Morning Chronicle,*
quoted by Mr. Shaw (November 13, 1849), recorded the
struggles of two women of forty-three and fifty-four, whose
earnings had shrunk so that, while in 1846 they had 4¼d. each
per day for food and clothing, in 1849 they had only 2½d.
For this pittance they worked eighteen and twenty hours daily,
including Sunday, when they had work. They lived in an attic

room, furnished with a chair and a bed. At times they lived entirely on oatmeal. They had sometimes fasted for thirty hours. They never had a fire in winter, and never a light except for their work.

Some of the women blamed their employers for the low prices; 297 worked for "sweaters", who took from 2d. to 4d. out of every shilling they earned. A few placed the responsibility on women who offered to work for less than the existing prices. There were many complaints about work returned as defective, which witnesses swore was satisfactory. Others had been forced to pay for buttons or parts of garments they had never received. Although they were expected to be at the shop to get work at a certain hour, they were kept waiting from an hour to half a day. Illness from getting wet was often a result, as well as loss of time. They were not paid promptly. They were fined for late work.

The competition of the workhouses was partly responsible for the fall in prices.[107] Female inmates were paid 1d. for three common shirts. *Punch*,[108] with its humour playing close to the tragedy of contemporary events, printed the letter of a fictitious needlewoman, who wrote: "I am a shirt-maker, and am desirous of getting into the Union or the Penitentiary (whichever you may advise as best), that I may be able to eat a little more from my needle and thread than I am able to do in my own garret." After the letter came a scornful item about the unfair competition of workhouse labour. The slop workers also suffered from the fact that large numbers of untrained women entered their ranks when sudden calamity forced them to be self-supporting. Prices were kept down by the constant surplus of women who could use a needle. In *Mary Barton* Mrs. Davenport, after her husband's death, did plain sewing at night of the variety "seam, and gusset, and band", words Mrs. Gaskell quoted from Hood's poem *The Song of the Shirt*, originally published in the Christmas number of *Punch* in 1843, the year the report of the Children's Committee appeared.

The Song of the Shirt is the most powerful picture of the slavery of these women.

> "With fingers weary and worn,
>   With eyelids heavy and red,
> A woman sat, in unwomanly rags,
>   Plying her needle and thread—
>   Stitch! Stitch! Stitch!
> In poverty, hunger, and dirt,
> And still with a voice of dolorous pitch
>   She sang *The Song of the Shirt*!"

Such lines as the following are a poetic representation of the appalling facts citizens were reading in the official Blue books :

> "Sewing at once, with a double thread,
> A shroud as well as a shirt.
>
> .   .   .   .
>
> Oh! God! that bread should be so dear,
> And flesh and blood so cheap!
>
> .   .   .   .
>
> And what are its wages?   A bed of straw,
>   A crust of bread—and rags.
> That shatter'd roof—and this naked floor—
>   A table—a broken chair—
>
> .   .   .   .
>
>   Work—work—work—
> As prisoners work for crime!
>
> .   .   .   .
>
> Seam, and gusset, and band,
> Band, and gusset, and seam,
>   Work, work, work,
> Like the Engine that works by steam!
> A mere machine of iron and wood
>   That toils for Mammon's sake—
> Without a brain to ponder and craze
>   Or a heart to feel—and break!"

Mrs. Caroline Norton in her *Child of the Islands*, published in 1845, in the division *Spring*, wrote of the seamstress who

could not enjoy it. In a footnote she explained that the first
case which made the public aware of the miserable wages
of sewing-women came up in the division of her husband,
George Norton, a metropolitan police magistrate.

A first reading of Kingsley's novel *Alton Locke* gives an un-
initiated reader the impression that the author is exaggerating
the horror of the haunts of tailors and slop workers. Only by
a comparison of the revolting descriptions with Government
reports and the articles in the *Morning Chronicle* is one convinced of the awful photographic truth. This is the description
of the den in which some of the slop workers toiled.[109]

"There was no bed in the room, no table. On a broken chair by
the chimney sat a miserable old woman, fancying that she was
warming her hands over embers which had long been cold, shaking
her head, and muttering to herself, with palsied lips, about the
guardians and the workhouse; while upon a few rags on the floor
lay a girl, ugly, small-pox marked, hollow-eyed, emaciated, her only
bedclothes the skirt of a large handsome new riding-habit, at which
two other girls, wan and tawdry, were stitching busily, as they sat
right and left of her on the floor."

One of them describes the life they lead:

" 'Night and day's all the same here—we must have this home by
seven o'clock to-morrow morning. My lady's going to ride early,
they say, whoever she may be, and we must just sit up all night. It's
often we haven't had our clothes off for a week together, from two
in the morning till two the next morning sometimes—stitch, stitch,
stitch. Somebody's wrote a song about that—I'll learn to sing it—
it'll sound fitting-like up here.' "

One of the inevitable consequences of such a sweating
system was prostitution. An article in *Fraser's*,[110] which
recorded the direct testimony of girls who did slop work,
gave an account of the struggles they made to keep chaste. One
told the investigator: "I don't know any that makes a practice
of walking the streets regularly of a night. They only go out
when they're in distress." Charles Kingsley shows the same
driving necessity of prostitution in *Alton Locke*. A sick girl has

been supported by money her companions had earned on the streets. From chance visitors she begged help in making her friends see that death was to be preferred.[111]

> " 'Tell them it'll never prosper. I know it is want that drives them to it, as it drives all of us—but tell them it's best to starve and die honest girls, than to go about with the shame and the curse of God on their hearts, for the sake of keeping this poor, miserable, vile body together a few short years more in this world o' sorrow. . . . It's no merit o' mine, Mr. Mackaye, that the Lord's kept me pure through it all. I should have been just as bad as any of them if the Lord had not kept me out of temptation in His great mercy by making me the poor, ill-favoured creature I am.' "

Lizzie, her companion, is more defiant:

> " 'I hate myself, and hate all the world because of it; but I must— I must; I cannot see her starve, and I cannot starve myself. When she first fell sick she kept on as long as she could, doing what she could, and then between us we only earned three shillings a week, and there was ever so much to take off for fire, and twopence for thread, and fivepence for candles; and then we were always getting fined, because they never gave us out the work till too late on purpose, and then they lowered prices again; and now Ellen can't work at all, and there's four of us, with the old lady, to keep off two's work that couldn't keep themselves alone.' "

The most revolting document concerning the enforced prostitution of slop workers is the letter of the Special Correspondent of the Metropolitan Districts in the *Morning Chronicle*.[112] A meeting was called of women reduced to prostitution, and twenty-five came, women and girls in rags, many with small babies. The majority of them told pitiful tales of living with men to divide expenses, the hand-to-mouth existence that left no balance for marriage fees, the unavoidable babies, and a life made up of months in the workhouse separated from their children, of infants already dying when their mothers recovered them. The death of little children figured largely in every tale. One baby was born in the street,[113] and a chance passer-by had pity on the mother. A mother with

twin babies in her arms sold matches on the street and begged.
One degraded creature told of a life which surpassed in horror
the worst of Dickens's slum stories,[114] a proof that Dickens,
like Kingsley, could document many of his tales, and was
less of a caricaturist than his critics have represented him. The
depths of this woman's misery were lighted only by a savage
love for her children. When they were starving she was
tempted to kill them. She was crazed when they were taken
from her. Slop work and the streets gave her at times a few
hard-earned pennies. All of the women who gave testimony
were prostitutes only intermittently, although most of them
had formed irregular unions.

Only one writer showed a different attitude toward the
temptations of underpaid sewing-women. John Crosswaithe in
an article in *Good Words* [115] attacked the maudlin sentimentality
about temptations, which he considered a bad influence. But
the sentiment notwithstanding, not many writers could advise
the course of starvation held up as the glorious alterna-
tive by the sick girl in *Alton Locke*. Only those close to death
can regard life so lightly.

6. THE RELIEF OF THE DRESSMAKER

Philanthropists in considering the gigantic problem of
sewing-women divided it into two parts, for the most part
dealt with separately, the relief of the dressmakers' and milliners' apprentices forming one kind of endeavour and that
of the slop workers another. The report of the Children's
Commission led directly to a consideration of the benefits to
be gained for the apprentices through legislation.

Before this document had been published, an article in
Fraser's in 1835 had predicted:

"If a commission were issued to inquire into the condition and
treatment of young girls in this metropolis who are apprenticed to
milliners, dressmakers, and other sedentary trades, we will venture

to predict that the publication of the report would occasion as much feeling of excitement in the public mind as the question of factory children has produced."[116]

The prophecy was fulfilled, but at first public indignation took the form of a desire to place the blame on a definite class of individuals.

In the record of misery examined in the textile and non-textile industries men had been largely responsible for the wrongs suffered by working women. But in the dressmaking and millinery business, as in the lace-finishing and the pin-heading trades, women were the executives, and their cruelty and injustice equalled anything earlier attributed to men. Dressmakers were more relentless toward the girls they hired than some of the most ignorant overlookers in Manchester factories. Girls were dismissed for giving evidence to the Commissioners.[117] The testimony of witnesses also showed that the wives and daughters of Tory land-holders, who had branded the slave-driving methods of Manchester mill-owners and Birmingham steel manufacturers, were indirectly responsible for the overwork of London apprentices. Their carelessness and indifference to the hardships the London season brought to young girls working at night to finish gowns for Court presentations and drawing-rooms was finally given a belated publicity. The *Edinburgh Review*[118] was emphatic in its denunciation of the women of leisure who brought about the suffering of other women.

Sir Robert Peel in the speech referred to in the preceding chapter (March 15, 1844) had remarked that there was a sentiment among Members of Parliament to pass laws to protect not only factory women, whose wrongs were then the immediate subject of discussion, but also workers in all the multifarious industries grouped under non-textiles and dressmakers and milliners. John Bright, in the midst of the discussion over the Factory Bill of 1844, had read a long quotation from the report of the Children's Commission to prove that dressmakers were in greater need of protective legislation than factory workers.[119] Lord Ashley on the same day urged the passing of a law to regulate this unrelieved toil.[120] But Lord Brougham in a speech in the House of Lords a few days later mentioned the fact that he had been asked to bring in such a bill, but had refused. The possibility of legislative restriction was given up then, and recourse to other methods of relief had to be made.

The first constructive suggestion for reform outside of Parliament had been offered by a milliner of Pall Mall, Ann L. Ollivier, who had outlined her scheme before the Commissioners. Her idea was that a few ladies known to one another should meet and have cards printed asking about the hours worked in different shops and sent to employers, who should be asked to keep an exact account of the hours for twelve months. The ladies joined in such a scheme should attempt the observance of a twelve-hour working day. Medals given to the best managers of establishments, she thought, would be a sufficient inducement for reform.[121]

In the definite programme for reform, the first project was the formation in 1843 of an "Association for the Aid and Benefit of Dressmakers and Milliners", often called the "Needlewomen's Benevolent Association", with Lord Ashley the President, and Mr. R. D. Grainger, one of the Commissioners, the secretary. The prime object of the society was to shorten the working hours of apprentices to twelve and to abolish Sunday work. The promoters of reform, however, directed their efforts to improve the ventilation of workrooms and sleeping-rooms, to induce customers to give time for their orders, to help deserving girls in periods of distress with loans, to supply good and cheap medical relief, and to establish a provident fund and registry for those who had finished their apprenticeship and were seeking work.[122] Two committees, one of women, including the Duchess of Sutherland and Argyll, the Countess of Shaftesbury, Lady Jocelyn, and Miss Burdett-Coutts, and the other of men, Mr. Grainger, Dr. Bissett Lawkins, and Mr. Tidd Pratt, met weekly and planned public meetings and prepared printed statements of the wrongs of these workers. Recognizing the fact that the blame for excessive toil was the divided responsibility of the heads of shops and also of the wealthy customers whose rush orders necessitated night and Sunday work, the Association laboured to give widespread publicity to the effects of such practices. Women were urged to find out the hours of work in the establishments they patronized and to refuse to deal with inhuman employers. Individual heads of shops were approached on the subject of overwork. Evidence against certain employers was collected. Through the department giving free medical assistance the doctors were able to contribute expert testimony concerning the effects of overwork.

The raising of funds to carry on this relief enlisted a certain amount of fashionable charity. *Punch* refers to the donation of £50 made by the Queen.[123] But Lord Ashley, who gave the society his support and spent time interviewing its officers, complained of the general indifference.[124] In his journal he recorded his belief that the clergy were either hostile or frigid on the subject.[125] In December 1844, when he took the chair of a meeting called for the relief of seamstresses, he wrote:[126] "Good heavens! that in such a cause there should have been so scanty an assemblage." But the society could show some improvements as a result of their activities. Sunday work in all the London shops was stopped,[127] and by 1853 the proprietors of many establishments had agreed to abide by the rules laid down by the Association.[128] Later, however, officers reported that some of these women had gone back to the old practice of sixteen and seventeen hours of work.[129]

But there was a sentiment favouring Government interference. The writer of the article "Milliners' Apprentices" in *Fraser's* went farther in suggesting reform than the Needlewomen's Benevolent Association. According to this plan[130] the legislature should interfere to prevent any young person from working more than twelve hours, extra work should be optional, with extra pay, the legislature should fix the length of vacation, and should determine the age of an apprentice. In addition, there should be agitation for other kinds of relief and relaxation, such as a hospital for workwomen, with a dispensary in connection, and lending libraries. The mistress of a dressmaking establishment should make Sunday a pleasant time for her girls by clearing the workroom for their use, giving them a better dinner than on weekdays, and inviting guests to dinner. She should also encourage them to go to church. Cleanliness of apprentices ought to be agitated, cold baths made popular, workrooms and sleeping-rooms improved as to ventilation.

In 1855, finding that conditions were not improved, reformers made a second attempt to secure parliamentary interference. Lord Shaftesbury introduced a bill into Parliament which proposed that between May 1st and August 1st work should be prohibited between 10 p.m. and 8 a.m., and for the remainder of the year between 9 p.m. and 8 a.m. An hour and a half was to be allowed for meals. All proceedings for the enforcement of penalties under the bill were to be taken at police courts before magistrates, to whom jurisdiction in these matters was to be exclusively committed.[131] Although Lord Shaftesbury made it clear he intended to reach only the slaves of the heads of the big fashionable establishments in London, and not the slop workers, sympathy in Parliament was clearly against him.[132] While evidence was being collected, only the *Standard* defended Shaftesbury's measure.[133] The greatest difficulty was confronted in getting evidence before the committee appointed. Apprentices stood in such fear of their employers that they preferred to suffer in silence.[134] The only real testimony secured was from women recently engaged in the trade. Another difficulty was that the most startling cases of oppression had to remain obscure because of the risk of libel. A Mr. Paget, who had published a book called *The Pageant*, in which he set forth parliamentary evidence about milliners and dressmakers, had been indicted for defamation.

In the face of general indifference and hostility, it was not surprising that the bill failed.

Once more the relief of young dressmakers was carried to individual effort. Mr. R. D. Grainger, when he found that in 1856 the apprentices were more abused than before,[136] saw no solution for the problem but that of giving the responsibility entirely to the ladies of England. An attempt was made to strengthen the influence of the Needlewomen's Benevolent Association by uniting it with the Early Closing Association. At a meeting, July 11, 1856, presided over by Lord Robert Grosvenor, Lord Shaftesbury, the Bishop of Oxford, Mr. Grainger, and other men prominent in social causes spoke. It is discouraging to note that there were three men to one woman present at the meeting.[137] It is equally discouraging that Lord Grosvenor's suggestion that his wife should have been in the chair in his place and that the Countess of Shaftesbury should have moved the first resolution instead of her husband was a bit of pleasantry received with cheers and laughter.

The result of this movement lies beyond the limits of this study. By 1850 the prevailing sentiment was that the relief of milliners' and dressmakers' apprentices was not the affair of Parliament, but of private individuals. Mrs. Tonna in *The Wrongs of Women* expressed this attitude.[138] Ann King is talking to the physician in the dispensary:

" 'Ah, sir, there was a beautiful young lady married to a great lord, and the wedding-dresses were so fine! We had all the millinery, and a house near us the dressmaking, and to my knowledge both houses were at work almost all Sunday to get the things done; and one girl, very weakly, came by her death through that.'

" 'Was the match so suddenly made?'

" 'It was in all the papers, sir, weeks and weeks before, and the time was fixed; but as some change might happen in the last fashions, the orders were put off to the latest; and then they were offered to those that would undertake them in least time.' "

In the closing paragraphs of her miserable tale, she stated that many employers would be glad to put an end to the evils of the present system, but that without the co-operation of the ladies of England they could do nothing.

That such co-operation resulted in many cases is proved by a letter written by a clergyman to Mrs. Tonna in praise of her book and published in the *Christian Lady's Magazine* in 1843.[139] He told of a society formed in a neighbouring town for the prevention of hurrying work and for the ordering of work some time before it was wanted. Doubtless there were numerous small agencies trying to better conditions. But nothing widespread resulted from the agitation. A magazine writer said plainly: "The ladies of England never did, and do not yet, as a body, thoroughly perceive how much it rests with them to improve or maintain the unhappy condition of the milliners' workwomen."[140] In 1863 the death of an apprentice from overwork stirred the public, and a new Royal Commission was appointed.[141] In 1908 girl dressmakers worked on gowns for Ascot from 8 one morning until 4 the following afternoon with only brief intervals for meals and rest.[142] Doubtless equally striking contemporary instances could be cited.

Some writers found that not only were employers and women of fashion to blame for bad conditions. The apprentices themselves were partly responsible. Harriet Martineau thought the needlewomen should resist every encroachment on their rights.[143] Another difficulty was the fact that many young women served a short apprenticeship in a shop to learn the business so they could sew for themselves. Their competition with others was a complication of the problem.[144] One fantastic writer, who used the *Edinburgh Review* for the exposition of his theory, divided all wrongs in society into those caused by fettered industry and by neglected education. A well-educated man would not, he contended, send his daughter to be worked to death in a dressmaking shop.[145] Another theorist urged a revolution against French style. With the freakishness of fashion removed, Society ladies would not wait until the last moment to order gowns in the latest Paris mode.

For the relief of the slop workers, whose sufferings were due in part to the deductions from their earnings by the "sweater" or middleman, an association was formed to eliminate this necessity. When Maurice and Kingsley planned the relief of tailors by an association of workmen[146] similar to the Associations Ouvrières described in *Fraser's Magazine*,[147] a similar association of needlewomen was formed in London. The superintendent gave out and allotted the work and had the power of dismissal, "subject to the ladies' committee or the lady visitor of the day". In 1860 a similar organization called the Institution for the Employment of Needlewomen was started, with a house where the women worked in light and airy rooms.[148] So successful was this that enlarged quarters were necessary. Five hundred women in 1861 were employed, out of a class, however, far above that whose sufferings were described in the *Morning Chronicle* articles. Wives of shopkeepers, decayed gentlewomen, and governesses out of work were the ones reached. The society paid 6d. for each shirt, instead of 4d. and 5d. Such schemes did not receive universal commendation. The *Edinburgh Review* was of the opinion that

"the benevolent men and women who are setting on foot these Associations of tailors, needlewomen, shoemakers, and bakers are merely aiding them to augment the produce of their several branches of industry, without augmenting the demand for this produce and the fund for the payment of it".[149]

Many commentators urged that the question of excessive competition, which affected all gradations of slaves of the needle, was forgotten by philanthropists who had schemes to lessen the misery of sewing-women. There were too many dressmakers and too many slop workers. If fewer women were competing for work, they could dictate prices, and their earnings would rise.[150] One solution was to increase the amount of sewing hired. Mary Lamb, herself a dressmaker for eleven years, had, some time before the period under observation, written a letter to the editor of the *British Lady's Magazine*, in which she had pointed out the injustice and false economy of a housewife's doing her own sewing. She showed very wisely that women would be better employed by trying to improve their minds instead of taking work away from a poor seamstress.[151] Another writer urged ladies to take up watch-making or engraving instead of sewing, so that when reverses came they would not crowd a market "already glutted with female labour". This has the ring of Miss Martineau under the anonymity.[152] Against this competition of women not entirely dependent upon sewing for self-support, the needlewomen themselves complained.[153] They wanted laws to protect them against such rivalry. The professional milliner, it was stated, had to compete with every woman having idle time on her hands. "A man does not make his own clothes; he finds a more valuable mode of occupying his time."[154] The small value of women's time was held responsible for the excessive competition that brought down prices. Census figures showed that from 1841–51 the number of women above twenty engaged in dressmaking had increased from 159,101 to 388,302. Although the latter figures, including women sewing part of the time, somewhat exaggerated the gains made, it revealed the disastrous results of a trade into which all untrained women crowded.[155]

Carlyle complained of another difficulty which complicated the problem:

"Shirts by the thirty-thousand are made at twopence-halfpenny each; and in the meanwhile no needlewoman, 'distressed' or other, can be procured in London by any housewife to give, for fair wages, fair help in sewing. Ask any thrifty house-mother, high or low, and she will answer. In high houses and in low, there is the same answer: no *real* needlewoman, 'distressed' or other, has been found attainable in any of the houses I frequent. Imaginary needlewomen, who demand considerable wages, and have a deepish appetite for beer and viands, I hear of everywhere; but their sewing proves too often a distracted puckering and botching; not sewing, only the fallacious hope of it, a fond imagination of the mind. Good seamstresses are to be hired in every village; and in London, with its famishing thirty-thousand, not at all, or hardly."[156]

To relieve the sewing-women, emigration was the most popular scheme. Charles Buller in a speech on emigration in Parliament, April 6, 1843, had brought forward this policy of relieving poverty in England. Sidney Herbert, through his Female Emigration Movement, gave a decided impetus to the plan of sending some of the excess of women to colonies where women were far below the men in number.[157] In 1847 in southern Australia, as the *Illustrated London News*[158] pointed out, there were 13,622 females to 17,531 males, and in New South Wales, 41,809 females to 83,572 males. Passage was furnished by the Government, to be repaid later. By January 1852 seven hundred girls had been sent. *Household Words* described the plan of Government emigration with "Clerks . . . ticking off as many single young women as they can afford to do for six shillings a day".[159] But there was some criticism of the Government scheme. On one journey the food was bad, and the berths of single women were open to the visits of the mate.[160] This, the writer in the *Illustrated London News* thought, the Female Emigration Society should assure emigrants would not happen again. A plan especially approved by *Household Words* in a series of articles[161] was Caroline Chisholm's scheme, carried out in the Family Colonization Loan Society. Mrs. Chisholm, who had lived in Sydney, Australia, in 1839 and 1840, had worked among women emigrants, founding a home for them and establishing a register for employment. When she returned to England she wanted to secure some way by which deserving families could be united in Australia. The Family Colonization Loan Society, which she announced in 1850, provided that the Society would assist persons to emigrate by lending them half the passage money without interest, to be repaid in four annual instalments.[162] A member, after he had been investigated, paid a shilling fee and was assigned to a group made up of from three to eight families, the group to be responsible for the loan made, each member paying from 6s. to 10s. weekly toward his passage. Every Monday night group meetings were held, so that the members became well acquainted before they sailed. Agents were appointed in different parts of Australia to keep in touch with the emigrants under the protection of the Society. When an emigrant had paid back his loan he had the privilege of nominating a relative or friend to be assisted in emigrating. The special advantage of this plan over that of the Government—at least so far as Victorian conventions were concerned —was that the group system offered protection to girls or single women, who would be looked after by the members of the group. Two years after the founding of the Society 2,000 members were enrolled. The first emigrant ship sailed September 28, 1850.[163] By 1852 four ships had sailed. The remarkable results of one woman's efforts were forcefully presented to the readers of *Household Words*:

"These emigrants have been collected by the exertions of a lady, living in a small house, rented at some thirty pounds a year, in an obscure street, at Islington, with one paid clerk and one old woman, at four shillings a week, to open the door. The letters, in answer to the inquiries of emigrants, have cost about one pound a week for ninety weeks; on the last week of January 80 letters were received in a day. The whole expenses—including four public meetings and twenty-four group meetings—have been under 400 pounds."[164]

Although the author of an article in *Fraser's Magazine* inquired somewhat sarcastically how many of the 1,500 needle-women must be exported to raise the wages of the remainder from 1s. 6d. a week to 7s.,[165] and sentimentalists objected that seamstresses "should be exported like so many bales of printed cotton",[166] *Household Words* wrote:

"The cry for wives, reaching England from Australia, also brought good tidings to many faint hearts; and hundreds of seamstresses were helped to ships that would carry them to comfortable homes. . . . Many seamstresses did embark, and are now happily married to prosperous colonists."

Charles Kingsley in *Alton Locke* expressed much the same sentiment:

" 'Oh! if that fine lady, as we're making that riding-habit for, would just spare only half the money that goes to dressing her up to ride in the park, to send us out to the colonies, wouldn't I be an honest girl there? Maybe an honest man's wife! Oh, my God, wouldn't I slave my fingers to the bone to work for him! Wouldn't I mend my life then! I couln't help it—it would be like getting into heaven out of hell.' "

Unfortunately, emigration offered itself only to the better class of needlewomen. The slop workers, it was admitted, were not fit material for emigration.[168] The charity offered to the miserable wretches as a result of the articles in the *Morning Chronicle* in 1849 gave temporary relief to a few, but the problem of the sweated worker is one still unsolved. Speculations were made as to the effect of the sewing-machine, invented in 1846, upon the hand-sewer.[169] *Household Words* in "The Iron Seamstress" described the machine in detail.[170] A writer in 1863 stated that the invention had compelled thousands of women to seek other employment.[171] The power-machine was later to make slop work a factory problem, to be remedied by legislation.

The real solution of the problem of the sewing-woman was wisely seen to lie in the relief of an overcrowded trade. The diverting of women into other occupations has been a partial solution. But the craft of the needle will always be the one to which women suddenly forced to support themselves will turn. The only effective legislation here, as in the case of many non-textile workers, was the establishment of Trade Boards in 1909 to fix a minimum wage for women engaged in tailoring, dressmaking, shirt-making, as well as in the occupations described in the previous chapter, with the duty of the Board to fix a minimum rate of wages for rate or piece work. In 1909 70 per cent. of the workers whose wages were improved by the Trade Boards Act were women.[172] What the factory has done to relieve the wretched shirt-maker has come indirectly to the dressmaker, who is now often an operative in shops manufacturing ready-made clothes. For the apprentice, who excited so much sympathy in 1850, there is little to record. In work so largely seasonable, the owners of fashionable dressmaking establishments are at the mercy of their customers. Generally their patrons lack that scientific training which replaces a vapid sentimentality by a sound social sympathy necessary to achieve permanent results. Lord Ashley's pleadings to the English Society women of his day fell upon deaf ears.[173] The present has changed little from the past.

7. THE LITERARY TREATMENT OF THE DRESSMAKER

The dressmaker was much more popular with authors than either the textile or non-textile women workers. This preference cannot be attributed entirely to an eagerness to rush to the succour of a class of toilers neglected by Parliament, since those in the non-textile trades were equally outside remedial legislation. With the dressmaker and her work, however, the writer, especially the lady writer, was at home. Needlecraft was, unlike cotton-weaving or nail-making, no mystery. It was old, familiar. It enforced no tiresome journeys to Manchester or Birmingham, no tours through cotton or steel mills. A dressmaker's labour was within the range of even masculine imagination. The apprentice, being young, was naturally the heroine *par excellence*. Plying a needle did not disarrange her curls, and long hours of toil brought a waxen pallor to her cheek and delicate frailty to her fingers that suited the style of maiden popular then. Since her skill with the needle enabled her to make simple but beautiful clothes for herself, and her trade acquainted her with the last whim of fashion, she was always attractive in appearance. When she went out to the shops to match silks or returned to her home late at night, she was exposed on the streets to the stares of young men. What pity could be expended on such an unprotected young female? Beautiful but poor, she met temptation on every hand. She was overworked by her employer. She sought distraction in her scant moments of leisure. She liked

pretty clothes, adornment. The favourite situation of a novelist was the temptation of such a heroine by a wealthy and idle
young man, her faltering on the brink of ruin, her noble
struggle against sin, her inevitable fall, her years of repentance
and atonement. In *Mary Barton* a humble lover and a murder
trial saved Mary from such an end. In *Ruth* the young dressmaker fled with her lover. In *David Copperfield* little Emily
could not resist temptation. Kate Nickleby was beset by a
band of adventurers, and saved only by miracle. One can
easily see that the dressmaker's life, unlike the mill girl's,
contained all the elements of romance. So conventionalized
had the dressmaker-tale become that the mocking author of
"The Novelist and the Milliner," probably Douglas Jerrold, in
Douglas Jerrold's Shilling Magazine,[174] represented a tired
seamstress reading a novel in which a toiler like herself was
beset by a lord with dishonourable, then honourable pro-
posals, became a fine lady, a joy to her parents, a torment to
her former friends. And, furthermore, the dressmaker was
generally a lady, at least in a novel. She could be represented
as toiling bravely with her needle the day after her husband or
father went into bankruptcy. Even if she were not a lady by
birth, the novelist could make her look like one. Mary Barton,
the daughter of a mill hand, had the beauty, the taste for
refinement and luxurious ways that characterize the gentle
born. The slop worker, usually a low character, was almost
totally neglected by novelists. Only an indomitable reformer
like Kingsley introduced her into fiction. She appeared in
several poems, as we have seen, but without much realistic
detail. The female novelists, especially, felt at home with the
dressmaker. She belonged more nearly to their class. She had
feelings akin to theirs. If she herself could not announce her
woes to the world, she had a sympathetic defender who could.
Then, the abuse apprentices suffered gave writers an excuse
to attack the aristocracy and the world of fashion, a solemn
Victorian duty. In studying the problem of relief for dressmakers they naturally gave hearty support to the philanthropic

schemes devised to reform conditions. These, too, harmonized with the taste of the first half of the nineteenth century. Colonization was the great movement. The Empire scattered widely over the seas needed good, steady, British inhabitants. What could arouse more enthusiasm among writers than the associations formed to send ladylike girls to remote British possessions where they could find husbands? Charles Dickens opened the pages of *Household Words* generously to long articles on emigration societies, and he sent Little Emily to Australia.

A comparison of the literary treatment of dressmakers with that of the workers already considered reveals a wealth of material concerning working conditions which is lacking for other classes of labour. Novelists give exact statements about the apprentice system, the hours worked, the bad seasons of overtime, the monotony of the sewing trade, the unventilated and crowded workrooms. Why, then, were they so concerned with these dull details when they, as a class, passed over similar material for the factory girl? The easiest explanation is that they had to reconcile both themselves and their readers to the dressmaker's downfall. They gave her every legitimate excuse for ruin. Sometimes they were forced to follow ruin with death, Mrs. Gaskell's procedure in *Ruth*. Even then, so sympathetic a picture of a fallen girl was reprehensible to many readers. Since a Victorian novelist dealt in moral and spiritual values, a dressmaker gave ample scope for literary powers. Unlike the factory and shop girls, she fitted in with the traditions of sentiment appropriated by the novel, and she was consequently a popular and useful heroine. Notwithstanding such explanations for the ulterior motives of fiction, the literature on the subject of dressmakers was invaluable for the effective publicity it gave to the injustice suffered by young girls. Mrs. Gaskell, both in *Mary Barton* and *Ruth*, has related the effects of monotonous excessive labour with power and excellent compression. Mrs. Tonna, by means of contrast in character and the skilful transformation of parliamentary evidence into conversation, gave to the drudgery of apprentices an unforgettable tragedy. Since Government legislation was unable to reach this oppressed class of workers, they were in greater need of the literary presentation which factory women were largely denied. Authors succeeded in demonstrating the truth that the proverbial loose morals of dressmakers and milliners were bound up with solid economic and social fact. That at the same time they were able to create such lifelike characters as Little Emily, Kate Nickleby, Little Dorrit, Jenny Wren, Mary Barton, Ruth Hilton, and Maggie Tulliver as representatives of those workers who live by their needle, is proof enough of the literary importance of the dressmaker heroine.

CHAPTER V

THE GOVERNESS

1. Her History

Mrs. Anna Jameson, herself a governess long before she became famous as an author, and, therefore, not entirely without authority, traced the genealogy of the governess back to Minerva. But if the stern-eyed Roman goddess was the tutelary spirit of those who instructed the young, her worship had degenerated on English soil. The meek young woman who served the intellectual needs of a Victorian household was the direct descendant of an almost unbroken line of ignorant servants who began as nurses to the girls in the household and then advanced to the responsibility of adviser and confidential friend, like the nurse in *Romeo and Juliet*. In Ford's *'Tis Pity She's a Whore* (1633) and in Fletcher's *Humorous Lieutenant* (1625?), such an attendant is called a governess. It is a safe conjecture that the mass of women who had the responsibility of moulding the young female mind were not superior to these famous representatives of the profession in drama. In the eighteenth century the intellectual demands upon the governess seem to have advanced little beyond those of the sixteenth. Of the pious old person who taught Lady Mary Montagu to read and write, her pupil wrote: "She took so much pains from my infancy to fill my head with superstitious tales and false notions, it was none of her fault I am not at this day afraid of witches and hobgoblins, or turned methodist."[1] But among all these governesses there were, no doubt, women of learning exceptional for their day. From Tudor times a few highly educated men and women had been engaged to teach the daughters in noble families. In the seventeenth century Bathsua Makin, who carried out ambitious educational schemes for the girls in her school at Putney, was governess to a

daughter of Charles I. In the eighteenth century Elizabeth
Elstob, an Anglo-Saxon scholar, taught the children of the
Duchess of Portland. The Puritan governess in Jasper Mayne's
The City Match (1639), who "works Hebrew samplers", and
teaches her pupil Dorcas to "knit in Chaldee" and to make
"religious petticoats", may have been introduced not as a
comic figure ridiculed for intellectual pretension and religious
bigotry, but as an alarmingly learned lady inspired by the
dramatist's acquaintance with a prototype of Mrs. Makin.
Mrs. Teachem in Sarah Fielding's *Little Female Academy* (1745),
and possibly Mrs. Norton in *Clarissa Harlowe*, also belong
to the class of superior governesses.

In the early period of her history, however, the governess
was, in general, the hireling of only the more aristocratic
families. In the average household the girls learned to work
samplers and knit garters under the direction of their mothers
or a servant too old for active service. But with the increased
interest in the welfare of children which characterized the
humanitarian spirit of the eighteenth century, it is highly
probable that many more parents than those who read the
ridicule of the ignorance of girls in Dr. Johnson's *Idler* of
1758,[2] decided that their daughters should be taught reading
and writing. A superior servant was found necessary for this
new responsibility, and the family governess became more
and more common. Daughters of the upper classes were no
longer the only girls who were taught by governesses. In
clergymen's families especially, a governess was employed
for the education of the daughters. While England remained
an agricultural country, with travel difficult and the female
population nearly stationary, such home instruction was a
practical procedure. But with the industrial development which
created cities and broke up the former rural isolation with
railroads, the governess was not, as might be expected, displaced. Manufacturers imitated the aristocracy and clergy
in having their daughters taught at home. The absence of
good schools for girls was not the only reason for adherence

to the old system. It had become the respectable thing for middle-class households to have a governess.

2. THE LIFE OF A GOVERNESS IN THE NINETEENTH CENTURY

In the nineteenth century the governess was a firmly established institution. Her importance is proved both by the census figures and by her frequent appearance as heroine or minor figure in the novels of the period. Although the census of 1841 does not list governesses apart from schoolmistresses and assistants, in 1851 they received separate attention. In 1850 over twenty-one thousand women were governesses.[3] The field of their employment was rapidly spreading. Mark Pattison, Rector of Lincoln College, Oxford, appearing before the Schools Inquiry Commission in 1865, explained that the daughters of the upper middle class, of professional men, and the clergy, were educated mainly by governesses, the middle class proper in boarding schools.[4] But other witnesses of broader experience reported that the fashion of educating girls at home had spread to the lower middle class. Farmers and tradesmen, because of the inadequacy of schools, had governesses.[5] Such a state of affairs was reflected in fiction. The family teacher had become too important a social figure to be neglected. That Lady Blessington, driven by her expensive manner of life to manage a successfully financial pen, should write a novel on the governess, suggests that such a theme was popular enough to be profitable. And that Anne Brontë, who wrote to satisfy a moral and spiritual restlessness, should also write a governess tale, indicates that the governess, in her earnest opinion, was in sore need of immediate relief. Other novelists took up the cause, and magazine writers and Government officials became seriously concerned with her. From all these sources, then, much can be learned about the economic and social status of these wage-earning women.

The social class of both the employer and the governess was

a primary consideration with all writers on the subject. Parents who employed a governess for their children, according to the novels at least, ought to belong to the aristocracy or the upper middle class. In *Agnes Grey*, by Anne Brontë, the Murrays of Horton belonged to the highly approved country families, although Mr Murray, a fox-hunting squire, whose children had acquired manners so tainted by the stable that their mother was forced to send for a governess to give them superficial attractions and showy accomplishments, showed few of the graces of a gentleman. Clare in *Wives and Daughters* (1865), by Mrs Gaskell, was employed by an aristocratic country family. Sir Pitt Crawley in *Vanity Fair*, Mr. Rochester in *Jane Eyre*, and Mr. Keeldar in *Shirley*, were all country gentlemen. In the professional class were the clergyman Dr. Kenn in *The Mill on the Floss*; the solicitor Mr. Wilkins in *A Dark Night's Work*, by Mrs. Gaskell; Mr. Gibson, a country physician in *Wives and Daughters*; and Major Ponto in Thackeray's *The Book of Snobs*. The Rivers sisters in *Jane Eyre*, and Clara Mordaunt in *The Governess* by Lady Blessington, had situations in families of great wealth. The manufacturers also hired governesses. Mr. Vincy in *Middlemarch*, Mr. Bradshaw in *Ruth*, the unnamed employers of Ruth Pinch in *Martin Chuzzlewit*, described as "perhaps the wealthiest brass and copper founders' family known to mankind", and Sir Brian and Hobson Newcome, were manufacturers. The only representative of the humbler ranks was Mr. Bloomfield, a retired tradesman, Agnes Grey's first employer, and his family life revealed the absence of the gentility and courtesy which Victorian novelists were too ready to make the peculiar possession of the landed aristocracy.

The governess herself, according to tradition at least, was supposed to be a girl of gentle birth. As a writer in the *Quarterly Review* stated the case:[6]

"The real definition of a governess, in the English sense, is a being who is our equal in birth, manners, and education, but our inferior in worldly wealth. Take a lady, in every meaning of the word, born

and bred, and let her father pass through the *Gazette,* and she wants
nothing more to suit our highest *beau idéal* of a guide and instructress
to our children. We need the imprudencies, extravagancies, mis-
takes, or crimes of a certain number of fathers to sow that seed
from which we reap the harvest of governesses. There is no other
class which so cruelly requires its members to be, in birth, mind,
and manners, above their station, in order to fit them for their
station."

Novelists represented these daughters of ruined gentlemen as
commonly becoming governesses. Maria Young in *Deerbrook*
(1839), by Harriet Martineau, Clara Mordaunt in *The Governess*
(1839), and Margaret Sutherland in *Tales of Woman's Trials*
(1835), by Mrs. S. C. Hall, were all the martyrs of wrecked
fortunes. The daughters of clergymen grew up with the fate
of governesses before them from their infant days. *Fraser's*
contended that the daughters of clergymen used to be housekeepers and ladies' maids, but that they now had loftier
pretensions. In the nineteenth century, then, Mrs. Slipslop,
the daughter of a clergyman and maid to Lady Booby, in
Joseph Andrews, would as a governess have had a broader
sweep for her grandiloquent vocabulary. Agnes Grey and the
Rivers sisters belonged, like their creators, to clerical households. Ruth in the novel *Ruth,* and Miss Monroe in *A Dark
Night's Work,* were clergymen's daughters. The *Christian
Lady's Magazine* referred to the sad circumstance of the
daughters of clergymen being "driven to the situation of
governess". So fixed had the future of clergymen's daughters
become that Tennyson in *The Northern Farmer—New Style*
(1870) wrote:

> "Parson's lass 'ant nowt, an' weänt a nowt when 'es dead,
>   Mun be a guvness [governess], lad, or summut, and addle
>   [earn] her bread."

Not all the governesses of fiction, however, were so irre-
proachably born. Esther Lyon in *Felix Holt* was brought up
as the daughter of a Dissenting minister. Becky Sharp was the

daughter of a Bohemian artist, Ruth Pinch of a gentleman's housekeeper, and Maggie Tulliver of a miller. Miss Eyre, Molly Gibson's governess in *Wives and Daughters*, was a shop-keeper's daughter. The *Quarterly Review* discovered that

"farmers and tradespeople are now educating their daughters for governesses as a mode of advancing them a step in life, and thus a number of underbred young women have crept into the profession who have brought down the value of salaries and interfered with the rights of those whose birth and misfortunes leave them no other refuge."[9]

The attitude of Society toward the profession of instructing the young had changed little since Jane Austen in *Emma* (1814) represented her heroine attempting to make a ladylike reference to the fact that Jane Fairfax was to become a governess.[10]

" 'You know Miss Fairfax's situation in life, I conclude—what she is destined to be.'
" 'Yes'—rather hesitatingly—'I believe I do.' "

In Maggie Tulliver's humbler circle of a later day, her mother's family felt the disgrace of Maggie's pedagogical employment. "Going into service" was the expression by which the Dodson mind represented to itself the position of teacher or governess.[11] The friends of Janet in *Scenes of Clerical Life*, excusing her marriage to a drunken scoundrel, remarked that she "had nothing to look to but being a governess".[12] Employers had an equally patronizing attitude toward the position of those who taught their children. Mrs. Vincy in *Middlemarch* referred to Mary Garth as " a dreadful plain girl—more fit for a governess".[13] Rosamond Vincy thought of the family governess, Miss Morgan, as "brown, dull, and resigned, and altogether, as Miss Vincy often said, just the sort of person for a governess".[14]

A girl who faced this occupation had no illusions. Jane Fairfax expressed the resigned fortitude of her Victorian descendants.[15] "With the fortitude of a devoted novitiate, she had resolved at one-and-twenty to complete the sacrifice, and retire from all the pleasures of life, of rational intercourse, equal society, peace and hope, to penance and mortification for ever." Clare in *Wives and Daughters* was "rather weary of girls as a class. All the trials of her life were connected with girls in some way. She was very young when she first became a governess, and had been worsted in her struggles with her pupils in the first place she ever went to. Her elegance of appearance and manner, and her accomplishments, more than her character and acquirements, had rendered it easier for her than for most to obtain good 'situations', and she had been absolutely petted in some; but still she was constantly encountering naughty or stubborn, or over-conscientious, or severe-judging, or curious and observant girls."[16] Mary Garth preferred the exacting task of taking care of a cross old man to that of going out as a governess. "I think my life is pleasanter than your Miss Morgan's", she told Rosamond Vincy. Jane Eyre, in choosing to teach in St. John Rivers's school, said: "It was plodding—but then, compared with that of a governess in a rich house, it was independent; and the fear of servitude with strangers entered my soul like iron." No heroine in fiction, however, rose to the heights of rebellion against the hardships of her employment as did the most brilliant and sharp-tongued of governesses—Charlotte Brontë. In a letter included in Mrs. Gaskell's *Life* she wrote: "I hate and abhor the very thought of governess-ship."[17] Again she wrote: "But no one but myself can tell how hard a governess's work is to me—for no one but myself is aware how utterly averse my whole mind and nature are for the employment."[18] She refers to her work as "governess drudgery",[19] which she would gladly have exchanged for "work in a mill".

From all the evidence at hand it is clear that girls were governesses when financial necessity drove them to self-support. Mrs. Jameson testified: "The occupation of governess merely through necessity is the only means by which a woman not born in the servile classes can earn the means of subsistence." She had never heard of a governess who was one by choice.[20] The same opinion is well stated by the author of *The Industrial and Social Position of Women.*

> "The situation of governess is the only other ordinarily available to any one wishing to retain her position in the middle ranks; and to it every young woman of spirit, intelligence, and education turns herself, when from unforeseen calamities she is driven to earn her own subsistence. Indeed, it forms the chief support of all that have a shadow of education."[21]

In *Fraser's* Miss Martineau is quoted as saying that there was no chance for the single woman but through ineffectual teaching.[22]

An examination of what Mr. Rochester in *Jane Eyre* called "governessing slavery" reveals an excuse for the panic of the wage-earning gentlewoman at the prospect of saving herself from starvation by such means. Young girls at nineteen, like Agnes Grey, and Clara Mordaunt at twenty, had had some free girlhood before they began their term of servitude. But records showed that girls at sixteen became governesses.[23] Wages varied. Agnes Grey's first post had a salary of twenty-five pounds yearly; Jane Eyre was paid thirty. The *Quarterly Review* gave one hundred or one hundred and twenty guineas as exceptional salaries.[24] *Fraser's* placed the usual annual rate at thirty-five pounds, although thirty was a common salary.[25] Wages as low as twelve pounds yearly were paid.[26] In a later article the equality of remuneration for the governess and the upper servants in a good family was commented on. Sir George Stephen, the legal champion of governesses, made a careful investigation of their wages, and found in 1844 one governess who was paid four hundred pounds yearly, three paid three hundred pounds, a few two hundred, and many eighty pounds.[27] Charlotte Brontë in her last situation received twenty pounds, really only sixteen, because the expenses of washing were deducted.[28] *Punch* began to conduct a vigorous campaign for the relief of governesses, showing the cruelty and ridiculousness of wages as low as eight and sixteen pounds per year.[29]

Many women, out of such stipends, had others besides themselves to support. Miss Maunsell, in Mrs. S. C. Hall's *Stories of the Governess*, cared for her mother and brother, with the result that she was penniless at fifty-two. A woman of sixty-two, according to the *Quarterly Review*, a governess all her life, had managed to educate two orphan nieces and a nephew.[30] So popular was the general theory of a bankrupt parent to be supported by a governess daughter that in *The Book of Snobs* Miss Wirt so represented her father, in reality a livery-button maker. Allowing her the scant comfort of an imaginary lost grandeur, Thackeray made her responsible for a bedridden father and for a young brother whose cadet's outfit she furnished. *Once a Week* summarized the situation thus:[31]

"She cannot avoid hearing the dreadful stories that we all hear, every year of our lives, of old governesses, starved, worn out, blind, paralytic, insane, after having educated nephews and nieces, put themselves out of the way of marriage, resisted temptations of which no one but the desolate can comprehend the force, and fought a noble fight, without receiving crown or tribute."

For a profession offering so little material reward, the advertisements for governesses exposed the impossible array of qualifications expected. *Punch*,[32] collecting some of the most ridiculous of these appearing in the *London Times*, the *Evangelical Magazine*, and other papers, constructed ironic replies. In answer to the following, published in *The Times*, June 27, 1845:

"Wanted, a Governess, on Handsome Terms. Governess—a comfortable home, but without salary, is offered to any lady wishing for a situation as governess in a gentleman's family, residing in the country, to instruct two little girls in music, drawing, and English; a thorough knowledge of the French language is required,"

Punch wrote:

"Sir,—Having a comfortable patrimony, and acknowledging that high and elevating necessity of our nature, that compels the heart to love something, I should feel myself selected by the happiest fortune did you think me worthy of fulfilling the serious, and no less delicious, duties of nursery governess to your interesting children (number no consequence).

"If I have any emotion in excess it is that of the love of children; a quality, perhaps, only second to that of plain and ornamental needlework. My activity never permits me to have a moment's leisure; and my good temper, from the time of my infancy, has passed into a family proverb.

"You state, Sir—and I admire the frankness—that 'no salary' will be given. I can fully understand, Sir, that the delightful privilege of dwelling under your roof, and enjoying the pure moral atmosphere of your hearth, must far exceed any value to be awarded by the coined dross of this selfish world. How happy am I that, possessing a sufficient competence of my own, I may give myself up heart, and soul, and pocket, to the formation of the minds of your children, and to the daily execution of your needlework. Deign, Sir, to consider my application with the most favourable grace; and, supplicating an answer,

"I remain your obedient and anxious servant."

Mrs. Jameson made as merry sport of the advertisements for governesses. *Fraser's* wrote, "such a catalogue of literary, ornamental, and moral acquirements as one would think no ordinary mortal would lay claim to". One mother, in search of an "all-accomplished and superior person", appealed to her brother by means of a letter stating her requirements in detail. The brother's answer is a delightful rebuke:

"MY DEAR SISTER,

"I have never yet met with such a woman as you describe; but when I do, I shall make her my wife, and not your governess."[34]

Heads of schools, desiring to place their trained pupils in good positions, wrote out pontifical credentials that might have impressed their patrons more successfully if they had followed the approved model adopted by a rhetorical conspiracy of head mistresses less rigorously. Miss Pinkerton in *Vanity Fair* used the following form:

"Either of these two young ladies is perfectly qualified to instruct in Greek, Latin, and the rudiments of Hebrew; in mathematics and history; in Spanish, French, Italian, and geography; in music, vocal and instrumental; in dancing without the aid of a master; and in the elements of natural sciences. In the use of the globes both are proficients. In addition to this, Miss Tuffin, who is daughter of the late Reverend Thomas Tuffin (Fellow of Corpus College, Cambridge), can instruct in the Syriac language, and the elements of constitutional law. But as she is only eighteen years of age, and of exceedingly pleasing personal appearance, perhaps this young lady may be objectionable in Sir Huddleston Fuddlestons's family. . . .

"Both ladies are endowed with every moral and religious virtue. Their terms, of course, are such as their accomplishments merit."[35]

Some sympathy must be granted these head mistresses and their proficient charges, for parents had such divergent views concerning what they wanted the instructor to be and to do that no training could meet all the demands. Mr. Gibson in *Wives and Daughters* feared lest his only daughter Molly become too learned.

" 'Don't teach Molly too much: she must sew, and read, and write, and do her sums, but I want to keep her a child, and if I find more learning desirable for her, I'll see about it to her myself. After all, I'm not sure that reading or writing is necessary.' "[35]

The wife of the retired tradesman in *Agnes Grey* demanded a young woman who would be a satisfactory nursery governess, washing and dressing and taking care of the clothes of the youngest child, would prepare the boy for school, and make over the diabolical dispositions of the two older girls. In her next situation Agnes was expected to make the girls "superficially attractive and showily accomplished without trouble to them". "I was", she records the programme pathetically, "to study and strive to amuse and oblige, instruct, refine, and polish, with the least possible exertion on their part, and no exercise of authority on mine."[37] The boys were to be taught the greatest quantity of Latin in the most painless way possible. The oldest daughter, encouraged by her mother, wanted only showy accomplishments—French, German, music, singing, dancing, fancy work, with the tedious parts done by the governess, and drawing, with the same kind of assistance.

Thackeray in *The Book of Snobs* makes an array of the ideal accomplishments of a governess.[38]

> " 'I asked this great creature in what other branches of education she instructed her pupils.' 'The modern languages,' says she modestly; 'French, German, Spanish, and Italian, Latin and the rudiments of Greek if desired. English, of course; the practice of Elocution, Geography, and Astronomy, and the Use of the Globes, Algebra (but only as far as quadratic equations); for a poor ignorant female, you know, Mr. Snob, cannot be expected to know everything. Ancient and Modern History no young woman can be without; and of these I make my beloved pupils *perfect mistresses.* Botany, Geology, and Mineralogy I consider as amusements.' . . .
>
> " 'But,' adds Mr. Snob, 'I looked in one of Miss Ponto's manuscript song-books and found five faults of French in four words: and in a waggish mood asking Miss Wirt whether Dante Algiery was so called because he was born at Algiers, received a smiling answer in the affirmative, which made me rather doubt about the accuracy of Miss Wirt's knowledge.' "

The governess Mrs. General in *Little Dorrit* seems to have been an ideal of Victorian pedagogical virtues, for she "varnished the surface that it might receive proper Society polish", and knew that opinions interfered with "perfect breeding".

The training of a governess could scarcely be arranged to meet these varied demands, and in too many cases the solution of no training at all was the easiest way out of the dilemma. If a girl of good family suffered financial reverses she automatically became a governess. If her antecedents were not too remarkable she might be expected to have had a little previous training. A writer in *Fraser's* asked:[39]

> "Is it not monstrous, that while a lady will not give her dress to be made to any one but a first-class dressmaker, she will give her children to be educated by a second or third-rate governess? That she will commit their training for this world and the next to a woman whose only qualification for the task is that she has had a twelvemonth's apprenticeship in an inferior boarding school, or that her father failed last week?"

Mrs. Gaskell described the hopelessness of improving the general character of governesses while the mothers themselves had low standards for the profession. Lady Harriet, in *Wives and Daughters*, in characterizing her governess said:[40] "She's not very wise, certainly; but she's so useful and agreeable, and has such pleasant manners, I should have thought any one who wasn't particular about education would have been charmed to keep her as a governess." Again, in *Ruth* an ex-dressmaker becomes a satisfactory governess in Mr. Bradshaw's family. Mrs. Jameson was disturbed by the new theory that colleges should be instituted to train girls for teaching. "For myself, I should not much like to take into my family a woman educated expressly for a teacher. I should expect to meet with something of a machine."[41]

The education of the governess was scantily referred to in various books of the period. Mrs. Jameson stated that she "was educated at some Ladies' Seminary or fashionable boarding school".[42] The Brontë sisters received training probably typical of that of many girls of their profession. After some preliminary study at home they went to Cowan's Bridge School, an institution for the daughters of clergymen, where they studied history, geography, the use of globes, grammar, writing, arithmetic, needlework, and housework such as getting up fine linen and ironing. Music and drawing were extras.[43] Charlotte, in addition to the one year she spent there, had two years at Miss Wooler's school at Roe Head, where she made up her deficiencies in geography and grammar. All three sisters knew French well enough to read it fluently, but not how to teach it. Emily and Anne had some musical training. Jane Eyre's education was almost an exact duplicate of her creator's. Esther in *Bleak House* was educated at Miss Donny's school to be a governess for six years as both pupil and apprentice teacher. Esther Lyon had the exceptional advantage of education in France. Rebecca Sharp was an articled pupil for two years in Miss Pinkerton's school, where she looked after the little girls in the lower school and talked French to the older girls. Of her education Thackeray wrote: "As she was already a musician and a good linguist, she speedily went through the little course of study which was considered necessary for ladies in those days",[44] in Miss Pinkerton's establishment consisting of music, dancing, orthography, every variety of needlework, and geography. Mary Garth in *Middlemarch* was educated in a provincial school as an articled pupil. Maggie Tulliver's education was of the scantiest, as she realized, for she would never get a better situation "without more accomplishments". The *Quarterly Review* described the governess with bald irony as "conversant with several languages—skilled in many accomplishments—crammed with every possible fact in history, geography, and the use of the globes—and scarcely the daily bread to put into her mouth".[45]

The governess in training frequently became an apprentice teacher, like Charlotte Brontë at Roe Head, Jane Eyre at Lowood, Esther, and Rebecca Sharp. The more conscientious young women studied by themselves after their schooldays were over. Mary and Diana Rivers in *Jane Eyre* took up German because they would be paid more if they could teach it. Miss Monro in *A Dark Night's Work* studied Spanish evenings. Miss Young in *Deerbrook* also studied German. But all of these were exceptional young women of intellectual interests and honesty.

When one comes to the subject of the sufferings of the governess, there is no dearth of material. The spirited writing denied the women in coal-mines or nail and chain works was given without stint to that ladylike heroine of delicate sensibilities and infinite capacity for forbearance, the Victorian governess; for what a coarse working woman could not feel was torture to her finer clay. But for all this sympathy there were powerful causes. "The hardships of the life of a governess are as widely known as the hardships of the life of a needle-woman; in biographies, in novels, in the newspapers, and from

the personal observation of everyone, they may be learned",
wrote one unusually sane commentator.[46]

A study of the daily life of these young women shows it to
have been one of general loneliness. Banished to remote rooms
in the top of the house, shared too often with the children,
and eating their meals in the schoolroom alone or, worse still,
with children as tormenting as Agnes Grey's pupils, who let
her food grow cold if they were in the midst of their games,
they had no escape from the cold depression which too often
settled upon them. Of such isolation Thackeray wrote: "She
sits alone in the schoolroom, high, high up in that lone house,
when the little ones are long since asleep, before her dismal
little tea-tray, and her little desk, containing her mother's
letters and her mementoes of home."[47] Charlotte Brontë
confessed in a letter:

"I used to think I should like to be in the stir of grand folks'
society; but I have had enough of it—it is dreary work to look on
and listen. I see more clearly than I have ever done before, that
a private governess has no existence, is not considered as a living
rational being, except as connected with the wearisome duties she
has to fulfil."[48]

Again, she characterized her profession as "dreary solitary
work". "You can tell as well as me the lonely feeling of being
without a companion."[49] In *The Professor* she wrote: "I
looked weary, solitary, kept down like some desolate tutor
or governess." Miss Monroe, Mrs. Gaskell portrayed as
talking aloud, a practice which "had become her wont in the
early years of her isolated life as a governess".[50] The *Christian
Lady's Magazine* mentioned the "awful isolation of governesses".[51]

The social discrimination inflicted by employers often of
no superior culture or refinement was commented on by
Mrs. Jameson, who knew that of which she wrote:

"The relation which exists between the governess and her
employer either places a woman of education and of superior

faculties in an ambiguous and inferior position, with none of the privileges of a recognized profession, or it places a vulgar, half-educated woman in a situation of high responsibility, requiring superior endowments."[52]

Diana and Mary Rivers worked in the fashionable homes of people "who neither knew nor sought one of their innate excellences, and appreciated only their acquired accomplishments as they appreciated the skill of their cook or the taste of their waiting-woman".[53] In *The Book of Snobs*, Major Ponto, discovering a well-treated governess, observed: "I, who have been accustomed to see governesses bullied in the world, was delighted to find this one ruling the roost."[54] So far was the stigma of being a governess carried that Harriet Martineau discovered "a suburb of London where the rules of the book-club contain, or did recently contain, a provision that no person engaged in education shall be admitted as a subscriber".[55] Even when employers were kind, as Clare expressed it in *Wives and Daughters*, "one has always had to remember one's position".[56] One of the newspaper advertisements reprinted in *Punch* is more powerful than pages of description :[57] "If a young lady, she would often be admitted into the parlour, and would have her meals in the school-room."

Servants, studying the attitude of their employers toward the governess, were insolent themselves. The porter told Clara Mordaunt when she arrived that she was no better than the servants, and immediately insulted her about her trunk. The lady's-maid made it her business to reprove her. The servants in the Sedley house were impertinent to Becky Sharp when she visited Amelia. The housekeeper, Mrs. Blenkinsop, said of her: "I don't trust them governesses, Pinner. They give themselves the hairs and hupstarts of ladies, and their wages is no better than you nor me."[58]

Petty discrimination and tyranny exaggerated the humble-ness of her position. Clara Mordaunt was given a tallow candle instead of a wax one. *Fraser's* relates an incident which proves that such a practice was common. A girl in a fashionable household, noting the absence of the tallow candle, remarked that "Calypso was not there". Upon being asked the meaning of her cryptic statement, she explained that Calypso was taller than her nymphs, just as the governess's tallow candle was taller than the wax ones used by members of the family and their guests.[59] Becky Sharp had orders to put out her candle at eleven. Agnes Grey had to ride to church with her back to the horses, even though it made her ill. When she walked with her pupils they ordered her to keep a few steps behind them so that they could talk without the restraint of her presence. Charlotte Brontë in a letter in 1839 wrote: "I had orders to follow a little behind."[60]

The fact was also emphasized by some writers that the governess had no equals and, therefore, no sympathy. In Society, says the writer in the *Quarterly Review*, she was a burden and a restraint.

"She is a bore to almost any gentleman, as a tabooed woman, to whom he is interdicted from granting the usual privileges of the sex, and yet who is perpetually crossing his path. She is a bore to most ladies by the same rule, and a reproach, too—for her dull, fagging, bread-and-water life is perpetually putting their pampered listlessness to shame. The servants invariably detest her, for she is a dependent like themselves, and yet, for all that, as much their superior in other respects as the family they both serve. Her pupils may love her, and she may take the deepest interest in them, but they cannot be her friends."[61]

This long passage from the article reviewing *Vanity Fair* and *Jane Eyre*, as well as the first report of the Governesses' Benevolent Association, to be treated later, Charlotte Brontë quoted exactly in Mrs. Pryor's bitter attack on the sufferings of governesses in *Shirley*.[62] Anne Brontë described Agnes as recording the names of the people who did not speak to her after church, including the clergyman, an incident bespeaking the author's proud resentment of her teaching days. Thackeray said, in emphasizing the kind nature of Colonel Newcome: "He behaves with splendid courtesy to Miss Quigley, the governess, and makes a point of taking wine with her, and of making a most profound bow during that ceremony."[63] When the sympathetic Thackeray invited Charlotte Brontë to meet some of his friends at his home, she, still smarting from the bitterness of her former misery, spent most of the evening conversing with the children's governess.[64]

The isolation of the governess was unnecessarily increased by the unwillingness of many employers to allow her visitors. When they were allowed, they were often rudely treated. Clara was given the privilege of callers once a month. Agnes Grey could not see her friends at the Murray house, and she had no opportunity to make new ones. When the curate showed a friendly interest in her, one of her pupils flirted with him and kept Agnes from seeing him. One must add, remembering the Victorian novelist's unshaken faith in the conquering power of true love, that in the end he succeeded in seeing her and finally in marrying her, but not until she was removed from the too stony soil of governessing. Tom Pinch, when he called upon his sister Ruth, was insulted first by the porter and the footman and then by her employers. The brassfounder delivered his social code for the family governess promptly: "I do not approve, as a principle, of any governess receiving visitors." Charlotte Brontë in one letter asked whether it was improper for governesses to ask their friends to come and see them. When her father was entertained by her last employers with charming courtesy, she was very much surprised.[65]

In the relation of the governess and the pupils writers, wisely enough, discerned the greatest problem. It was one of severe strain because of the enforced daily intimacy. Anne Brontë's description of the behaviour of the children in *Agnes Grey* would seem ridiculous exaggeration were it not corroborated by other writers. The young teacher was at the mercy of the children, like a slave. She had to run, walk, or stand in the garden, according to their fancy. When she

wanted them in the schoolroom she had to run after them
and catch them. "The task of instruction", the gentle Anne
explained, "was as arduous for the body as the mind."[66] One
would smile, if the sufferings of a frail girl in this confessional
book of hers were not so starkly revealed. There were no
settled hours of study. Tom pretended to weep when he was
forced to learn his lessons. His governess had to hold his
hand to make him write. Mary Ann lay on the floor in stubborn
rebellion against any form of instruction, and her screams
could be heard from afar. The youngest child was mischievous,
intractable, deceptive; she had the inconvenient habit of
spitting in the faces of those who opposed her, and she could
bellow like a bull. The children made teasing their governess
a daily occupation. They threatened to throw her work-bag
in the fire. They ran out in the snow. Agnes used the weapons
"Patience, Firmness, and Perseverance". Timid and inex-
perienced, she embarked on a deliberate campaign to conquer
her unruly charges. She resolved that she would make the
children stay in the schoolroom until they got their lessons,
that she would fulfil all the threats and promises she made,
and that she would keep her temper. At night she would
remind them of their sins, and would choose hymns penitential
or cheerful according to their behaviour. She prayed for help
daily in a task that finally was too much for her. In her second
situation Agnes Grey had less physical strain, but she was
equally tyrannized over by her pupils.

In *Jane Eyre* Mr. Rochester's guests amused themselves one
evening by reminiscences of the tricks they had once played
on their governesses. Blanche Ingram related of Madame
Joubert: "I see her yet in her raging passions, when we had
driven her to extremities—spilt our tea, crumbled our bread
and butter, tossed our books up to the ceiling, and played a
charivari with the ruler and desk, the fender and fire-irons."
Her brother then told how they "sermonized her on the presumption of attempting to teach such clever blades as we were,
when she was herself so ignorant". Another governess was

described as more amiable: "We might do what we pleased—ransack her desk and her work-box, and turn her drawers inside out; and she was so good-natured, she would give us anything we asked for."[67]

The Victorian child, banished from the drawing-room, apparently ruled the nursery. In *Pendennis* Frank Clavering, "in his disputes with his governess over his book, . . . kicked that quiet creature's shins so fiercely that she was entirely overmastered and subdued by him".[68] Clara Mordaunt was told by the porter that the children would "worry her worse nor ever a cat did a rat", and his prophecy was fulfilled. Charlotte Brontë had some difficult experiences with her pampered pupils, and she confessed "it was hard to repel the rude familiarity of the children".[69] Thackeray is one of the few writers who showed the gentler moments of the unruly English child. In *The Newcomes* Maria Newcome, as the dishes were brought from the dining-room, used to take the sweet things and give them to her governess, an unamiable woman described by Clive as "a great cross French governess, who is always crying, shrieking after them, and finding fault with them".[70] The assertive governess was apparently more successful than meek Agnes Grey.

For the difficulties the teacher had with her pupils, the mother of the children was generally blamed. In *The English Governess* by Miss McCrindell the governess was sent away merely because the pupil was tired of her lessons. Interference with discipline was a frequent complaint. Mrs. Bloomfield informed Agnes Grey that she was not to punish the children. She later complained that they got worse under the governess. Mrs. Murray, her next employer, gave her grandiloquent advice. She urged her to keep her temper and to be mild always, quoting St. Matthew's approval of a meek and quiet spirit to prove that her sons must have gentle treatment. When remonstrance failed, the mother was to be used as a court of appeal. Mrs. Murray soon was scolding Miss Grey for not trying to improve the tastes of the hoydenish Matilda.

She dropped hints that Agnes was not devoting all of her energies to the education of the children. She was hard and unsympathetic when the young governess heard of her father's death. Charlotte Brontë bitterly resented the attitude of the women who employed her. One reproved her for being depressed. Of her she wrote: "I have never had five minutes' conversation with her since I came, except while she was scolding me",[71] and "she cares nothing about me, except to contrive how the greatest possible quantity of labour may be got out of me". Complaints to the mother about the behaviour of the children had no effect. They were to do as they pleased.[72] She related an incident to Mrs. Gaskell which illustrated the unfortunate snobbery of Victorian matrons. The small boy in the family threw a stone at Miss Brontë, but she concealed his offence. In gratitude he said before his mother, "I love 'ou, Miss Brontë". To this the mother "exclaimed before all the children, 'Love the governess, my dear!' "[73] Of the general situation Charlotte Brontë said: "None but those who had been in the position of a governess could ever realize the dark side of 'respectable' human nature; under no great temptation to crime, but daily giving way to selfishness and ill-temper, till its conduct toward those dependent on it sometimes amounts to a tyranny of which one would rather be the victim than the inflicter."[74] The father received less criticism. Charlotte Brontë praised the husband of the woman who was unkind for his unfailing courtesy to her. In *Agnes Grey*, however, Mr. Bloomfield was as unjust as his wife. In *Pendennis* it was the older sister, Blanche Amory, who "sent the governess crying away from the dinner-table",[75] and would give herself "imperial airs of command" and "send that young lady upon messages through the house to bring her book or to fetch her pocket-handkerchief".[76] The effect of the parents' attitude removed any authority the governess might have had. The writer in *Fraser's* showed[77] the consequent demoralization of the children. Ruskin in *Queen's Gardens* wrote:

"But what teachers do you give your girls, and what reverence do you show to the teachers you have chosen? Is a girl likely to think her own conduct, or her own intellect, of much importance, when you trust the entire formation of her character, moral and intellectual, to a person whom you let your servants treat with less respect than they do your housekeeper (as if the soul of your child were a less charge than jams and groceries), and whom you yourself think you confer an honour upon by letting her sometimes sit in the drawing-room in the evening?"[78]

Unsatisfactory as were the relations between the governess and her pupils and their parents, her position was made even more onerous by the indefiniteness of her duties. Earlier pages have shown the conflicting opinions employers had about what they wanted a governess to teach. Their demands upon her time placed her in a situation where she had no stated duties, but was expected to be generally useful. Any leisure from her schoolroom tasks could be filled with needle-work for a thrifty housewife like the one Charlotte Brontë described: "She overwhelms me with oceans of needlework; yards of cambric to hem, muslin nightcaps to make, and, above all, dolls to dress."[79] Much of the sewing was done at night. Clara Mordaunt in *The Governess*, in addition to the sewing, had to read aloud to the mother of her pupils in her spare time. Often a governess was hired, not because she knew anything about teaching, but because she was a clever needlewoman. Ethel Newcome's governess made purses, anti-macassars, guard-chains for Ethel to give Colonel Newcome. In *Middlemarch* Rosamond Vincy called upon the family governess to help her with her trousseau.[80] Clare in *Wives and Daughters* was called away from the schoolroom to write notes for Lady Cumnor and to add up her accounts. No governess in fiction proved more useful than Becky Sharp. She "wrote Sir Pitt's letters, did his business, managed his accounts—had the upper hand of the whole house",[81] a temporary slavery her detractors too easily forgot. She at least worked for her triumph. As one observer said of such duties: "They work as hard as any servant, besides teaching what they can to the children, with no moment of peace either night or day, and for wages which would not be high for a kitchen-maid."

A further hardship was that the governess lived in constant fear of dismissal. A woman in the same family for fifteen years was sent away with a recommendation describing her as a treasure, but with no provision made for her.[82] Women of sixty-two and sixty-seven, who had earned salaries too small to permit savings for old age, were cast off. Some found a little needlework to do. An occasional present helped others. But many women were left totally destitute. Mrs. Jameson stated that the rewards of the governess were "a broken constitution and a lonely unblessed old age".[83] Mrs. Hall's tale *The Old Governess*, a plea for the feeling of responsibility an employer should feel toward the person who has taught his children faithfully, may lay too much stress upon the possibility of universal gratitude in mankind, but it is a moving portrayal of helpless old age.

The effects of such a profession upon women were described by various writers. Mrs. Jameson wrote:

"Now everyone has a just horror of a nervous governess; complaints of the ill-health of governesses, as a class, are so common, one meets with them at every turn; and let the physician speak of what he knows! He could make fearful revelations, if he dared, of the constitutions of young women ruined through fatigue, confinement, anxiety, in a sphere of life somewhat above those who make shirts and fit on finery."[84]

The mental suffering of an isolated situation was inescapable. "It is usual to talk contemptuously of the stiffness and ungenial strictness of a governess: whence have these come?" demanded one student of the general problems of working women.[85] The result of a succession of morbid days was, in extreme cases, insanity. Harriet Martineau suggested the seriousness of such results: "Let philanthropists inquire into the proportion of governesses among inmates of lunatic asylums."[86] Later she stated that servants and governesses formed by far the largest proportion among the insane, both the victims of overwork and underpay. *Punch*, *Fraser's*, and the *Quarterly Review* all gave the same tragic verdict.

In the face of this unrelieved gloom of fact, it is not surprising that governesses struggled to escape. The ambition of most young women seems to have been somewhat lacking in originality. They plotted deliverance by setting up a school, or by marrying a curate. Agnes Grey and Clare did both. Jane Eyre had the same plan as the Brontë sisters of opening a school, but unlike them was, with St. John Rivers's help, successful in carrying it out. David Copperfield's mother was released from her bonds by the gallantry of his father. Becky Sharp contrived to set herself up in the good graces of her employer. An even greater genius among governesses, Charlotte Brontë, retired to a Yorkshire vicarage and satirized her employers in three remarkable novels, before she married her father's curate. Unfortunately, there was escape for only the most energetically ambitious and attractive women. The rest had to be saved in other ways. To the improvement of the condition of the governess both writers and social and educational reformers directed their energies, and contrived a programme of reform that was both intelligently constructive and far-reaching in its effects.

3. The Relief of the Governess

In a study of the general situation the reformers of the time made a careful analysis of the reasons for the widespread misfortune of the governess. Mrs. Jameson took upon herself the duty of rousing the mother to a consciousness of a responsibility toward the woman who taught her children. She wrote eloquently upon the necessity employers should feel to give the governess facilities for change of employment, variety, and rest. She preached the advantages of a large airy schoolroom, and a comfortable bedroom away from the children at night. She urged the mother to visit the schoolroom daily and to co-operate with the teacher.[87] A writer in *Fraser's* dwelt upon the importance of teaching children respect for their teachers.[88]

Advice was also given to the governess about her short-comings. A young woman like Miss Wade in *Little Dorrit*, who prided herself on her determination to resist all the kind overtures of her employers, must have been a prickly inmate of any household. The *Christian Lady's Magazine* suggested that the governess "ought not to stipulate for unlimited access to the evening circle".[89] Harriet Martineau, guided always by common sense, scolds the governesses who want to sit at the table when there are dinner-parties and insist upon a permanent invitation to the drawing-room.[90] In *Deerbrook* she has Miss Young, the governess, say: "Let a governess learn what to expect; set her free from a hankering after happiness in her work, and you have a happy governess." But the gospel of work which Miss Martineau doubtless learned from Carlyle is too stoical for general acceptance, as she probably knew.

Recognizing that the relationship could not be made ideal without the radical reform of human nature, the most sensible critics believed that some practical improvement could nevertheless be made. The decision was first reached that governesses should be pitied less and paid more.[92] The wells of pity had evidently been pumped nearly dry, according to *Fraser's*: "The frequent appeals to public compassion made in behalf of governesses—the 'fancy fairs', 'shilling subscription cards', got up with a view to their benefit, are calculated to fill a thinking mind with painful reflections". The main difficulty, according to Mrs. Jameson, was that too many poorly educated young women hired themselves out as governesses at low wages, with the result that the supply always exceeded the demand, and a governess could be obtained for less than a good servant.[93] There was no premium offered for exceptional ability. Until half-educated instructors were excluded, salaries would remain low, and governesses be treated with contempt.

The foundation of the Governesses' Benevolent Association was the beginning of a definite reform in the educational equipment of governesses. From the first, this organization in its provision for temporary relief and gradual improvement, was the decisive force in attacking a long-standing evil with sympathetic intelligence. In 1841, the year it was started, nothing was accomplished except the collection of one hundred pounds. With the appointment of the Reverend David Laing as honorary secretary in 1843, the new society became more active. For a year the meetings were held in his home. A report of the work was made at the end of nine months, and such writers as Mrs. S. C. Hall, who manufactured tales embodying every aspect of their programme, and magazines like the *Quarterly*, *Fraser's*, and *Punch*, gave publicity to the purposes of the new society.

From such sources one gathers the necessary information concerning its actual programme. For the temporary relief of governesses a fund was raised to help women out of work. A home opened in 1846 at 66 Harley Street, in London, with accommodation for twenty-five women during their unemployment, was sufficiently spacious for the ground floor to be used as a registry office without expense to those enrolled. The same building held a bank, where they could invest their money in Government securities in their own names, the society taking all the responsibility, and with another department reserved for small savings. Assistance was also planned for women too old to work; annuities were to be raised, and an asylum built for these helpless, aged workers. By November 1847, four annuities of fifteen pounds had been secured, but there were ninety candidates. The next year the increase to thirty-two annuities was still insufficient.[95] A home in Kentish Town was finally erected, mainly, it would seem, with funds raised by "fancy fairs" at Chelsea Hospital. The general success of this part of the work of the Association is shown by the results in 1862. *Saint James Magazine*[96] reported that £180,000 had been accumulated in Government securities, one hundred annuities for aged governesses had been provided—some of these raised to twenty-five pounds—three thousand women had used the home for unemployment, and fourteen thousand had found engagements through the registry office. The Kentish Town asylum was also in successful operation.*

The most remarkable and enduring project, however, was that of a college which should make it practicable, in time, for all governesses to be required to have a certificate guaranteeing the proper qualifications for their work. A house was taken in Harley Street adjacent to the governesses' home, with the permission of Queen Victoria called Queen's College, and formally opened in 1847. With the humour which relieves so much of the barrenness of historical fact, the date of the opening of this humble school for governesses is now given as the beginning of college education for women. Although Queen's and Bedford College, founded in 1848, in their beginning were only secondary schools with a cumbersome and ineffectual lecture system, they manifested an altogether new consciousness of the importance of intellectual training for women. Men like Maurice and Kingsley, who lectured in King's, offered their services to Queen's. Between 1847 and 1850 nearly two hundred women were given certificates of qualification in various branches of study. After 1862 the College became entirely separate from the Association, except that the latter maintained a system of scholarships whereby sixteen pupils would be trained for governesses.

The *Quarterly Review* in 1850 contained an article of twenty pages, combining reviews of the introductory lectures delivered at Queen's College during 1849, a book describing the origin and progress of Queen's, the report of the Governesses' Benevolent Association for 1848, and also a book about governesses.[97] It offers a picture full of interest for the historian of women's education, and also gives the essential facts about the beginnings of Queen's. The classes open to all girls over twelve were conducted by means of the lecture system, and

* The institution is still flourishing.

divided into junior and senior groups. There were also preparatory classes for girls from nine to twelve. Moderate fees
were charged for such instruction. But the evening classes for
governesses hired during the day were free, and were attended
in 1849 by seventy students. Lady visitors to chaperon the
girls during the lectures by male professors show the rigid
conventions observed. Mrs. Marcet was one of these chape-
rons. The criticism of the College as a training school for
governesses was very intelligent. In the first place, girls
were admitted too young. For the girls under sixteen the
writer showed the advantages of a boarding school or a
governess. Then, the professors did not examine the pupils
on the lectures, so the results were superficial. Much of the
teaching was not suited to governesses. The College itself,
with its connection with the Governesses' Benevolent Association, had a dual purpose, which in its early stages was
considered difficult to execute. The professors, self-constituted
and self-elected, under no superior authority, were not amenable
to any definite policy.

The results of the training at Queen's were naturally not
immediate. The important recognition of the principle of
certificated governesses slowly gained ground. As Queen's
College trained such women as Miss Emily Davies and Miss
Dorothea Beale, and the Home and Colonial School produced
Miss Frances Mary Buss and Miss Annie Clough, all of
them prominent in the movement to give a real education
to English girls, and as training colleges increased rapidly in
England between 1840 and 1850,[98] governesses, as well
as teachers, were forced to equip themselves for their
jobs. Governessing grew into a profession instead of a misfortune.

The kind of preparation designed for governesses is best
presented in connection with the testimony given by prominent
educators before the Schools Inquiry Commission in 1865.
Miss Emily Davies, at the time a lady visitor of Bedford
College, who later was one of the founders of Girton College,

Cambridge, described the training in the special classes for governesses offered by the Home and Colonial School Society. She praised the excellent instruction in elementary subjects, but wanted more advanced studies in the curriculum.[99] Miss M. E. Porter[100] gave an account of her school for training private governesses in Devonshire, limited to the daughters of professional men, in which instruction in English, French, German, drawing, and elementary Latin was offered for a yearly fee of £18. A practising school where the students taught children was an excellent provision. Of two hundred pupils, she stated, one hundred and fiteen had been successful as governesses. Miss Porter herself had been educated at Queen's College. In a second school she conducted in the north of England she offered a two-year course for governesses. It was her opinion that better education would be the most powerful means of improving their social condition.

Conflicting views about the improvement in governesses prove that instructors of the young did not immediately become vessels of wisdom. Miss Davies insisted that as a class they were unfit. Most of them were weak in arithmetic.[101] Miss Gertrude King, secretary of a society for the employment of women, received misspelt letters from governesses applying for situations.[102] But much real gain was discerned. Miss Davies noted some evidences of greater efficiency in their teaching.[103] "At any rate", she stated, "there is a great deal of stir, and they are very anxious to improve themselves, the better sort." Some of the reform she attributed to Queen's College, which had "raised the standard and tone". Governesses joined the classes of drawing and designing in the Government School of Design.[104]

But the idea of certificated governesses continued unpopular in many quarters. A writer in the *Quarterly Review*[105] objected to the system of examinations deciding the merits of governesses : "We would only observe that, as the real and highest responsibility and recommendation of an *English* governess must ever rest more upon her moral than her literary qualifications, the plan of subjecting her to an examination upon the latter appears to us neither wise nor fair." There were also differences of opinion about the kind of education they should have long after it had been generally decided that they ought to be educated. Miss Frances Martin, superintendent of Bedford College School,[106] did not favour a special kind of training for governesses. Miss E. E. Smith, a member of the council of management of Bedford College, agreed that their education should be that of well-educated women.[107]

The solution of the problem was found not to lie in better training alone. In 1844 Sir George Stephen pointed out the fact that "the absence of combination which servants and artisans have" was a source of weakness.[108] The *Quarterly Review* expressed the same opinion.[109] Contemporary reformers in education have placed more and more emphasis upon the necessity of effective organization in all ranks of the profession. In the second place, more efficient means for employment were needed. The registry office at Queen's College and the formation of a society for the employment of women in 1860 were steps in the right direction. With the profession over-crowded as it was, some reformers studied other openings for middle-class girls. Designers for the improvement of manufactures, with training in the Government schools, as well as clerks, book-keepers, housekeepers, were suggested. Harriet Martineau hoped for the opening of more extensive industrial occupation to women. She also described a system of insurance in Denmark which protected a girl from sudden poverty. A society, the Danish Maiden Assurance Company, was founded on the principle that a father, on the birth of a daughter, should register the infant and deposit funds in the society. Each girl then received 4 per cent. interest on the deposit until marriage.[110] But these various suggestions, all given by writers in connection with the governess question, will receive more extended treatment in the part of this study dealing with the whole problem of the middle-class woman.

By comparing the status of the governess in the eighteenth century, the early nineteenth, and the period after 1841, the year the Governesses' Benevolent Association was started, one gets some idea of the changes in the attitude adopted toward her and the rapidity with which her cause gained public notice and intelligent comprehension. Starting as a servant who relieved the mother of the responsibility of the daughters in the household, she advanced to an indefinable condition deemed appropriate for a lady of fallen fortunes, where she was regarded with contempt by her employers and with pity by herself, because she must be self-supporting. From such an anomalous rank the reformers raised her to a position which must be prepared for with adequate education, be decently paid, and receive dignified treatment. By 1850 she belonged to what is still one of the most important occupations for middle-class women. But the question of the governess has not been entirely solved. In the delicate complexities of the relation between the mother and the teacher of children, there is an immortal difficulty which will never be entirely settled while human nature is what it is. Mothers, past and present, have almost unanimously resented criticism of their children. Even the most honest parent has a suspicion that her child is understood by no one but herself. When the critic is a dependent young woman, rendered super-sensitive by enforced self-support in a profession which has had little respect, and when mother and governess live in daily contact, brought about by necessity, not choice, and seldom with congeniality, there is generally friction. In the Victorian period the awkwardness of the case was intensified by the fact that the mother had only a meagre education and no pedagogical standards, and the governess was only slightly her intellectual superior. With the better education for girls, those who were to become mothers and those trained to be teachers, an improvement has resulted. The attitude toward self-support has also grown less apologetic among wage-earning women of the middle class. But not until women are proud of their professions, not merely tolerant of them, will the governess receive the valuation from society she deserves. Too many women become governesses because they can think of no better way of earning a living. During the World War some of those not attached to their jobs escaped temporarily to more vigorous and congenial work. Too many have returned once more to their schoolrooms. One looks forward to the day when men and women will be found only in the work which is theirs by temperamental equipment and training. But such a fitting of round pegs in round holes must be left to the psychologists and the remote future. In the meantime there will be many an unhappy child in the bondage of a woman held to the schoolroom by economic necessity and by lack of freedom in the choice of a profession.

4. LITERARY USE OF THE GOVERNESS

In the relief of the governess fiction played an important part. Although much of the improvement which has been sketched in the preceding pages must be assigned to a new interest in education and the child mind, and to the persistent efforts of some of the most intelligent men and women of the age to better conditions, the widespread publicity gained for the governess and her wrongs is largely the work of novelists. Of all wage-earning heroines in early nineteenth-century literature, the governess occupied by far the most conspicuous place. A variety of causes contributed to her importance. Like the non-textile worker and the dressmaker, she had presented problems insoluble by Parliament. Like the dressmaker, she gained the interest of private organizations; unlike her, effectual aid from them. But with the governess, literature worked side by side with the reformers. It is an interesting coincidence that both *Jane Eyre* and *Vanity Fair* appeared the same year that Queen's College was founded. But the governess as a heroine had claims to popularity superior to those of any working woman so far considered. If the dressmaker's life had tragic elements tempting for fictional treatment, so had hers. Her gentility was easier to demonstrate. If her beauty did not shine upon the gloom of a crowded workshop, it languished alone in an attic schoolroom. She was oppressed not only by her employers, but by her pupils and by the servants. She was insulted by rude guests. Equal to her employers in birth and intelligence, often superior, she was treated worse than a servant. But love came to her, in spite of her sad fortunes. At best, an aristocratic caller saw her drooping figure and instantly loved her. This is the plot of Lady Blessington's novel *The Governess*, and is not far removed from *Jane Eyre*. A humbler fate was that of wife to a curate. Anne Brontë preferred this second type of ending in *Agnes Grey*. But a greater force than these elevated the governess to her supremacy as heroine among working women. Her peculiar good fortune was that she had a governess for her historian. Mary Wollstonecraft had already demonstrated the power of an educated woman turned author. Her years as a governess brought a gleam of passion to her *Vindication of the Rights of Woman*. She knew from experience the farce of domestic education for girls. Mrs. Jameson wrote her essays on governesses and other working women with the same fire. Charlotte Brontë finally proved that it takes a governess to write about governesses. The great governess-tales are not, therefore, those of Lady Blessington, but of Charlotte Brontë. With her comes a type of heroine altogether new—plain, passionate, intelligent, witty. One might almost say—even at the cost of the undying hostility of Jane Austen admirers— that the governess brought the intelligent heroine into the place of honour she has since occupied. Pamela had a low cunning; Elizabeth Bennett and Emma a sprightly charm; but the woman of brains was ushered into fiction with Jane Eyre, Lucy Snowe, and Becky Sharp. She was a creature as entirely outside the realms of Victorian conventions as the independent mill girl, and, therefore, not approved. Harriet Martineau wrote:[111]

"I have too much sympathy with the class which suffer keenly and indignantly under such picture-drawing as the Brontës, and many other novelists, have thrust into every house. Keenly indignant women may reasonably be, who know that the Brontës' prodigious portraits and analyses of love-lorn governesses have been read by their employers, and their pupils, and every visitor who comes to the house. . . . They have no gratitude for the Brontës; and will have none for any self-constituted artist, or any champion, who raises a sensation at their expense, or a clamour on their behalf."

But in spite of the displeasure the governess in fiction aroused, she was an alluring heroine then, and so she has remained. In the late nineteenth and even in the twentieth century, she has held her own, in spite of the arrival of the typist. The number of governesses in Henry James's novels is legion. He has also given one glorified representative in the teacher of the children in *The Turn of the Screw*. Ethel Sidgwick is also a good friend to the governess. For writers dealing with the leisure class, children creep into the picture of life, and with them their governesses. They are, perhaps, less cloyingly feminine than their predecessors, as portrayed by Lady Blessington, Mrs. Hall, and Anne Brontë, and they no longer marry the heroes. Their compensation is an increase in energy and in efficiency, as Miss Wilkinson, an admirable teacher in *Of Human Bondage*, testifies, and, one suspects, a better understanding of children. On account of their favourable situation for observation they can always be made an important part of the machinery of the social novel. But at the present time the fact that the governess in fiction is no longer pitied is eloquent testimony to her bettered fortunes.

The result of the wealth of literary material concerning the governess between 1832 and 1850 was a wider interest in all classes of working women. From her the reader turned to the dressmaker, often of the same social class and suffering more acute misery. That the governess was represented in fiction with a vividness and passion lacking in the pictures of other working women, was mainly due to the favourable circum-

stance that a woman equipped to be a governess had the education, as well as the talent, to be a writer. Charlotte Brontë
was able to make the governess something greater than a
clothes-horse upon which she hung her personal wrongs.
She created a woman of dignity and force who did not allow
her lowly occupation to deprive her of the esteem of her
employer. Jane Eyre is the proud working woman who
respects herself and makes others respect her. That labour
should be no disgrace was the final accomplishment of the
governess in literature.

CHAPTER VI

THE IDLE WOMAN

1. The Origin of the Idle Woman

ABOVE this great army of labourers, ranging from the girl in the cotton mill to the governess in her lonely schoolroom, were the ladies of England, the idle women. In an age when women of the lower ranks were notoriously overworked, not only the aristocracy but both the upper and the lower middle classes protected the females of their households from any kind of useful employment.

The bustling dames of the age of Chaucer, of Queen Elizabeth, of Cromwell, had long since passed away.[1] Then spinning and weaving, the care of dairies, the compounding of medicines, the management of large estates while husbands were away at wars, at the Court, or engaged with judicial duties, had been the responsibility of ladies in the manor-houses. The direction of large forces of servants and retainers, the entertainment of distinguished visitors, had called forth executive powers. But with the Restoration women of the upper classes more and more gave up their homely activities for the fashionable shows of Society. At first idleness was confined to aristocratic circles in London close to the Court. The lady in the country manor continued her former occupations. But as the improvement of roads in the eighteenth century made travel easier, and countrywomen formed the habit of visiting the baths at Bath, Cheltenham, and Tunbridge Wells, and more often accompanied their husbands to London, they began to imitate the fashions of the nobility. The stirring activity which Miss Alice Clark in *Working Life of Women in the Seventeenth Century* describes in her historical account of women in the sixteenth century, had already begun to break down in the seventeenth. By the eighteenth the triumph of the useless woman was complete.

With the changes of the nineteenth century, the conditions
of life for a woman of the middle class were much altered.
The use of machinery for making textiles took away her
occupation at the spinning-wheel. Elias Howe's invention of
the sewing-machine was soon to make her beautiful stitches
a superfluous art. With marriage postponed from the former
age of fourteen or fifteen to twenty or twenty-one, she was
kept at home for a period of years after she left school. If
she did not marry, there were no longer nunneries where she
could retire. The Industrial Revolution had increased the
urban population. A new class of wealth had sprung up.
Manufacturers and City bankers, envying the established social
class, imitated their aristocratic superiors who kept their wives
and daughters in an elegant bower of ease. Women-folk who
did not have to work represented the success of the men
of the family. The practice of female idleness spread through
the middle class until work for women became a misfortune
and disgrace. Only financial ruin, as the study of the governess
conclusively shows, sent a girl out of her home to seek employment. She was pitied. She pitied herself.

What the proper state for womankind in the reign of Queen
Victoria had become is well portrayed by a full-page repro-
duction, in the *Illustrated London News*[2] for June 16, 1849, of
the bazaar given in the grounds of Chelsea Hospital for the
building and endowment fund of an asylum for aged governesses. Crowded into the tents set up and equipped with
booths for the fancy articles to be sold are ladies wearing
feathered bonnets draped often with floating veils, shawls
modestly drawn over their shoulders, and flounced hooped
skirts with great bustles. The faces, with soft curls falling
over them, have the pensive and gentle sweetness familiar in
the books, magazines, and paintings contemporaneous with
Melbourne and Disraeli. Some of these delicate creatures are
attended by gentlemen with swallow-tailed coats and stiff hats.
With their own dainty fingers they had made the embroidered
slippers, the dressing-gowns, the guard-chains, the antima-

cassars, the samplers which comprised the feminine art of
those days when bazaars were a part of religion.

But why should these idle wives and daughters be introduced into a study of working women? What have they to
do with factory girls or nail workers? Little, one would say,
except that all were alike women. Together they give a com-
posite picture of the life of the time, with its dramatic contrasts
and ironic illogicality. With such delicate values and balances,
however, interesting as they might be, we are not concerned
here. But the question of idleness is fastened inextricably with
that of labour. The working woman was not independent
of the female leisure class. It was a constant menace to both
dressmakers and governesses, as we have already seen. Daily
the labour market was glutted with girls and women trained
to do nothing, but through adversity suddenly forced to earn
money. Why, then, were they not educated for some definite
occupation not already overstocked by those born into the
expectation of self-support? An answer to such a question goes
down deep into the roots of nineteenth-century life. Another
influence bringing working and idle women together is the
fact that many from the leisure class were beginning to seek
employment. They were looking for new occupational
opportunities. As they discovered their own limitations they
exerted themselves in reforms which affected all classes of
women. An examination of the literature dealing with the
idle woman is, moreover, a negative test of the point of view
adopted toward female labour. Whether writers have a
critical or approving attitude toward leisure forms the natural
conclusion to a study of working women.

One of the problems presented to the already burdened
reformer was: Is too much labour for women worse or better
than none? For the first time one heard the revolutionary
doctrine advanced that the labouring woman was happier than
her idle sister. In *Shirley* Charlotte Brontë wrote:[3]

" 'Caroline,' demanded Miss Keeldar abruptly, 'don't you wish
you had a profession—a trade?'

" 'I wish it fifty times a day. As it is, I often wonder what I came into the world for. I long to have something absorbing and compulsory to fill my head and hands, and to occupy my thoughts.'

" 'Can labour alone make a human being happy?'

" 'No; but it can give varieties of pain, and prevent us from breaking our hearts with' a single tyrant master-torture. Besides, successful labour has its recompense; a vacant, weary, lonely, hopeless life has none.'

" 'But hard labour and learned professions, they say, make women masculine, coarse, unwomanly.'

" 'But what does it signify whether unmarried and never-to-be married women are unattractive and inelegant, or not?—provided only they are decent, decorous, and neat, it is enough.' "

When Mrs. Jameson showed this passage to two men, one said such a girl should emigrate, the other that she should marry.[4]

From the conventional point of view the ladies who compressed their waists, pinched their feet, loaded themselves down with a weight of skirts, were not idle. Masculine philosophy had decreed the sanctity of motherhood and designated them potential mothers. In the face of statistics which proved that many women would be neither wives nor mothers, girls continued to be educated for functions they would never perform. The question then arises : Is there any useful purpose in society these single women of the middle class could fulfil? And here again the reformers of the time had something to say.

2. The Life of a Victorian Girl

For a study of the middle-class woman the fiction of the period yields far more satisfactory results than for the working woman. The Victorian heroine was an almost standardized product. Her function was courtship, marriage. Novels like *Vanity Fair* began with the day a girl left school. Unlike *Vanity Fair*, the average novel ended with the heroine's wedding. "My third volume ended when I was sixteen, and was married to my poor husband", confided a widow in *The Newcomes*.[5] All girls from infancy, if they were born above the level of

poverty, had the dream of marriage, successful marriage, held
before their dazzled eyes. By marriage alone a girl could rise
to higher rank. Ethel Newcome, the daughter of a manufacturer
descended from a weaver, by marrying Lord Farintosh would
enter the charmed highest circles. Rosamond Vincy, daughter
of a provincial silk manufacturer and a vulgar mother, had to
content herself with a doctor who was cousin to a lord.

To get ready for the marriage market a girl was trained
like a race-horse. Her education consisted of showy accomplishments designed to ensnare young men. The three R's
of this deadly equipment were music, drawing, and French,
administered by a governess at home, as has been shown in the
preceding chapter, or, for girls below the aristocratic and the
higher professional ranks, by mistresses in an inferior boarding-
school. Miss Pinkerton's academy described in *Vanity Fair*
was probably typical of the more ambitious girls' school.
Amelia Sedley for six years studied music, dancing, orthography, every variety of embroidery and needlework—in all
of which, according to Miss Pinkerton's testimonial, she
"realized her friends' fondest wishes"—and geography, which
she less completely mastered.[6] Formal walks, stigmatized by
Alfred Garth in *Middlemarch* as "such a set of nincompoops,
like Mrs. Ballard's pupils, walking two and two", gave the
only outdoor relief from the confinement of the schoolroom.[7]

Concerning education at home an earlier chapter has
described the general merits and shortcomings of the governess
system. For girls whose mothers could not afford a governess
irregular instruction at a minimum of expense for a maximum
of show was contrived. Mrs. Mackenzie got Miss Cann for
"five shillings for an hour and a half" to teach her daughter
music.[8] "If Rosey played incorrectly, mamma flew at her with
prodigious vehemence of language, and sometimes with a
slap on poor Rosey's back." Mrs. Bute Crawley was also a
hard taskmistress. Of her daughters Thackeray wrote sym-
pathetically:[9] "Those unfortunate and well-educated women
made themselves heard from the neighbouring drawing-room,

where they were thrumming away, with hard fingers, an elaborate music-piece on the pianoforte." They were "drumming at the duets in private . . . mamma drilling them rigidly hour after hour".[10] Mrs. Crawley also tortured her daughter with the backboard,* that indispensable instrument frequently mentioned by novelists. Jane Eyre had heard it spoken of as part of school discipline.[11] Miss Pinkerton recommended to Amelia, upon her leaving school, the "undeviating use of the backboard, for four hours daily during the next three years" "for the acquirement of that dignified deportment and carriage so requisite for every young lady of fashion".[12]

Life at home continued the routine begun at school, for the education of the Victorian young lady was never completed until she married. Her first duty was to keep the rust from gathering on her accomplishments. Accordingly the leisure for which she had been educated did not immediately begin. Music—that elusive art so painfully gained, so easily lost—must be struggled with constantly. The daughters of Sir Pitt, chronicled Thackeray, "took exercise on the pianoforte every morning after breakfast".[13] Blanche Amory, to quote her unsympathetic stepfather, was "sweeching from morning till night".[14] Rosamond Vincy went on studying with the town organist after she left school, and practised her repertoire of " Meet Me By Moonlight", "Black-Eyed Susan", Haydn's canzonets, or Italian songs.[15]

Drawing and painting also filled many hours. Caroline Helstone, driven to desperation for want of employment, "sat endeavouring to find some pleasure in painting a little group of wild flowers, gathered under a hedge at the top of the Hollow fields".[16] Dora Spenlow in *David Copperfield*, when she was not playing on her guitar, was painting flowers. Blanche Amory devoted much time to drawing. But she was one of Thackeray's most accomplished young ladies, versatile in all the arts. "Miss Amory paints, Miss Amory writes poems,

* The backboard: a board worn or fastened across the back to give erectness to the figure.—THACKERAY.

Miss Amory composes music, Miss Amory rides like Diana Vernon. Miss Amory is a paragon, in a word."[17] Yet prominent as this feminine devotion to Art is, novelists did not make any of their heroines artists, even though Rosa Bonheur was at the time painting in France. Too much skill would not have been ladylike. The only relic of this Victorian avocation is the presence to-day in English houses of prim pencil-drawings of castles on the Rhine, mountains in Switzerland, or faded water-colour sketches of primroses or thatched cottages made by some deceased relative and kept apologetically, in the guest-chamber generally, out of respect for the grandmother or great-aunt who "did all that work".

Fancy work as a womanly accomplishment was tiresomely prominent in all chronicles of feminine lives. Worsted work was a favourite use for knitting-needles. Jane Eyre and Lucy Deane made worsted flowers for rugs.[18] Fanny Thornton's "interminable piece of worsted work" is mentioned in *North and South*.[19] Amelia Sedley worked muslin collars.[20] Rebecca Sharp netted a green silk purse while she was visiting her friend Amelia, as did Jane Eyre sitting in a corner of a drawing-room full of guests.[21] Indeed, all the heroines plied their needles with admirable industry. Much of this sewing was dedicated to the Church. Indeed, the most powerful result of the Oxford Movement, so far as women were concerned, appeared to be the embroidering of altar-cloths and other ecclesiastical furnishings. Maude de Mowbray in *Sybil* embroidered a banner. Of Eliza Reed, Charlotte Brontë wrote: "Three hours she gave to stitching, with gold thread, the border of a square crimson cloth, almost large enough for a carpet."[22] Church bazaars made heavy demands upon female time. Lucy Deane and Maggie Tulliver made articles for one.[23] Rebecca in her last days had stalls at fancy fairs for the benefit of the poor. Caroline Helstone "sat in the room, and seemed to find wondrous content in the stitching of Jew-basket *

---

* See Shirley, ch. vii. Miscellaneous articles of women's handiwork were sold to helpless gentlemen and the proceeds used for the conversion of the Jews.

pin-cushions, and the knitting of missionary-basket socks". She also made children's dresses for this same Jews' basket, for which piously minded women contributed articles later sold at large prices to helpless men in the cause of charity. Sewing for the poor was also a duty of Victorian maidens.[24]

The Church was an important interest in most feminine lives. In *Pendennis* Lady Lucy read volumes of sermons.[25] Mr. Honeyman, the clergyman in *The Newcomes*, was very popular with the women of his parish, who wrote notes commending his sermons and even read those he printed. He was the recipient of many fruits of their industry: purses, pen-wipers, portfolios, even braces. They made him presents of flowers, grapes, jelly, lozenges, a silk cassock, and a silver teapot filled with sovereigns. Although Eliza Reed in *Jane Eyre* was one of the few religious zealots on novelistic record, Lady Maud in *Sybil* was a moderate devotee, and one of the Foker daughters made the cupboard in her room into an oratory, and fasted on every Friday in the year.[26] Teaching in the Sunday schools was a duty.[27] Closely allied to piety were the social duties of the moment. Dorothea Brooke interested herself in infant schools and in the improvement of cottages on her uncle's estate. Lady Emily in *Vanity Fair* wrote tracts, hymns, and spiritual pieces, and was deeply concerned with the negroes.[28]

With the coming of the penny post in 1838, a girl, without too great expense, could indulge in the writing of lengthy letters to fill up any gap in her round of occupations. But even before this date long, gushing epistles passed between young ladies. Becky Sharp in her girlhood was an industrious letter-writer. Amelia Sedley wrote to her "twelve dearest friends at Chiswick Mall" in empty intervals before luncheon.[29] Her letters, later, to George Osborne would have filled volumes, crossed and recrossed, with words underlined, poetry quoted, full of repetition, and sometimes with doubtful grammar. Mrs. Carlyle, as Jane Welsh, wrote letters which probably illustrate the higher standards of correspondence, with accounts of love-affairs interspersed with enthusiastic comments upon Rousseau and Byron. Girls with a taste for writing or intro-spection kept diaries. Miss Mills in *David Copperfield*, Eliza Reed, Jane Eyre, were all faithful in keeping up daily records.

Circulating libraries were well stocked with the reading-matter popular among ladies of all ages, ministering as do Mudie's or Boots to a novel-reading public referred to by a contemporary English novelist as "the lady on the suburban sofa". Victorian women had an insatiable appetite for novels. Sometimes they fell asleep over them, like Georgiana Reed on her sofa.[30] Blanche Ingram, when utterly bored, "having fetched a novel from the library, had flung herself in haughty listlessness on a sofa". Rosamond Vincy "found time also to read the best novels, and even the second best, and she knew much poetry by heart". She also had a weakness for the Annuals and for Lady Blessington and L.E.L., but she knew when to feign higher tastes. Mary Garth had a liking for Scott. Miss Rebecca Linnet's "reading had been more extensive than her sister's, embracing most of the fiction in Mr. Proctor's circulating library". Of Blanche Amory, Thackeray recorded: besides devoting herself to her favourite bard, Lamartine, she "had subsequently improved her mind by a sedulous study of novels of the great modern authors of the French language. There was not a romance of Balzac and George Sand which the indefatigable little creature had not devoured by the time she was sixteen." Her knowledge of life was gained from her devotion to the printed page. Pious books were considered the most appropriate mental food for a young girl.[31] Amelia Sedley read religious tracts like the *Washer-woman of Finchley Common*. George Eliot mentioned such volumes as *Female Scripture Characters* as the conventionally esteemed pastime. Maggie Tulliver read Thomas á Kempis. There were a few young women who had serious intellectual interests, but too often the men novelists laughed at them.[32] Blanche Amory's French and German took an unfortunate turn for the extremes of romanticism. One of Foker's cousins was "blue and a geologist". Joan de Mowbray in *Sybil* knew Arabic and Hebrew. She had an observatory and was "the first person to discover the comet". Mrs. Gaskell was fond of employing her heroines with Italian.[33] In *Mary Barton* she represented a manufacturer's daughter as trying to read Emerson, but not succeeding. Becky Sharp for her own amusement read French and English works with her pupil, Miss Rose—Smollett, Fielding, Crébillon, and Voltaire. Mrs. Browning relates with delicate humour her banishment from the shelves of her father's library :

> "Papa used to say . . . 'Don't read Gibbon's *His'ory*—it's not a proper book. Don't read *Tom Jones* and none of the books on this side, mind!' So I was very obedient and never touched the books on *that* side, and only read instead Tom Paine's *Age of Reason*, and Voltaire's *Philosophical Dictionary*, and Hume's *Essays*, and Werther, and Rousseau, and Mary Wollstonecraft . . . books which I was never suspected of looking towards, and which were not 'on that side' certainly, but which did as well."[34]

With the additional devices of card games, backgammon, and billiards, rainy afternoons and dull evenings might be devoured.[35] Gossip and fashion were dependable subjects for feminine conversation, and were, according to George Eliot, the "usual occupations of women's leisure moments".[36] Georgiana Reed "would chatter nonsense to her canary bird by the hour". She "spent most of her time in lying on the sofa, fretting about the dullness of the house, and wishing over and over again that her Aunt Gibson would send her an invitation up to town".

Of course the real moments in a girl's life were those spent at balls, with much sleep before and after, as Blanche Amory's custom helped to prove. Seated at the piano with an enraptured swain bending over her while she sang, or enthroned on the sofa with him beside her, turning over the pages of the latest *Keepsake*, examining his sketches or hers, she was also content. But because these uplifted periods did not fill up all her waking hours, even with the choice of occupations already enumerated at her disposal, the Victorian heroine found a day hard to get through with.

Everything was, after all, subsidiary to the main business in life, that of marriage. One must tolerate a few months or years of preliminary boredom. The *Westminster Review*[37] stated that girls were brought up with no other thought. "Marry your daughters when you can, and your sons when you will." The burden of disposing of a daughter in the safe harbour of matrimony fell upon the mother. When a parent had unattractive daughters to dispose of, too many of them, or no money for a tempting dowry, her efforts had a feverish activity dangerous to a young man. Mrs. Hawxby, who intended Arthur Pendennis for her "poor little Beatrice, who has one shoulder higher than the other", "caused her Beatrice to learn billiards from Mr. Pendennis, and would be driven by nobody but him in the pony-carriage, because he was literary and her Beatrice was literary too".[38] Only the watchfulness of the worldly Major Pendennis saved his nephew. A poor widow like Mrs. Mackenzie, dubbed the Campaigner for her conscientious interpretation of a mother's duties, captured Clive Newcome for Rosey. Lady Dorking, with "a brood of little chickens to succeed Clara", and with more aristocratic blood than middle-class gold, could take no account of the fact that Clara's heart was already given to Jack Belsize, but was forced to arrange an alliance with the son of a prosperous manufacturing family like the Newcomes. A clergyman's wife was often placed in a most embarrassing situation. Mrs. Bute Crawley, with four daughters, short, poor, plain, and with bad complexions, "could think of nobody but the curate to take one of them off her hands". But she "took them about to balls and public places". . . . "They appeared perseveringly at the Winchester and Southampton assemblies; they penetrated to Cowes for the race-balls and regatta-gaieties there; and their carriage, with the horses taken from the plough, was at work perpetually." Mrs. Hardyman performed a mother's duties for her sisters, thirteen of them, "daughters of a country curate, the Rev. Felix Rabbits, and married eleven of them, seven high up in the service". But this happened in India, where men seemed to be more plentiful, or, at least, more amenable to marriage, than in England.

Fortunately, daughters in those days obeyed their parents in the big issues of life as well as in the small.[39] Lady Jane Southdown let her mamma manage everything for her. Lady Southdown "ordered her dresses, her books, her bonnets, and her ideas for her". Lady Clara Pulleyn's attitude to penniless but handsome young men was carefully directed. Rosey Mackenzie was so obedient that she "acquiesced gladly enough in her mamma's opinion, that she was in love with the rich and handsome young Clive, and accepted him for better or worse". When a girl was intractable like Ethel Newcome, a mother was sometimes reinforced by a grandmother.

One must not conclude from this maternal interest in marriage that the Victorian heroine, about whom has gathered a faded aroma of shyness about love and reluctance to accept the most ardent lover without the proper preliminaries of artful refusals, took no active interest in her own fate. The defenders of romantic tradition will insist that some girls had no mothers to conduct for them the less ethereal arrangements. Becky Sharp, Thackeray said mischievously, had to be her own mamma.[40] Blanche Amory was unfortunate in Lady Clavering, who blundered sadly, so that she had to depend upon her own cleverness. But with others also, the plain truth is revealed that maidenly dreams, stolen glances at cavaliers, and whispered confidences to an intimate friend, were not all. The Victorian heroine was a husband-hunter. In *Shirley* Charlotte Brontë wrote: "They scheme, they plot, they dress to ensnare husbands." Ethel Newcome described the procedure in great detail. "Those Miss Burrs, you should have seen them at the country houses where we visited together, and how they followed him; how they would meet him in the parks and shrubberies; how they liked smoking, though I knew it made them ill; how they were always finding pretexts for getting near him!" The Lord Farintosh in the case was aware

"that every daughter of Eve was bent on marrying him. . . . Everybody hunted him. The other young ladies, whom we need not mention, languished after him still more longingly. He had little notes from these; presents of purses worked by them, and cigar-cases embroidered with his coronet. They sang to him in cosy boudoirs—mamma went out of the room, and sister Ann forgot something in the drawing-room."

According to satirists like Thackeray, it was not love, but the commercial and social aspects of marriage which held first place with both parents and daughters.[41] Such sacrifice of sentiment some women defended on the grounds of family duty. Lady Newcome said to her recalcitrant daughter: "Every young lady in your position in the world has sacrifices to make, and duties to her family to perform. Look at me. Why did I marry our poor dear papa? From duty." Lady Clara Pulleyn had duty preached to her. Ethel Newcome had no illusions about the trafficking of marriage. "I think, grand-mamma", Ethel said at a picture exhibition, "we young ladies in the world, when we are exhibiting, ought to have little green tickets pinned on our backs, with 'Sold' written on them; it would prevent trouble and any future haggling, you know. Then at the end of the season the owner would come to carry us home!" Of Miss Maria Osborne's engagement Thackeray wrote:

"Miss Maria Osborne, it is true, was 'attached' to Mr. Frederic Augustus Bullock, of the firm of Hulker, Bullock and Bullock; but hers was a most respectable attachment, and she would have taken Bullock senior, just the same, her mind being fixed—as that of a well-bred young woman should be—upon a house in Park Lane, a country house at Wimbledon, a handsome chariot, and two prodigious tall horses and footmen, and a fourth of the annual profits of the eminent firm of Hulker and Bullock, all of which advantages were represented in the person of Frederic Augustus."

"Of what else have young ladies to think, but husbands?" inquired Thackeray.[42] In all Becky Sharp's castles in the air, "a husband was the principal inhabitant". In maidenly dreams lovers were handsome, brave, devoted, and, of course, they ought not to be poor or have impossible family connections. No one has diagnosed the day-dreaming heroine better than George Eliot in describing Rosamond, "who had neither any reason for throwing her marriage into distant perspective, nor any pathological studies to divert her mind from that ruminating habit, that inward repetition of looks, words, and phrases, which makes a large part in the lives of most girls". Thackeray has presented with equal skill the pathetic dreams of Amelia, with no thought but her lover.

In spite of this concentration of action and imagination upon marriage, the girl waiting for a husband was given no training for her practical duties as a wife, even in many lower middle class families.[43] Girls like Nancy Lammeter, skilled in butter- and cheese-making, and Laura, in *Pendennis*, who studied housekeeping along with dancing and singing, were rare exceptions. A few voices were raised against this lack of preparation. The Rev. Helstone preached the importance of sewing and cooking. Dr. Helper in *The Newcomes* asked the mother of one marriageable heroine: "Has Miss Ann a genius for sewing buttons and making puddens?" But Dickens was not exaggerating the usual distaste for the domestic arts when he represented Dora as receiving David's suggestion that she study housekeeping with "something that was half a sob and half a scream", and finally with hysterics. Nor is Mrs. Gaskell's description of Mrs. Hale's distress that her daughter should be working in the kitchen overdrawn. The daughter's reply, "I am myself a born and bred lady through it all, even though it comes to scouring a floor or washing dishes", reveals the middle-class attitude toward household labour.

In the end, however, it was the young men who had the most direct effect upon the matrimonial market. They had their dreams of feminine beauty and grace which must, in

some measure, be satisfied. If the ladies who decorated the
novels and the verse can be trusted, heroines belonged to
two schools:[44] the statuesque brunettes represented by
Blanche Ingram, Charlotte Brontë's caricature of the reigning
belle in *Jane Eyre*; Ethel Newcome, "of a countenance somewhat grave and haughty", "rather taller than the majority of
women", with hair and eyebrows "jet black", grey eyes and
red cheeks; Tennyson's imperial Eleanore, Maud "tall and
stately"; and the petite blonde, "fair as a lily", like Rosamond
Vincy or Lucy Deane. Green-eyed Becky Sharp and the
brown-eyed Blanche Amory offer a slight variation. Curls,
real like Ethel Newcome's, or like Shirley's or Glorvina
O'Dowd's, resulting from a previous arrangement in "innumerable little bits of paper", fell over the ideal heroine's
lily neck. Rosebud lips, pearly teeth, were stock terms used to
enumerate her charms. Tennyson, being a poet, had the
advantage of such phrases as "baby roses in her cheeks";
"crimson-threaded lips"; and "little head, sunning over with
curls". The young lady perfect, in the eyes of the average
young man at least, was delicately proportioned. In height
she ought, like Amelia Sedley, to reach a man's heart. Laura
Bell, with a height of five feet four inches, was considered too
dangerously tall to achieve marriage easily. Of course, a few
stately girls like Ethel Newcome were allowed to decorate
both fiction and verse. A slender figure was greatly admired.
Lilian's "tiny hands", and Rosey Mackenzie's hand "like a
little white bird lying in mine", were Tennyson's and
Thackeray's additions to the ideal picture of femininity.
Small feet were greatly esteemed by the young men. Becky
had "the prettiest little foot", her author assures us. Tennyson's
Maud had feet "like sunny gems", and her step, so light she
"left the daisies rosy", might be confused with "the dry-
tongued laurel's pattering talk". Dora Spenlow, with her
dimpled chin, her curls hiding a blushing face, her little hands
and feet, was as clearly a young man's perfect dream as Blanche
Amory was a caricature of it.

"Blanche was fair and like a sylph. She had fair hair with green reflections in it. But she had dark eyebrows. She had long black eyelashes, which veiled beautiful brown eyes. She had such a slim waist, that it was a wonder to behold; and such slim little feet that you would have thought the grass would hardly bend under them. Her lips were of the colour of faint rosebuds, and her voice warbled limpidly over a set of the sweetest little pearly teeth ever seen. She showed them very often, for they were very pretty. She was always smiling, and a smile not only showed her teeth wonderfully, but likewise exhibited two lovely little pink dimples, that nestled in either cheek."

White muslin, typical of virginal innocence and purity, clothed many a heroine, with delicate shades of blue and pink next in popularity.[45] Dobbin remembered Amelia as a "girl in white, with large ringlets". Even stately dusky heroines like Maggie Tulliver and Blanche Ingram were clothed in white muslin. If her curls were long enough to cover her neck and her muslin dress was "fashioned modestly as a nun's robe", she could, like Caroline Helstone, "dispense with the encumbrance of a shawl".

Young men approved of the accomplishments. Never had the adage "Music has charms to soothe a savage breast" exhibited such force of truth as in the early years of the nineteenth century.[46] Young men and old men alike sat quiet under its spell. Rosey Mackenzie captivated Colonel Newcome and his friends with her Scottish songs and ballads. She always sang "very sweetly" any two of the five songs she had worked over. And Clive's cousin Maria, at her mother's orders, performed in Hungarian, Polish, German, Spanish, and Italian for his amusement. Stephen Guest sang duets with Lucy Deane, as a succession of suitors sang with Blanche Amory. David Copperfield bragged to his friend Traddles about Dora's guitar playing and singing. The weight of evidence goes to show that Victorian young men had an almost universal love of music, at least that produced under feminine fingers or by a light girlish voice. They turned the pages and complimented the skill of a performer, even if like Lydgate they were "entirely ignorant of music". There were a few hard-headed men whose hearts were not moved by dulcet strains. Becky Sharp tried both French songs and sentimental ballads upon Joseph Sedley in vain. Glorvina O'Dowd failed to capture Dobbin with song.

The stamp of masculine approval was placed upon innocence, ignorance of the world, meekness, lack of opinions, general helplessness and weakness; in short, a recognition of female inferiority to the male. David Copperfield's Dora was a "pretty toy or plaything"; Rosey Mackenzie was a "pretty little tender nursling", "like a little song-bird . . . a tremulous, fluttering little linnet". Amelia Sedley's weakness was "her principal charm—a kind of sweet submission and softness, which seemed to appeal to each man she met for his sympathy and protection". Men in the society of the pure creatures they idealized modified their conversation. There was a definite line drawn concerning what an unmarried lady could hear.[48] Not only was the impure barred, but also anything requiring intelligence. Caroline Helstone's uncle kept the conversation in domestic channels. Politics were not for women. Charlotte Brontë ridiculed the prevailing manly attitude in the person of Joe, "holding supercilious theories about women in general", convinced that in talking politics with women "you are sure not to be understood". When men introduced weighty matters into the talk which fell upon womanly ears, George Eliot accused them of liking to talk on what women knew nothing of. Stephen Guest summarized the popular sentiment of resistless femininity in his description of Lucy as "accomplished, gentle, affectionate, and not stupid". One of the few dissentients was Browning's Andrea Del Sarto, with his reproof,

> "Had you, with these the same, but brought a mind!
> Some women do so",

voicing the sentiment of one of the few Victorian gentlemen who tolerated cheerfully a wife with more than the average of intelligence. Too often the superior girl was unpopular. Ethel Newcome scared off men. Dorothea Brooke didn't "look at things from the proper feminine angle".

Accordingly, the usual girl, with all hope gone if she failed to make a successful marriage, tried hard to please the exacting young male.[49] Not many young ladies had the spirit of Priscilla Lammeter.

" 'I've no opinion o' the men, Miss Gunn; I don't know what you have. And as for fretting and stewing about what they'll think of you from morning till night, and making your life uneasy about what they're doing when they're out o' your sight—as I tell Nancy, it's a folly no woman need be guilty of, if she's got a good father and a good home. . . . As I say, Mr. Have-your-own-way is the best husband, and the only one I'd ever promise to obey.' "

Most heroines made an effort to conform with manly standards. To keep the befitting slenderness and a reputation for fragility, they curbed their appetites. But Thackeray suspected these dainty creatures. "When nobody was near, our little sylphide —who scarcely ate at dinner more than the six grains of rice of Amina, the friend of the Ghouls in the *Arabian Nights*— was most active with her knife and fork, and consumed a very substantial portion of mutton cutlets: in which piece of hypocrisy it is believed she resembled other young ladies of fashion." So common was tight-lacing that the editress of the *Christian Lady's Magazine* waged an earnest campaign against it. Tight shoes were another sacrifice. Rosey stamped "on her little feet if they refused to enter into the slipper", and submitted when "mamma insisted upon lacing her so tight as nearly to choke the poor little lass". Since she found opinions and intelligence an incumbrance, the wise girl like Rosamond Vincy got rid of them, or gave up timid attempts to develop her mind. In the process of trying to be what Society expected, she became unhealthy from lack of exercise and tight-lacing. Many a family, like that of Traddles's Sophie, had its invalid. The Victorian girl was hysterical, taking frequent "recourse to the waterworks", to quote Thackeray's phrase. She fainted easily. She had fits of sentiment, rather than any deep feeling. She formed habits of idleness or gave herself up to gossip, social life—if she were favourably situated, or stupid calls— if fate had placed her in a vapid small town. Her only escape was a vague day-dreaming, that habit so beset with dangers the Freudians tell us, which George Eliot, long before the discovery of their terminology, realized was as bad for Dorothea Brooke as for Rosamond Vincy. She was a slave to the will of her parents. She was forced into the prevailing commercial view of marriage and accepted the social snobbery of her day. Jane Welsh kept a man like Carlyle dangling to protect herself from her mother's displeasure. Elizabeth Barrett, at the age of forty, had to elope to marry the man she loved.

A few rebels against the game of marriage uttered bitter protests. Nowhere is the commercial marriage attacked more violently than in a scene between Shirley and her uncle.[50] Charlotte Brontë understood the indefinite position of the unmarried woman. She wrote to her former teacher:

"I speculate much on the existence of unmarried and never-to-be-married women nowadays; and I have already got to the point of considering that there is no more respectable character on this earth than an unmarried woman, who makes her own way through life quietly, perseveringly, without support of husband or brother."

But such a philosophic attitude was not that of the average woman. For those young ladies trained in the graces who, in the end, did not marry, girlhood was indefinitely prolonged.[51] "The farce of youth is enjoined upon some, and played, alas! by many more", recorded one sad critic. Thackeray described them in *The Newcomes*. "The Misses Gandish came to one of Mrs. Clive's balls, still in blue crape, still with ringlets on their wizened old foreheads, accompanying papa." Women cheated of marriage, the hope dangled before their eyes from their cradles, not only lied about their age, but made use of kittenish tricks more attractive at eighteen than at forty. Their parents treated them like children.

"It is common", wrote an intelligent woman, "to see young women, and women no longer young, kept dependent in every movement, with a moderate allowance for dress, from which not unfrequently they hardly dare to economize for any other object. They are without the power of making a journey, of engaging in any undertaking, unless it is to cost nothing beyond their own trouble, and to square exactly with the most trifling arrangements of the rest of the family, without even a quiet room of their own in which they may if they choose enjoy solitude and their own pursuits. . . . In many wealthy houses the daughters could no more venture to order a fire in their own apartment, to avoid the talk and interruptions of the drawing-room, than they could order from the bookseller a work from want of which some favourite study is arrested."[52]

Thackeray described the not uncommon life of such women. Mr. Osborne

"tyrannized over his unmarried daughter at home. She had a fine carriage and fine horses, and sat at the head of a table loaded with the grandest plate. She had a cheque-book, a prize footman to follow her when she walked, unlimited credit, and bows and compliments from all the tradesmen, and all the appurtenances of an heiress; but she spent a woeful time. The little charity-girls at the Foundling, the sweeperess at the crossing, the poorest under-kitchen-maid in the servants' hall, was happy compared to that unfortunate and now middle-aged young lady."

He then gave an extended explanation for her misery. Fear of her father, the loneliness of the empty house, the lack of any real occupation, were her daily portion. At the pompous dinner-parties her father gave she seldom met a man under sixty. A clandestine affair with her drawing-master was violently interrupted by her father, who threatened to cut her off without a shilling if she married without his consent. Hereafter, in Thackeray's words, "she was content to be an old maid". But she was a "lonely, miserable, persecuted old maid". Lady Julia in *The Newcomes* suffered a similar slavery under her mother. "Being always at home, and under her mother's eyes, she was the old lady's victim, her pin-cushion, into which Lady Kew plunged a hundred little points of sarcasm daily."

Too often the tyranny of home was increased by that of a

clergyman who sent meek women "to distribute tracts and teach Sunday schools".[53] A Victorian lady directing a rebellious pen wrote of this ecclesiastical direction of her sex: "He rules their lives for them; he portions their days and hours." Clearly such rumblings threaten a new generation of women. The same lady stigmatized visiting the poor as "meddling" with them. Intelligent social work was not for "weak characters and suppressed minds", but for those who had studied the "causes operating upon social and national welfare and the laws operating". Here again one discerns the modern spirit.

3. The Life of the Married Woman

From such an eventful existence women accepted almost any kind of a marriage offered them.[54] After the excitements of courtship and marriage, life resumed the unchanged, dull ways. The miracle had not happened. The wife was untrained in household management. She had servants she could not manage. Dora Copperfield used the cook-book David gave her for her dog Jip to stand on, and she never learned how to add up her accounts. She continued to make flower drawings and to play on her guitar instead of looking after a flighty servant. The tragedy of David's comic description of their housekeeping is another of Dickens's contributions to the cause of reform. Because the average middle-class matron had not been self-supporting before her marriage and her expenditures had been directed by her parents, she had no idea of the value of money and squandered what her husband gave her, like a heedless child. Rosamond wrecked Lydgate's usefulness in his profession by her extravagance and her complete indifference to her part in the management of their affairs. If a woman lived in the country, her days were probably not far from Becky's account of life on five thousand pounds a year:

"I could dawdle about in the nursery, and count the apricots on the wall. I could water plants in a green-house, and pick off dead leaves from the geraniums. I could ask old women about their rheumatisms, and order half-a-crown's worth of soup for the poor. . . . I could even drive out ten miles to dine at a neighbour's, and dress in the fashions of the year before last. I could go to church and keep awake in the great family pew; or go to sleep behind the curtains."

In the City she made calls and did shopping in her carriage, like Mrs. Sedley or Mrs. Clive Newcome. She took almost no exercise indoors or out. George Eliot wrote: "Women of her generation . . . were not given to much walking beyond their own house and garden." Foreign missions, astronomy, labouring classes, Thackeray enumerated as the solace of a few married women, but these were the strong-minded. The sofa, as an article of furniture, was an indispensable part of daily life. Mrs. Carlyle, Mrs. Browning, and Mrs. Tennyson are intimately associated with sofas. During pregnancy, referred to as an "interesting condition" or a "most interesting period"—and for Victorian ladies a lengthy procession of such events made up a large part of married life—wives took to the sofa and a French novel, expected sentimental pampering, and were privileged to go off into frequent hysterics. Mrs. Clive Newcome performed all the fitting preparations incidental to her situation. During these months on the sofa the visits of the doctor, referred to as "that Lady's Delight" by Thackeray, furnished the chief excitement. After the birth of the children the mothers could not direct them wisely, but appealed to their emotions in disciplining them. Before any crisis they were first in tears, then in hysterics. Margaret Hale in *North and South* remarked that the custom of not attending funerals of their own dead had risen because women were ashamed to exhibit their inability to control their feelings. One commentator wrote:

"It was very unusual for ladies at this date to attend funerals: it was an emotional, sentimental period for women, and they were supposed to be liable to make 'scenes' on occasions of this sort. As an old domestic in my family used to say, when describing a funeral she had particularly enjoyed: 'The scenery at the graveside was terrible.' "[55]

The number of women who shrieked in fits of hysterics through the pages of novels and poems is legion. Even Thackeray approved of Amelia's seizures as a sign of deep feeling. Mrs. Copperfield, Mrs. Nickleby, Rosey Newcome, have too many prototypes in literature to seem exaggerated. Meekness and tears were their stock in trade. The sweetness admired in a maiden was treasured as humility in a wife.

A girl on her marriage often passed from dependence upon parents to submission to a husband. Thackeray in *The New-comes* speaks of a woman as "well broke". Disraeli shows Lady Marney cowed by her husband. In *Middlemarch* George Eliot wrote: "A woman dictates before marriage that she may have an appetite for submission afterward." Wives took their husbands' opinions in politics and religion. Lydgate wanted to find in marriage "an accomplished creature who venerated his high musings and momentous labours, and would never interfere with them". Marriage was seldom a relation of frank comradeship. In *Shirley* Charlotte Brontë records: "A wife could not be her husband's companion, much less his confidante, much less his stay." Often a husband waited until the eve of ruin to inform his wife of his desperate affairs. Such a scene was a favourite for novelists. That a higher relationship between men and women could exist than in the usual marriage George Eliot knew: "the delight there is in frank kindness and companionship between a man and a woman who have no passion to hide or confess", but she represented it as existing in friendship only. Where equality was lacking in marriage, partnership could not exist. Both Barnes Newcome and Sir Pitt Crawley beat their wives. Of Lady Crawley her creator wrote: "When her husband was rude to her, she was apathetic: whenever he struck her, she cried. She had not character enough to take to drinking, and moaned about, slipshod and in curl-papers all day."

In the year 18... the laws of England gave women little protection. Mrs. Hugo Reid in *A Plea for Woman*, published

in 1843, made a scornful attack upon the injustice of laws
relating to women, as later Barbara Leigh Smith (Madame
Bodichon) in clearer form showed in her pamphlet *A Brief
Summary in Plain Language of the Most Important Laws Concerning Women* (1854). A woman of twenty-one could inherit
and administer her own property, over which her father had
no power. But "on marriage", wrote Miss Smith, "she is
legally an infant". As a wife she had no right even to her
clothes. After she was engaged, she could not dispose of
property without the consent of her fiancé. Her personal
property, her real property, passed into her husband's possession. Without his permission she could not make a will
concerning even her personal property. Mrs. Reid, and later
the *Westminster Review*,[56] cited the case of a husband who
willed his wife's property to his illegitimate children. She
had no control over her earnings, which were her husband's.
In a period when women of the lower classes commonly
worked and middle-class women earned large sums as writers,
this was a grave handicap. The legal custody of the children
was the father's. Until 1840 a small infant dependent upon a
mother could be taken from her. A husband had the right over
his wife's person. He could lock her up. He could compel
her to return home if she ran away from him. On the other
hand, a husband had to support his wife, her right to support
being enforced by ecclesiastical and magistrates' courts. He
was liable also for his wife's debts, even those contracted
before marriage. A married woman could not sue or be sued
for contracts, nor enter into them. She could not be a witness
against her husband nor he against her. Divorce was almost
impossible for a woman. On grounds of adultery, cruelty,
or unnatural practices she could be given separation from
bed and board by the ecclesiastical courts. But an absolute
divorce, which was granted by Act of Parliament, with the
investigation resting by usage with the House of Lords alone,
was granted to a woman very seldom, and only in cases of
aggravated adultery. A husband frequently got a divorce for

a wife's adultery. In a divorce suit a wife could not be plaintiff, defendant, or witness. The expenses of divorce, between £600 and £700, multiplied to £1,000 and £1,500 by Dickens in *Hard Times*, placed it above the reach of the poor. Before the law, then, a married woman was a chattel, an infant, made helpless by a system designed for primitive society.

The force of these legal restraints was dramatically illustrated by the sufferings of Mrs. Caroline Norton, the beautiful and clever granddaughter of Sheridan, who was not only a prominent social figure of the time, but also a successful contributor to the fashionable Annuals, and later editor of the *Keepsake*. In 1835 she finally left her husband, from whose cruelty she had previously fled. Later she offered to return for the sake of her three small children, but he refused to take her. Encouraged, it was thought, by Lord Melbourne's political enemies, he tried to divorce his wife, naming Melbourne as co-respondent. During the divorce proceedings she could not appear to defend herself, and her children being in her husband's possession, she could see them only by stealth. Once she tried to steal them. Finally she was allowed to see them for half an hour at a time in the presence of two witnesses chosen by her husband. Although the suit failed, she could not divorce Norton because in previously returning to him she had condoned his worst acts of cruelty and infidelity. Lengthy disputes over the children and money arrangements followed. In 1853 the Norton quarrels were once more aired in the Press, when the husband refused to honour a previous financial settlement he had made with her and claimed a share of her earnings. Such were the complexities of the Victorian system of marriage.

The history of idle women, then, both the unmarried and the married, had far-reaching effects upon Society as a whole, and all of them were bad. The fashions designed for leisure were imitated by working women, for whom long, flowing skirts and elaborate headdress were dangerous. The point of view of women of the leisure classes in regarding self-support as degrading detracted from the dignity of labour. Mrs. Vincy, the daughter of an innkeeper, in despising Mrs. Garth because she had been a teacher before her marriage, was reflecting the popular attitude. The widespread commercializing of marriage, with its petty bargaining, which aroused so much of Thackeray's bitterness, was a direct result of women's helpless condition and forced both men and women into bitter quarrels and a dreary life together. Unions often without love on either side encouraged the wife to adopt an exalted spiritual attitude which rebelled against the physical side of marriage and drove the husband to less fastidious women. The economic dependence of women upon men kept them living with partners they despised. Widows like Mrs. Nickleby threw themselves upon the nearest male relative for support. Unmarried women had to submit to the lordly parents who doled out money. If the head of the family died penniless or lost his money through bad trade or speculation, his daughters glutted the labour market and brought down the wages of dressmakers and governesses, trained for this kind of work.

Who was to blame? anxious writers asked their readers. The wisest pointed out the fact that men's ideals for women and a faulty system of education were mainly responsible. But since schools are easier to change than men, the reformers began with attacks upon the conventional modes of training a girl for life. All of their efforts, however, were directed toward the relief of middle-class women. Daughters of the aristocracy were left with no salvation from the commercial marriage which joined Lady Clara Pulleyn to the son of a wealthy bourgeois family. Even the most cheerful critics failed to prophesy the coming of an age when duchesses and countesses should manage tea-rooms, hotels, and hat-shops, or lend their proud beauty to the stage and the cinema. Only the daughters of professional and business families concerned the Victorian reformer.

4. The Relief of the Idle Woman

Against a showy educational system for girls which was designed to capture a husband, the Victorians were making a belated protest. All that women of the upper classes had gained during the sixteenth century when noblemen, following the example of Catherine of Aragon, secured real scholars as teachers for their daughters, had been sacrificed when the accomplishments came into fashion with the life of leisure of the Restoration. There were no successors to Lady Jane Grey and Margaret Roper. At the close of the seventeenth century Mary Astell and Defoe protested against the shackling of women's powers. Girls in the eighteenth century, even in the upper ranks, were grossly ignorant.[57] Adam Smith, observing that daughters in middle families were acquiring "accomplishments" to imitate the rich, advised domestic training, but he received no serious attention. Rousseau, whose *Emile* preached reform in boys' education, was content that Sophie should be trained in accomplishments. With Mary Wollstonecraft, however, the most advanced revolutionary theories about feminine education were presented. Her *Vindication of the Rights of Women* (1790) proposed the same education for girls as for boys, and her imitators continued to ridicule the accomplishments. The moral of Mrs. Inchbald's *A Simple Story* (1791) was the "pernicious effects of an improper education", and one of the characters, Matilda, had substantial learning besides the usual music and drawing. No sharper or more discerning comment on the state of female education in the late eighteenth century can be found than that of Jane Austen. The ideals of a girl's education she satirized in *Mansfield Park*. The Bertram daughters had discovered their cousin Fanny's lamentable ignorance. Fanny could read, work, and write, but she had been taught nothing more.

" 'Dear mamma, only think, my cousin cannot put the map of Europe together—or my cousin cannot tell the principal rivers in

Russia—or she never heard of Asia Minor—or she does not know
the difference between water-colours and crayons! . . . How long
ago it is, aunt, since we used to repeat the chronological order of
the kings of England, with the dates of their accession, and most
of the principal events of their reigns! . . . And of the Roman
emperors as low as Severus, besides a great deal of the heathen
mythology, and all the metals, semi-metals, planets, and distinguished philosophers.' "

What was worse, Fanny announced that she did not want
to learn either music or drawing. In the horror of such ignorance the Miss Bertrams went back "to exercise their memories"
and "practise their duets", and "their father saw them becoming, in person, manner, and accomplishments, everything that
could satisfy his anxiety". Two famous contemporaries of
Miss Austen also had their fling at the "accomplishments".
In his essay *Mackery End, In Hertfordshire*, Charles Lamb wrote
of his sister:

"Her education in youth was not much attended to; and she
happily missed all that train of female garniture, which passeth by
the name of accomplishments. She was tumbled early, by accident
or design, into a spacious closet of good old English reading,
without much selection or prohibition, and browsed at will upon
that fair and wholesome pasturage. Had I twenty girls, they should
be brought up exactly in this fashion. I know not whether their
chance in wedlock might not be diminished by it; but I can answer
for it, that it makes (if the worst comes to the worst) most incom-
parable old maids."

De Quincey rejoiced that Dorothy Wordsworth was
"thoroughly deficient . . . in ordinary female accomplishments". Unfortunately, match-making mothers would never
hold up either Mary Lamb or Dorothy Wordsworth, among
the most charming women of their age, to their daughters
for emulation.

In the early nineteenth century Mary Wollstonecraft's bold
demand was replaced by the more timid contention that
women ought to be given a better education.[58] One of the
best articles on the subject was that of Sidney Smith in the

Edinburgh Review in 1810. Instead of the ineffectual training in music, drawing, painting, and dancing, which he said embellished only a few years of life, he would equip a girl for Society by cultivating her mind so that she could contribute real charm of conversation. Not only would the education of women improve that of men, but it would result in a higher type of marriage with intellectual understanding between husband and wife. With his characteristic facetiousness he insisted that no educated woman would desert a baby for a quadratic equation. *Blue Stocking Hall* (1827) argued that girls could study Latin, Greek, modern literature, mathematics, and a little botany, and still remain attractive.

After 1832 serious attacks upon the follies of feminine education grew in number.[59] A witness before the Commissioners of 1833 examining factories had suggested that they consider the condition of schoolgirls, especially those at finishing schools, who needed relief from overwork and unwholesome living conditions as much as children in the cotton mills. *Fraser's* made a lengthy criticism of girls' boarding-schools. "Girls should be trained", the author began, "to a sense of high moral responsibility and self-dependence." Instead they were taught "to view education as a preparation for an ambitious marriage". The object of most girls' schools was "fine ladyism". In a more detailed way the author stigmatized the houses used for schools as unfit; there were no playgrounds, so that the only exercise was walks along public roads two by two; the food was poor; the sleeping-quarters were crowded; the girls had no privacy; and their surroundings, the bare walls, and scanty furniture, were cheerless. The intellectual equipment was as discouraging as the physical. Too much memory work, the grammar and music badly taught, and a general smattering in many subjects characterized most of these institutions. Girls were overworked to the detriment of health. The use of pupil teachers was bad. The general policy was a disgrace. "Rivalry, shame, display, marriage—these are the motive forces which make the wheels

of school discipline go round." In an age when "English
women, married and single, must have a share in the work of
life", education did not fit "women's extended responsibilities".
At the end of her schooldays a girl with a superficial education
and described as "accomplished" became the wife of a man
with whose mind she had no sympathy, and sank "gradually
into the dull commonplaces of housekeeping and nursery
matters". The *Christian Lady's Magazine* observed that girls
were taught "to sing, to play, to dance, to paint, to embroider,
but not to think". They needed mental discipline that would
not leave them children, but would "prepare them efficiently
for life". The *Westminster Review* (1849–50) attacked a system
which allowed girls the gossip of history and literature, but
considered political economy and logic improper. It also
ridiculed the prejudice against exercise. "Girls would be
thought mad to run, leap, or engage in any kind of active
game in the open fields."

The most powerful attacks upon the education of girls,
however, came from the novelists. Much before the investigations of Parliament had exposed long-existing evils to the
nation, Thackeray, Dickens, Charlotte Brontë, and George
Eliot had already used the weapons of ridicule and biting
satire upon the follies of parents in equipping their daughters
for life.

In Thackeray the realistic description of education and its
caricature are so intermingled that the two can scarcely be
distinguished.[60] On the accomplishments he was especially
remorseless. "For she [Amelia] could not only sing like a
lark, or a Mrs. Billington, and dance like Hillisberg or Parisot,
and embroider beautifully, and spell as well as the Dictionary
itself, but she had such a kindly . . . heart . . . as won the
love of everybody who came near her." The craze for teaching
girls French reached such extremes that Colonel Newcome
upon his return from India, greeted by his young niece with
"a glib little oration in French", was so bewildered that he
began to think "perhaps French was the language of the polite

world". Of the usual French learned by English schoolgirls, Thackeray wrote concerning Becky: "It was only from her French being so good, that you could know she was not a born woman of fashion." He also ridiculed the memory work exacted by having Becky say after her marriage: "Who'd think the moon was two hundred and thirty-six thousand eight hundred and forty-seven miles off? . . . Pooh! we learned it all at Miss Pinkerton's." To reproduce a young lady's music, he described Betsy Horrocks, a servant, "seated at the piano with the utmost gravity, and squalling to the best of her power of imitation of the music which she had sometimes heard". Amelia Sedley on her return home from school confessed to her mother that the drawing-master "used to do all the best parts of our drawing".

" 'My love! I'm sure I always heard Miss Pinkerton say that he did not touch them—he only mounted them.'

" 'It was called mounting, mamma,' Amelia explained."

Of Miss Pinkerton, Thackeray wrote: "She no more comprehended sensibility than she did Algebra"; and again: "Miss Pinkerton did not understand French; she only directed those who did". From Rebecca the reader learns what Thackeray's candid opinion was of the academy on Chiswick Mall. "The rigid formality of the place suffocated her: the prayers and the meals, the lessons and the walks, which were arranged with a conventual regularity, oppressed her almost beyond endurance": "The pompous vanity of the old schoolmistress, the foolish good-humour of her sister, the silly chat and scandal of the elder girls, and the frigid correctness of the governesses equally annoyed her." In *The Newcomes* he is equally satirical about the education at home. Ethel Newcome "had had so many governesses . . . that the poor child possessed none of the accomplishments of her age. She could not play on the piano; she could not speak French well; she could not tell you when gunpowder was invented; she had not the faintest idea of the date of the Norman Conquest, or whether the earth went round the sun, or vice versa. She did not know the number of counties in England, Scotland, and Wales, let alone Ireland; she did not know the difference between latitude and longitude." Of her cousins in Bryanstone Square, Thackeray wrote: "If they have been lectured, and learning, and backboarded, and practising, and using the globes, and laying in a store of 'ologies . . . what a deal they must know!" Equally amusing are the satiric sketches Clive and his friend J.J. draw, "representing the life of a young lady as they imagined it, and drawing her progress from her cradle upwards; now engaged with her doll, then with her dancing-master; now marching in her backboard; now crying over her German lessons; and dressed for her first ball finally, and bestowing her hand upon a dandy of preternatural ugliness, who was kneeling at her feet as the happy man". Finally he asks in *Vanity Fair* what is the purpose of all the labours endured in the name of education. "What causes them to labour at pianoforte sonatas, and to learn four songs from a fashionable master at a guinea a lesson, and to play the harp if they have handsome arms and neat elbows, and to wear Lincoln green toxophilite hats and feathers, but that they may bring down some 'desirable' young man with those killing bows and arrows of theirs?"

Dickens, who had undertaken an ambitious programme of reform, had some criticisms to make concerning the education of girls.[61] In *Sketches by Boz* he describes one of the female institutions of learning: "Minerva House, conducted under the auspices of the two sisters, was a 'finishing establishment for young ladies', where some twenty girls, of the ages of from thirteen to nineteen inclusive, acquired a smattering of everything and a knowledge of nothing; instruction in French and Italian, dancing lessons twice a week; and other necessaries of life." He laughed at Mrs. General's labours with the Dorrit sisters: "If Miss Amy Dorrit will direct her own attention to, and will accept of my poor assistance in, the formation of a surface, Mr. Dorrit will have no further cause of anxiety." But Fanny was a difficult pupil who formed too many opinions. "A truly refined mind", in the words of Mrs. General, "will seem to be ignorant of the existence of anything that is not perfectly proper, placid, and pleasant." Little Dorrit, in addition to her consciousness of suffering around her, had the added vice of slowness in acquiring the necessary French and Italian. Estella in *Great Expectations* was educated with the object of breaking hearts, and was first sent abroad "educating for a lady" as a prerequisite for her undertaking. In describing Mrs. Wackles's school in *The Old Curiosity Shop* Dickens wrote: "The several duties of instruction in this establishment were thus discharged: English grammar, composition, geography, and the use of dumb-bells, by Miss Melissa Wackles; writing, arithmetic, dancing, music, and general fascination, by Miss Sophy Wackles; corporal punishment, fasting, and other tortures and terrors, by Mrs. Wackles." In *Bleak House* Caddy Jellyby asks enviously of Miss Ada Clare: "But knows a quantity, I suppose? Can dance, and play music, and sing? She can talk French, I suppose, and do geography, and globes, and needlework, and everything?"

Thomas Hardy, in reconstructing the first half of the nineteenth century for the scene of the *Mayor of Casterbridge*, gave Elizabeth Newson the correct historical viewpoint.[62] "If they only knew what an unfinished girl I am—that I can't talk Italian, or use globes, or show any of the accomplishments they learn at boarding-schools, how they would despise me! Better sell all this finery and buy myself grammar-books and dictionaries and a history of all the philosophies!"

Charlotte Brontë and George Eliot, being women and feeling the tragedy of educational folly more personally, adopt a less lightly mocking tone than the men. Miss Brontë is, at times, bitter. Like Thackeray, she made fun of the test of ladyhood which rested in the possession of accomplishments.[63] In *Jane Eyre* an old servant is questioning Jane about what she knows:

" 'I dare say you are clever, though,' continued Bessie, by way of solace. 'What can you do? Can you play on the piano?'
" 'A little.'

"There was one in the room; Bessie went and opened it, and then asked me to sit down and give her a tune: I played a waltz or two, and she was charmed.

" 'The Miss Reeds could not play as well!' said she exultingly. 'I always said you would surpass them in learning; and can you draw?'

" 'That is one of my paintings over the chimney-piece.' It was a landscape in water-colours, of which I had made a present to the superintendent, in acknowledgment of her obliging mediation with the committee on my behalf, and which she had framed and glazed.

" 'Well, that is beautiful, Miss Jane! It is as fine a picture as any Miss Reeds' drawing-master could paint, let alone the young ladies themselves, who could not come near it; and have you learnt French?'

" 'Yes, Bessie, I can both read it and speak it.'

" 'And you can work on muslin and canvas?'

" 'I can.'

" 'Oh, you are quite a lady, Miss Jane!' "

Later in the same novel Mr. Rochester makes cynical remarks about the playing and sketching of young ladies. In *Shirley* Miss Brontë describes Mr. Helstone as doubtful of the value of a girl's learning French. " 'The language,' he observed, 'was a bad and frivolous one at the best, and most of the works it boasted were bad and frivolous, highly injurious in their tendency to weak female minds. He wondered (he remarked parenthetically) what noodle first made it the fashion to teach women French; nothing was more improper for them; it was like feeding a rickety child on chalk and water-gruel.' " When Caroline was asked by Robert Moore: "What will you do with your French, drawing, and other accomplishments when they are acquired?" she could not answer. Again, in analysing the education of the Sympson daughters, she wrote:

"They had been educated faultlessly. All they did was well done. History, and the most solid books, had cultivated their minds. Principles and opinions they possessed which could not be mended. More exactly regulated lives, feelings, manners, habits, it would have been difficult to find anywhere. They knew by heart a certain young-ladies'-schoolroom code of laws on language, demeanour, etc.; themselves never deviated from its curious little pragmatical provisions; and they regarded with secret, whispered horror all deviations in others."

George Eliot also ridiculed the graces.[64] Of Milly in *Amos Barton* she comments: "You would never have asked, at any period in Mrs. Amos Barton's life, if she sketched or played the piano. You would even, perhaps, have been rather scandalized if she had descended from the serene dignity of being to the assiduous unrest of doing." And she described Countess Czerlaski, the former governess of Caroline Bridmain, as not having "any very ripe and comprehensive wisdom, but much external polish". In *Janet's Repentance* she referred to the young ladies of the 'thirties as speaking "French, indeed, with considerable facility, unshackled by any timid regard to idiom", an art acquired at "distant and expensive schools", where they had been "finished". George Eliot directed some of her most powerful educational sarcasm against Rosamond Vincy, whose brother described her course of study as "certain finicking notions which are the classics of Mrs. Lemon's school". The institution followed the rigorous Victorian ethics for girls by cherishing as its ideal the maintenance of maidenly purity. "At that time young ladies in the country, even when educated at Mrs. Lemon's, read little French literature later than Racine." Rosamond "was admitted to be the flower of Mrs. Lemon's school, the chief school in the county, where the teaching included all that was demanded in the accomplished female— even to extras, such as the getting in and out of a carriage. Mrs. Lemon herself had always held up Miss Vincy as an example; no pupil, she said, exceeded that young lady for mental acquisition and propriety of speech, while her musical execution was quite exceptional." To her music, however, her creator made a subtle objection. "Rosamond played admirably. Her master at Mrs. Lemon's school . . . was one of those excellent musicians here and there to be found in our provinces, worthy to compare with many a noted Kapellmeister in a country which offers more plentiful conditions of musical

celebrity. Rosamond, with the executant's instinct, had seized
his manner of playing, and gave forth his large rendering of
noble music with the precision of an echo. It was almost
startling, heard for the first time." Her singing, since it was
not too expressive, was all the more correct, for as Charlotte
Brontë inquired in *Shirley*: "Was it proper to sing with such
expression, with such originality—so unlike a schoolgirl?"
Celia Brooke's music was probably more typical of the average
young lady. "Celia was playing an 'air with variations', a
small kind of tinkling which symbolized the æsthetic part of
the young ladies' education". Her sister Dorothea, that heroine
dear to her author, revolted from "domestic music and fine
art", stigmatized as "small tinkling and smearing". One of
Casaubon's recommendations as a husband was that he was
"not fond of the piano". "I never could look on it", he says
for himself, "in the light of a recreation to have my ears
teased with measured noises", and consequently he did not
ask her to "play *The Last Rose of Summer*".

With Dorothea and Maggie Tulliver in *The Mill on the Floss*,
George Eliot went beyond a flippant attack upon "accomplishments". For those who were content to equip themselves with
artifices pleasing to prospective husbands, like Rosamond or
even Celia and Lucy Deane, there was no personal tragedy.
But where an ardent nature aspiring vaguely to some kind
of higher use was caught in the net of French, drawing, music,
and general superficiality, the lack of real mental equipment
and of intellectual judgments could ruin an entire life. Dorothea,
noble as she was, could not escape the evils of her deficiencies,
many of them due to improper education.[65] When she con-
templated marriage with a scholar, Casaubon's vast learning,
"something beyond the shallows of ladies' school literature",
gave her the ambition to be more worthy of him; consequently
she was "getting down learned books from the library and
reading many things hastily", in the haphazard fashion of her
schooldays. Her desire to learn Greek and Latin was only
partly for her husband's sake, that she might read to him as

Milton's daughters had read to their father. It was also for her own. "Those provinces of masculine knowledge seemed to her a standing-ground from which all truth could be seen more truly." Superior ladies of her generation frequently sought deliverance through Greece and Rome. But Dorothea found herself a stupid pupil. She finally suspected that "there might be secrets not capable of explanation to a woman's reason". After her marriage, although there is no evidence of Casaubon's continued instruction, his book "after that toy-box history of the world adapted to young ladies which had made the chief part of her education" gave her glimpses of the great philosophers, and she thought marriage would give her "higher initiation in ideas". But her husband, finding her of little use except for mechanical secretarial duties, shut himself up with his great work. Lydgate found her half-education annoying. "It is troublesome to talk to such women. They are always wanting reasons, yet they are too ignorant to understand the merits of any question, and usually fall back on their moral sense to settle things after their own taste." Her lack of any appreciation of art was in the beginning a barrier to her friendship with Ladislaw. The drawing she had studied in school—"chiefly of the hand-screen sort"—did not protect her from being shocked in Rome by the "severe classical nudities and smirking Renaissance-correggiosities", although her natural honesty did keep her from trying to admire what she did not understand. In a final estimate of the failure of Dorothea's marriage to Casaubon, George Eliot gives one the basis for conjecturing that her ignorance made her idealize a man who had only knowledge, that she looked to marriage chiefly as a means of service and unfortunately chose a husband for whom her lack of classical training made her a vexation, and that not until Ladislaw revealed the chaos and uselessness of her husband's studies could she see she had dedicated her youth to a dust-heap.

Maggie Tulliver had the same intellectual strivings as

Dorothea, and a far better mind.[66] Her eyes, Philip Wakem early observed, were "full of unsatisfied intelligence". Her education was not a subject of deep family concern, as was that of her stupid brother Tom. When she returned from school, she "wished for books with more in them" than those she had used, with the "hard dry questions on Christian doctrine". But like Dorothea she could not give herself up to studies for their own sake. They must serve some high purpose in life. Because books made her restless, conscious of the world, and impatient of home, she swayed between the zeal of renunciation, which Evangelicism encouraged in women, and her mental hunger. In the end, renunciation triumphed. Again one is tempted to moralistic summaries with Maggie as with Dorothea, and to conclude that no discipline had tempered the emotional excesses of a generous nature, nor did she attain the breadth of intellectual outlook Philip Wakem had desired for her, which would have prepared her to judge the provincial triviality of Stephen Guest.

Two books which appeared close to 1850, *Thoughts on Self-Culture* by Mrs. Maria Grey and her sister Emily Shirreff, and *Intellectual Education* by Miss Shirreff, who later helped to establish Girton College for women at Cambridge, demonstrate the sad truth that so late as the middle of the century education for girls remained "a mere blank, or worse, a tissue of laboured frivolities under a solemn name; a patchwork begun without aim, fashioned without method, and flung aside, when half-finished, as carelessly as it was begun".[67] No scientific investigation of the subject was made, however, until 1867, when the Schools Inquiry Commission published its report on both boys' and girls' schools. Only at the instigation of a committee of ladies, with Miss Emily Davies as secretary, had girls' schools been included in the educational investigations. A comparison of what was revealed to the conscientious gentlemen on the committee with the mass of criticism already before the public in the form of novels and magazine articles, proves not only a long-standing consciousness of the need of reform, but also the social reliability of the fiction examined.

The Government investigations were made with the greatest difficulty. Even the larger girls' schools were conducted with such privacy that hunting down satisfactory information was almost impossible. The report was also incomplete, because it excluded facts concerning the training of the daughters in wealthy and upper middle-class families carried on at home and also of those in schools "too small to be entitled to the name". The most valuable evidence came from the new generation of schoolwomen : Miss Emily Davies, Miss Dorothea Beale, and Miss Frances Buss. Although the reforms they made came after 1850, their criticisms of schools in general and prevailing standards of education dealt with the deep-rooted evils of the earlier period.

The prevailing opinion of the heads of schools who were called as witnesses was that the main responsibility for the ignorance of girls went to the parents. As a class they seemed indifferent to the education of their daughters; those who would make any sacrifice for their sons sent the girls to the cheapest schools.[68] They were convinced that "solid attainments are actually disadvantageous to marriage", and "accomplishments and what is showy and superficially attractive are really essential".[69] Then there was masculine concern about the effects of study upon a girl's health.[70] Miss Beale was asked concerning the question of girls' taking certain qualifying examinations : "You have never found any reason to suppose that any peculiarity in girls' physical or mental constitution makes it dangerous to apply the principle of emulation to them?" It is also evident that the fears of parents about educating their daughters at the risk of sacrificing marriage for them had some foundation. Mark Pattison, the Rector of Lincoln College, Oxford, stated that the average man of the middle class disliked an educated woman, because she made him too conscious of his own want of instruction.[71] But according to the discouraging reports before the Committee, the middle-class man was to have a few more comfortable years in feminine society. The whole plan, from the bottom up,[72] seemed designed to protect girls from the shock of any real mental struggle. During their early years they were taught by incompetent governesses at home or sent to schools from which they emerged in a state of "unfathomable ignorance".[73] Arithmetic was the stumbling-block, as many teachers of the higher schools stated. Girls with this faulty preparation, even when they went to better schools at the age of ten or twelve, lacked all mental discipline and had no desire for study. Generally, however, the second school was little better than the first. The majority of schools for these older girls were so small that efficient management was difficult, and heavy fees had to be charged to get the better class of teachers. Fees ranged from £25 to £98 annually in boarding-schools—as high as £112 in Lancashire—and from £3 to £22 yearly in day schools.[74] Competent teachers were not easily secured at any price. Few of them knew enough arithmetic to teach it. Miss Emily Davies showed the reason for the lack of good teachers.[75]

"There is no examination for girls above eighteen, except that, I believe, Queen's College and the College of Preceptors have some kind of examinations for schoolmistresses and governesses, but they are not much known. They are not of sufficiently high standing to be at all on a par with a University examination, for instance. If you want to appoint a schoolmistress to a school analogous to a public school for boys, you have no sufficient means of ascertaining her qualifications or attainments."

Poor teachers, inferior school-books, uninteresting lessons, with much memorizing of rules, conspired to kill any small interest in study. Instead of playing in the fresh air, young schoolgirls bent over needlework. The general result was utter futility. It was the opinion of Miss Buss that the majority left school without even a taste for reading. The minority who had intellectual tastes,·with all "stimulus and motive for studies after leaving school" lacking, found it impossible to go on cultivating their minds after they returned home. Serious study would be considered "unnecessary and unsociable". As one teacher concluded : "I only wish further to insist once more on the great evil of girls spending ten important years of life, seven to seventeen, in learning not to understand French and not to play the piano."

But women writers refused to give up the hope of some kind of intellectual stimulation for their sex. Mrs. Maria Grey and Miss Shirreff were among the first to see reform in a kind of mental discipline, which would prepare girls for life. They wanted to show women how to get self-culture. Miss Shirreff, taking the spinster as her natural province, based her plan of education upon her view of the general hopeless condition of unmarried women. She writes that since a woman in marriage "can have none but a negative choice, it is far from likely, if feelings, character, and taste are to be considered, as well as mere worldly considerations, that she will have it in her power to make a really suitable marriage".[76] She wants girls to look forward to "single life as the probable, marriage only as the possible, contingency". Nor does she see any chance that an unmarried woman can find "a career of honourable activity analogous to men's professions". But the proper education has not the power to make woman, with her "clinging, trusting tenderness", living in "the sunshine of an approving smile", equal to man, who will "eagerly brave toil and danger, and bear the heaviest burdens of life, sooner than the loved one should feel the 'breath of heaven visit her cheek too roughly' ". Education, as she views it, consists of those subjects which will give solace to a spinster's lonely existence. To show the empty life dragged out by the majority of women, she compared the faces of an old man and woman. "He has ripened through the course of years—she has withered; his powers have enlarged and gained in firmness and weight what they may have lost in fire and brilliancy; hers have been smothered under small cares, small pleasures, and small interests." In her book she outlined a course of subjects, including higher mathematics, the natural sciences, literature, and history, which would give a woman the mental equipment to be a friend to men.

Mrs. Grey, with the married woman as her special interest, devoted a chapter of *Thoughts on Self-Culture*, a joint undertaking with her sister, to the sins of women.[77] They lacked method, reason, truth, independence of opinion, justice, tolerance, accuracy, self-control. They deceived themselves; they abounded in vanity. All these vices she hoped a vigorous discipline of education would help to correct. She wanted a training which would enable a woman to bring charm to domestic life, make her intelligent enough to listen to the results of her husband's scientific investigations, and become a real wife, "the most valued of companions, the most loved and trusted of friends". To her children she will give more than natural affection; she will direct both their physical and mental welfare. A "purer atmosphere must surround the cradle" for the "regeneration of society". To her sister's list of studies she added politics and political economy, subjects which both Charlotte Elizabeth Tonna and Harriet Martineau judged necessary for women. She also emphasized the necessity of critical reading and comprehension instead of memory work. The basis of all her educational theory is the development of women's judgment, rather than their emotions.

Even more powerful and courageous are the words of the anonymous author of *The Industrial and Social Position of Women in the Middle and Lower Ranks*, ready for the press, the writer explained, some years before its publication in 1857. No document examined reveals greater insight or clearer thinking than this remarkable book. In her opinion, the ultimate tragedy of middle-class women lay not in their misdirected aims, their lost talents, much as she regretted these.[78] It was their estrangement from men, a tragedy for men as well as for women. She writes:

"In spite of the happiness that must establish itself within the domestic circle in the midst of all obstacles, there is, in the relation of the sexes in the middle ranks, an incongruity of taste, a diversity of pursuit, a clashing of sentiment, a want of common ground in matters of reasoning, that are only repressed, or kept out of view, in order to prevent the still greater evils that their free development would inflict. . . . How impossible is it for the sexes to break ground on any but the most commonplace topics of conversation!"

This estrangement she sees begun by the traditions of English education. Before schooldays there is childish companionship between boys and girls. Their early education is the same. Then the boy goes to his public school, the girl devotes herself to accomplishments. As another writer comments: "That rascal Smith is educating boys and girls together. . . . I am surprised that Nature should produce us boys and girls to grow together in one family . . . but that little girls should play and learn with little boys . . . my modesty is overcome by the idea." Finally, continues the first writer,

"the university comes, and the fate of woman is sealed. Debarred from an institution that has done so much for the youth of the other sex, woman sees her brother going forward step by step in his haughty career of knowledge and ambition; she, left on her father's threshold, can but gaze after him, or turn back to weep."

In the future relations of men and women there is nothing but the deference men pay to women. "It is but an equivocal compliment to woman that man should treat her like a doll he is in constant fear of breaking; that he should be ashamed to appear to her anything but a trifler; that he should so seldom speak to her naturally and truthfully." She believes women's influence on society is nothing. Even more deliberately than George Eliot she pleads for friendship between young men and women. For a better state of society she sees a partial remedy in an improved education for girls, with instruction in the natural sciences and classical literature which was given to men. Of marriage she writes: "Not even the gift of children can remedy the sad blank of want of true mental companionship betwixt husband and wife."

Before 1850 agitation for colleges for women, as well as for better preparatory schools, was advanced. Mrs. Hugo Reid definitely urged the necessity of college training.[80] Queen's College had attracted not only governesses, but girls of the leisure class, who came to hear Maurice lecture. Bedford College, established in 1849 with Harriet Martineau as secretary and George Eliot as one of the students attending lectures, was offering a more advanced grade of education than that available in the ordinary girls' school. The movement to start good, cheap day-schools came much later. Although the paramount idea in both schools and colleges was equipment for teaching, some of the students had the desire for culture which Mrs. Grey and Miss Shirreff emphasized in their projected reforms.

But not all ladies wanted to be teachers. What women needed was work, plenty of work; not the kind with which they had formerly played fitfully, but employment which would demand all their energy. Arthur Clough in *Bothie of Tober-na-Vuolich* expressed the new point of view.

> "But ye, ye spurious ware, who
> Might be plain women, and can be by no possibility better!
> Ye unhappy statuettes and miserable trinkets,
> Poor alabaster chimney-piece ornaments under glass cases,
> Come, in God's name, come down! the very French clock by you
> Puts you to shame with ticking; the fire-irons deride you.
> You, young girl, who have had such advantages, learnt so
>   quickly,
> Can you not teach? O yes, and she likes Sunday school extremely,
> Only it's soon in the morning. Away! if to teach be your calling,
> It is no play, but a business: off! go teach and be paid for it.
> Lady Sophia's so good to the sick, so firm and so gentle.
> Is there a nobler sphere than of hospital nurse and matron?
> Hast thou for cooking a turn, little Lady Clarissa? in with them,
> In with your fingers! their beauty it spoils, but your own it
>   enhances,
> For it is beautiful only to do the thing we are meant for."

In the same poem he says:

> "Labour, and labour alone, can add to the beauty of women."[81]

Charlotte Brontë in *Shirley*, already referred to, had emphasized the necessity of work. Again and again in her letters she mentioned the importance of a girl's being self-supporting. Both men and women should have the power and the will to work for themselves.[82]

"Girls without fortune should be brought up and accustomed to support themselves." "One great curse of a single female life is its dependency. Your daughters—no more than your sons—should not be a burden on your hands. Whenever I have seen, not merely in humble, but in affluent homes, families of daughters sitting waiting to be married, I have pitied them from my heart." "Lonely as I am, how should I be if Providence had never given me courage to adopt a career? . . . How should I be with youth past, sisters lost, a resident in a moorland parish where there is not a single educated family? In that case I should have no world at all: the raven, weary of surveying the deluge, and without an ark to return to, would be my type. As it is, something like a hope and motive sustains me still. I wish all your daughters—I wish every woman in England, had also a hope and motive. Alas! there are many old maids who have neither."

Charlotte Brontë's friend Mary Taylor, the Rose Yorke of *Shirley*, emigrated to New Zealand because, Charlotte wrote to her sister Emily, she "has made up her mind she cannot and will not be a governess, a teacher, a milliner, a bonnet-maker, nor housemaid".[83] Miss Taylor did not think that *Shirley* went far enough in advocating work for women.

"I have seen some extracts from *Shirley* in which you talk of women working. And this first duty, this great necessity, you seem to think that some women may indulge in, if they give up marriage, and don't make themselves too disagreeable to the other sex. You are a coward and a traitor. A woman who works is by that alone better than one who does not; and a woman who does not happen to be rich and who still earns no money and does not wish to do so, is guilty of a great fault, almost a crime—a dereliction of duty which leads rapidly and almost certainly to all manner of degradation. It is very wrong of you to plead for toleration for workers on the ground of their being in peculiar circumstances, and few in number or singular in disposition. Work or degradation is the lot of all except the very small number born to wealth."

Of herself Miss Taylor wrote: "I have wished for fifteen years to begin to earn my own living; last April I began to try". This courageous pioneer, who kept a store in Wellington, New Zealand, finally wrote a series of articles for the *Victorian Magazine*, reprinted under the title *The First Duty of Women*, which is "the duty of earning money".

But what were women to do? So few employments were as yet open to them. As Charlotte Brontë wrote to her friend Mr. W. S. Williams, of Smith and Elder:[84]

> "It is true enough that the present market for female labour is quite overstocked, but where or how could another be opened? Many say that the professions now filled only by men should be open to women also; but are not their present occupants and candidates more than numerous enough to answer every demand? Is there any room for female lawyers, female doctors, female engravers, for more female artists, more authoresses? One can see where the evil lies, but who can point out the remedy?"

Deerbrook[84] by Harriet Martineau gives the governess Miss Young such words:

> "A woman from the uneducated classes can get a subsistence by washing and cooking, by milking cows and going to service, and, in some parts of the kingdom, by working in a cotton mill, or burnishing plate. . . . But, for an educated woman . . . there is in all England no chance of subsistence but by teaching—that almost ineffectual teaching, which can never countervail the education of circumstances, and for which not one in a thousand is fit—or by being a superior Miss Nares—the feminine gender of the tailor and the hatter."

In *Bleak House*[85] the question arises as to what Mr. Vholes's daughters are to become. "Are they to be shirt-makers, or governesses?" In *Martin Chuzzlewit* Pecksniff is speaking of Mary Graham.

> " 'If her position could be altered and defined, sir?' Mr. Pecksniff hinted.
> " 'How can that be done? Should I make a seamstress of her, or a governess?'
> " 'Heaven forbid!' said Mr. Pecksniff."

Other writers make the same disheartened lament.

Upon the enlarging of vocational opportunity depended the employment of middle-class women. Because the textile industries held first place in the public attention, one of the most often repeated suggestions was that ladies could be employed in the mills as overseers, "overlookers", to use the technical term.[86] Miss Emily Davies wrote in *The Higher Education of Women*: "Might it not be possible to bring them [factory women] again under womanly influence, and at the same time find fit work for their brains, by introducing women of the employing class into factories?" She advocated women both as directors and overlookers of female labour. In this connection another woman writer became even more eloquent.[87]

"When women of the middle ranks have established for every few streets a room where women of the working classes may be taught a few simple lessons in cookery, in mending, cleanliness, and nursing; when women of the middle ranks, in place of the present dilettante mode of dealing with the working classes, either train themselves at a normal school to be able to instruct their sisters of a humbler rank in the duties of domestic economy, or get others to train themselves for the duty; then, and only then, having done their part, can women of the middle ranks cast a stone at the shortcomings of the ranks beneath them."

She was convinced that mill women needed the sympathy and understanding of women to whom they could look for guidance and encouragement. But she went even farther, farther than any of her contemporaries. Middle-class women with superior training could protect the workers from the employers' attempts to keep down women's wages, and thus serve a definite industrial function. Because she believed the rise of factory workers to the higher branches of industry impossible, she looked forward to their being filled by middle-class women. Reformers thought that if the daughters of mill-owners could be instructed in their fathers' business, their contact with the degraded "hands" would result in moral uplift.

Occupation for women in a variety of social work, a sphere

so largely to become theirs in later years, was a theory much
agitated around 1850. For English ladies nursing was discovered
as a suitable profession. But as *Fraser's* pointed out in an article,
"Hospital Nurses as they Are and Ought to Be",[88] the care of
the sick was still given over to servants and women of doubtful
character totally without training. Mrs. Jameson described
English nurses as too often drunken, profligate, violent-
tempered, and brutal in language.[89] When Florence Nightingale informed her parents that her ambition was to become a
nurse, "it was as if", she said, "I had wanted to be a kitchen-
maid".[90] While the magazines[91] were still referring vaguely
to training in nursing at Kaiserwerth, Germany, and to the
work of sisters of charity in France, Miss Nightingale had
personally investigated the *Sœur de Charité* in Paris, and
had worked for three months at Kaiserwerth. By 1852 she
had overcome family opposition and was superintendent of a
nursing-home in Harley Street, London. Her departure for
the Crimea in 1855 was the beginning of the dignity of nursing.
Even though Miss Shirreff in the same year could not think
it "desirable that women of education and refined habits
should devote themselves to menial offices, however ennobled
by charity",[92] the care of the sick became and still remains
one of the most popular employments open to women of the
middle class. To the work of Miss Nightingale, who triumphed
"at the seat of war over highly placed officers and hoary
military traditions", a historian of nineteenth-century England
considers, "was due a new conception of the potentiality and
place of the trained and educated woman".[93] In fiction the
change is reflected in the years between the appearance of
Sairy Gamp in *Martin Chuzzlewit* (1843), with her deliberate
cruelty to her patient, and that of Ruth in Mrs. Gaskell's novel
(1853), who, after her trials as dressmaker and nursery
governess, became a devoted nurse.

Public opinion was also roused to the need of a higher class
of women in the public institutions which cared for the dependent members of society. *Fraser's* informed its readers that

statistics showing an infant mortality of 34 per cent. in an industrial town as compared with 20 in a non-industrial demonstrated the necessity of day nurseries for children, whom old women drugged with Godfrey's Cordial while their mothers were away at work.[94] Mrs. Jameson, taking advantage of the public excitement following Miss Nightingale's Crimean mission, delivered two lectures to show the necessity of better machinery for social work and to urge a substitute for the orders of the Catholic Church, which not only gave to unmarried women the occupation they were fitted for, but trained nuns for the hospitals and for charity and prison work. She commended the labours of Mr. Fliedner at Kaiserwerth, where a refuge for women discharged from prison had been opened in 1833. Later, a general hospital, lunatic asylum, orphan asylum, and infant school had been developed, all of them serving at the same time as training schools for nurses, teachers, and visitors of the poor. Similar institutions for the training of nurses and teachers had been started at Paris, Strasbourg, Berlin, and Dresden. All of these could serve as models for similar institutions in England.[95] In a later lecture she called the attention of her audience to the fact that Mrs. Fry's prison work and the Act of Parliament she succeeded in getting passed, ordering the appointment of matrons and female officers in all prisons, had become ineffective, because no women with the proper training could be provided. She suggested a superior order of female superintendents and lady visitors, with the necessary equipment. In the prisons of Piedmont trained sisters of charity had been successful; in Newdorf, prisons were governed chiefly by women. She also spoke at length concerning reformatories and workhouses. For young criminals she suggested the employment of the best men and women as teachers, with penitentiaries and houses of refuge for delinquent girls. In the workhouses she described the low state of general management. The master was often an ex-policeman, the keeper of a public-house, or a porter. The matrons were of low class. One had died from intemperance. The nurses were often chosen from the pauper women, in age between sixty and eighty, unsuited for their duties, and paid a penny a week with extra beer, at most a shilling a month. Little wonder that in 1856 nearly five hundred women were sent from the workhouse to prison. The whole workhouse system, with such harpies as Mrs. Corney and Mrs. Mann in control, Dickens had already exposed in *Oliver Twist*. A re-reading of the novel corroborates all that Mrs. Jameson was declaring from a public platform eighteen years later. Between the delivery and the publication of Mrs. Jameson's lectures, the prisons at Brixton and Fulham were organized under female management, and in 1857 the Workhouse Visiting Society began its work. The labours of Mary Carpenter for delinquent children, of Sarah Martin and Mrs. Gaskell in prisons, of Caroline Chisholm and Lady Jane Kinnaird for emigration societies for women, reveal the opportunities which were discovered in a variety of social service. Although little of this activity found expression in literature, Mary Carpenter was a prolific writer of books dealing with delinquent children, which roused public opinion, and she was considered an expert witness in parliamentary investigations on the subject. With the Oxford Movement, religious orders, notably Clewer, established in 1849, trained women for charity.[96] Disraeli represented Sybil in a Catholic convent as a visitor of the poor. The trained nurse and the social worker, however, have more and more taken hold of the management of public charitable institutions.

Finally, women began to clamour for professional and business opportunities. The author of *The Industrial and Social Position of Women* not only wanted women to be made superintendents of hospitals, workhouses, and reformatory prisons, but was ambitious to see them in the higher offices of education, in the pulpit, and in medicine. In business she saw their usefulness in the management of shops and warehouses, as overseers, book-keepers, tellers in banks.[97] The Dissenters had already encouraged women as preachers. Dinah Morris in *Adam Bede* was a Methodist preacher. Elizabeth Blackwell,* the first woman physician, was a pioneer in the profession at the time *Household Words* was indulging in humour about the danger of pretty women doctors. "More Work for the Ladies" in *Household Words* mentioned the existence of a woman dentist in France and also lady daguerreotypists. Miss Mitford, writing in 1849, referred to women just below the gentry in France employed as book-keepers. Charlotte Brontë portrayed Caroline as longing to be a clerk in a counting-house. In England, unlike France and the United States, women did not find a ready place in business. Miss Gertrude King, secretary of a society for the employment of women, established in 1860, stated before Parliament in 1867 the fitness of women for clerkships, secretaryships, etc., from which they were barred by the jealousy of men. The society had a book-keeping class and also a class to train girls to copy law papers. She mentioned the fact that one telegraph office employed only women. But as the *Edinburgh Review* pointed out in 1859, one great impediment to their success in business, especially in shops, was their almost universal ignorance of accounts. Considerable training must precede such employment. That occupations were greatly extended, however, is proved by the fact that by 1863 Virginia Penny could enumerate five hundred kinds of work available for women.

Economic independence was, unfortunately, no solution for the complications of the married woman, since a husband had a right to his wife's earnings. There were women, in spite of this handicap, who stood for the employment of married women in the middle class. Charlotte Brontë in *The Professor* has Frances say:[98]

"'Well, Monsieur, I wished merely to say that I should like, of course, to retain my employment of teaching. . . . Think of my marrying you to be kept by you, Monsieur! I could not do it; and

---

* Elizabeth Blackwell (1821–1910) was a practising physician in New York in 1851; in 1868 she was established in London.

how dull my days would be! You would be away teaching in close, noisy schoolrooms, from morning till evening, and I should be lingering at home, unemployed and solitary; I should get depressed and sullen, and you would soon tire of me. . . . I have taken notice, Monsieur, that people who are only in each other's company for amusement, never really like each other so well, or esteem each other so highly as those who work together, and perhaps suffer together.' "

In a letter to Mr. Williams she wrote:

"I think you speak excellent sense when you say that girls without fortune should be brought up and accustomed to support themselves; and that if they marry poor men, it should be with a prospect of being able to help their partners."

Although she was aware that "a woman may be so placed that she cannot possibly both 'guide the house' and 'earn her livelihood' ", her residence in Belgium had demonstrated the capability of a woman like Madame Heger to be a wife and mother at the same time she was managing the *pensionnat*. But with Charlotte Brontë a wife's work was not a means to independence, but a help to her husband and a pleasant occupation. She had adopted the Continental attitude of joint responsibility of husband and wife.

Nor did spinsters or married women look at Women's Rights as a solution for their troubles with the enthusiasm those in the United States rallied about a new cause. There Mrs. Bloomer was agitating not only votes for women as early as 1849 in her paper the *Lily*, an organ of both temperance and women's rights, but was preaching the adoption of bloomers, a costume consisting of skirts reaching just below the knee, worn with Turkish trousers. Frances Wright had emigrated to America to enjoy the greater freedom she considered possible there. But in England the women's rights movement had, at least, a feeble existence. In 1841 the *Edinburgh Review* listed six books on the subject, published in 1839 and 1840.[99] In 1843 Mrs. Hugo Reid wrote:

"The consciousness of responsibility which the possession of a vote would bestow, the dignity of being trusted, the resolution to justify the faith placed in her truth and judgment, would all call forth, in woman, noble powers which, hitherto, have been too much suffered to lie dormant."

She also wanted women in Parliament, where they could legislate for their own sex and its interests. Men had passed too many unjust laws for women. She had nothing but ridicule for the sentimental attitude of men who objected to women's overhearing debates in Parliament, because they might be exposed to something indelicate. In the next year Helene Weber wrote a book, *Woman's Rights and Wrongs*, which advanced the theory that women were the intellectual equals of men and should have political and legal equality. She agitated male attire for single women. In accordance with her belief that agriculture was the most suitable employment for women, she bought a farm and worked in men's clothes.

The subject had the misfortune to be rich in material for humour. Mrs. Jellyby, Dickens used in *Bleak House*[100] to ridicule the whole crew of female reformers who, like her, sacrificed their children to Africa. Miss Wish, who declared that "the idea of woman's mission lying chiefly in the narrow sphere of home was an outrageous slander on the part of her Tyrant, Man", performed a similar function for the cause, Women's Rights. The *Comic Almanac*, to which Thackeray, Cruikshank, and other wits contributed, was especially concerned with the new woman. A poem, *The Woman of Mind*, has the lines:

> "But she loves the whole human fam'ly,
> For she is a woman of mind."

In 1848 the *Almanac* records: "The ladies are invading everything." In 1849 four pages of drawings and appropriate texts describe the

> "Frightful State of Things
> If Female Agitation is allowed only for a Minute".

In 1852 a drawing by "Cruikshank" is entitled "Bloomerism in Full Blow". Women on juries and voting only for handsome candidates inspire a flood of jokes that seem somewhat forced to a later generation.

The most influential women of the time failed to support the movement in its earlier stages.[101] Mrs. Jameson's point of view was expressed in her first lecture on women's employments.

"I think that on this question [women's rights] our relations across the Atlantic have gone a mile beyond the winning-post, and brought discredit and ridicule on that just cause which, here in England, prejudice, custom, ignorance have in a manner crushed and smothered up."

Harriet Martineau had unqualified scorn for the women who forced the question of their "rights" before the public. Only gifted women, she was convinced, could demonstrate the importance of the sex.

"The best advocates", she wrote, "are yet to come—in the persons of women who are obtaining access to real social business, the female physicians and other professors in America, the women of business and the female artists of France; and the hospital administrators, the nurses, the educators and substantially successful authors of our own country. . . . Women, like men, can obtain whatever they show themselves fit for. Let them be educated, let their powers be cultivated to the extent for which the means are already provided, and all that is wanted or ought to be desired will follow of course. Whatever a woman proves herself able to do, society will be thankful to see her do, just as if she were a man."

It is possible Miss Martineau's success came too easily for her to doubt the entire truth of her statements. Even Mrs. Norton in her appeals to her public contended not for sex but for financial rights. In a letter to *The Times* she wrote:

"The wild and stupid theories advanced by a few women of 'equal rights' and 'equal intelligence' are not the opinions of their sex. I, for one (I with millions more), believe in the natural superiority of man, as I do in the existence of a God."

For relief the married woman in England looked first to the reform of the laws. When Mrs. Norton was separated from her children she began her spirited attempt to change the law which kept them from her. In 1837, when the Infants' Custody Bill had been brought up before Parliament by Sergeant Talfourd, she wrote a pamphlet, *Observation on the Natural Claim of a Mother to the Custody of her Children as affected by the Common Law Right of the Father, illustrated by Cases of Peculiar Hardship*, which she distributed among Members of Parliament. The next year the Bill was passed by the Commons, but rejected by the Lords. At this juncture she wrote another pamphlet, *A Plain Letter to the Lord Chancellor on the Custody of Infants*, under the pseudonym Pearse Stevenson, "as I feared, if they knew it was a woman's writing, it would have less weight". *Fraser's* in February of the next year[102] reviewed this letter.

Largely as a result of her influence, it is now thought, the Infants' Custody Bill was passed in the summer of 1839. The Act permitted any mother deprived of her children, if she could prove her irreproachable character, to petition the Lord Chancellor for a hearing before a special court. In 1842 she brought her suit in Chancery to have her children in order to direct their education, and was finally granted limited control of them.

Mrs. Norton next directed her pen to a reform of the antiquated divorce laws. In 1850 a Royal Commission had been appointed to examine the whole subject, but nothing had been done. In 1854 she published her spirited *English Laws for Women in the Nineteenth Century*, which covers the same ground as Madame Bodichon's pamphlet. As a text she used Dickens's words: "It won't do to have Truth and Justice on our side. We must have Law and Lawyers." After she had outlined other abuses which had been corrected, such as the improvement in the care of the insane and the reform of prisons and of the education of the poor, she demonstrated from her own unfortunate history the need of change in a law which made a husband's contract with his wife not binding and also of legislation which would give her "the right to her own brains". Then in scathing words she summarized the existing laws. A month after her pamphlet appeared, Lord Cranworth brought forward a bill in the House of Lords to reform the English marriage and divorce laws, but it asked for little more than a transfer of divorce cases from the ecclesiastical courts to a special court consisting of the Chancellor and other legal dignitaries. It made a woman's chance of getting a divorce or even legal separation more difficult than before. In a speech before the Lords, Lord Cranworth, in defending the part of a bill which denied divorce to a woman for mere infidelity of her husband, said: "If a woman could divorce on small ground, a man who for some reason wished his wife to divorce him had only to be a little profligate to get his freedom at his wife's expense." Mrs. Norton replied with a pamphlet, *A Letter to the Queen on Lord Cranworth's Marriage and Divorce Bill*, which was privately circulated at first and then published in 1855. Not until 1858, however, was a divorce law passed which made any real reform. One of its most important provisions was that which not only protected the earnings of a deserted wife and made provision for separate maintenance, but also made possible the wife's inheritance and possession of property, and gave her power of contract, of suing, and being sued in any civil proceeding.* She had at last become an adult before the law. Another equally important law for women was the Married Women's Property Act, first brought forward in 1856,† but not fully passed until 1882. For such a law Barbara Bodichon had long laboured.

Mrs. Norton's importance in the reform of laws affecting

---

* Mrs. Gore in *Men of Capital* had introduced the deserted wife whose child was taken away from her.

† In the petition sent to Parliament urging the Married Women's Property Act, signed by Mrs Browning, Mrs. Carlyle, Mrs. Gaskell, Mrs. Jameson, Harriet Martineau, Bessie Rayner Parkes, Mrs. Hugo Reid, and Barbara Leigh Smith, the earnings of working women were emphasized. See *Westminster Review*, 1856, p. 338.

women cannot be overestimated. As she had written in her *Letter to the Queen* :[108]

"My plea to attention is, that in pleading for myself I am able to plead for all these others. Not that my sufferings or my deserts are greater than theirs [other women's], but that I combine, with the fact of having suffered wrong, the power to comment on and explain the cause of that wrong, which few men are able to do.

"For this, I believe God gave me the power of writing. To this I devote that power. I abjure all other writing till I see these laws altered. . . . If I could be justified and happy to-morrow, I would still strive and labour in it; and if I were to die to-morrow, it would still be a satisfaction to me that I had so striven."

But the old order was soon to become as unfair to the husband as to the wife. For the husband to be liable for debts contracted by his wife, when she was capable of earning £1,400 annually, as Mrs. Norton asserted she did, was a turn of affairs destined to change rapidly the former relation of husband and wife. If Mrs. Norton's earnings had tempted her husband to air their private quarrels, they also stood as the symbol of the new importance of women. As a wage-earner, then, not as the idle woman she might have been with a more successful husband, she had emerged into a recognized place in the world.

By 1850 the idle women were crying out for a chance to work; they were proclaiming their need of a better education to fit them for profitable employment; they were revolting against legal subjection to a husband. They wanted idleness to be the choice of the women who desired it, not the lot of all middle-class women.

5. Literary Materials concerning the Idle Woman

In the study of the idle woman, one observes that the literary overbalances the non-literary material. Such a reversal of the proportions examined for working women is easily comprehensible. The idle woman, not the worker, was the real Victorian heroine, entirely within the traditions of the age. She alone had infinite leisure to play the game of love. Her unoccupied girlhood was a brief prelude to marriage and motherhood, the real function of women. Here the novelists dealt with the heroine they saw most of and understood best. But the real importance of this part of our study lies in the fact that many writers saw the tragedy of idleness. The men, married, perhaps, to girls with the conventional faulty training of the day, had suffered from their partners' incompetence. Many of the women had escaped the fate of idleness only because they could write. Charlotte Brontë's cry in *Shirley* has the epic sweep of emotion which comes from personal defeat:[104]

"Men of England! Look at your poor girls, many of them fading around you, dropping off in consumption or decline; or, what is worse, degenerating to sour old maids, envious, backbiting, wretched, because life is a desert to them: or, what is worst of all, reduced to strive, by scarce modest coquetry and debasing artifice, to gain that position and consideration by marriage, which to celibacy is denied. Fathers! cannot you alter these things? Perhaps not all at once; but consider the matter well when it is brought before you, receive it as a theme worthy of thought: do not dismiss it with an idle jest or an unmanly insult. You would wish to be proud of your daughters and not to blush for them: then seek for them an interest and an occupation which shall raise them above the flirt, the manœuverer, the mischief-making tale-bearer. Keep your girls' minds narrow and fettered—they will still be a plague and a care, sometimes a disgrace, to you: cultivate them—give them scope and work—they will be your gayest companions in health; your tenderest nurses in sickness; your most faithful prop in age."

CHAPTER VII

CONCLUSION

IN tracing the emergence of the working woman in literature, one observes that her prominence in *belles-lettres* is in proportion to the degree of her conformity with the traditional patterns of her age. Only when the writer and the wage-earner have been one, as in the case of the governess, does the new heroine come forth. Elsewhere the worker is either neglected or presented in a way not wholly justified by the facts. Such a condition has complicated a study of working women.

The non-literary material necessary to supplement the literary in building up a complete structure of fact, often overshadowed it. When *belles-lettres* were available, one sometimes questioned their veracity. The only course, then, was to test all secondary material by means of primary sources in order to separate fact and fancy, and next to analyse the sources of error. Writers were seldom deliberate deceivers. But in too many cases they were unable to understand the changes of the Industrial Revolution. They either adopted a superior attitude to cotton factories and Birmingham steel which enabled them to pass over the complexity of women's employment in new industries, or they praised the traditional and attacked the new. They were agitated by the appearance of women as labourers in mills and shops, although they had made no protest against their long-established overwork in domestic manufacture. They criticized new standards of conduct without trying to understand why the old had disappeared. Such prejudices led many earnest writers to conclusions totally unjustified by the facts they took the trouble to collect. Because they discovered certain intolerable conditions in industries which hired women, they argued, first, that women should be kept at home, and second, that they wanted to stay there, entirely disregarding the traditional and necessary family wage, and the absence of sentiment among the lower classes for the hovels writers deified as home. Artistic necessity, as we have seen, caused a further departure from truth. In their search for a new model of villain, novelists fastened upon the manufacturer. Because the reading public had a taste for moral and spiritual victories, they directed their attention to the dressmaker, wavering between the support of a lover and her own hard labour, or the mill girl preferring spiritual salvation and persecution to degradation and the approval of her mates. The results were violent contrasts in virtue and vice, heroic disregard of personal comfort and gain, and recurrence of certain romantic situations. Women writers further complicated the problem. Not only did they possess most of the mental and literary vices of the time in an exaggerated degree, but their interest in their own sex tended to obscure certain issues. Their treatment of women had the reality and intensity which come from personal experience; they made exhaustive studies of a great variety of female occupations; they exposed unsanitary modes of life as few men could have done; they steadily concerned themselves with the constructive aspect of working women's difficulties. But they lacked the intellectual aloofness which eliminates hysteria and bigotry. As a consequence, then, the real working woman was lost often in a mass of literary incompetence and sentimental misrepresentation, and the investigator was driven back to the chroniclers of fact.

Such difficulties lead inevitably to the query as to the value of strictly literary material in giving a reliable social picture of any age. The slowness of *belles-lettres* to register sudden changes, joined with the mental limitations and prejudices of the writer and his public, are together grave disqualifications. But let us imagine for a moment the elimination of all literary aids to an understanding of certain aspects of early nineteenth-century life. Could the ignorant and inarticulate mill girl called in as a witness by Government officials have revealed her life to us without other means? Neither side understood the significance of many of her answers. Often the questioners found only what they were searching for. What seemed not pertinent to them was either passed over or given scant attention. Clearly enough, primary sources alone are insufficient. One needs the interpretation and drama of such writers as Mrs. Tonna and Mrs. Gaskell to make the mill girl and dressmaking apprentice flesh and blood figures. Contemporary comment is equally necessary. What another age thinks of itself is surely as important as what we think about it. That primary sources alone are unsatisfactory is further emphasized by the novels of Charlotte Brontë; her individual experiences as a governess need checking with the detached observations of such secondary agents as Thackeray, George Eliot, or the educational committees. A study of primary sources, together with literary data, has demonstrated the incompleteness of each. All this argues a plea for the historic method as applied to the study of literature.

The literary critic, unlike the historian, has preferred his own æsthetic individualism to a procedure of detailed comparison of primary and secondary sources. But if literature is to be judged in part by its value as social criticism, such methods are inadequate. At the moment the æsthetic critic appears at a special disadvantage. The twentieth century offers a violent contrast to the nineteenth in its canons of critical as well as of creative literature. The modern critic is subjective; he is not searching for touchstones in criticism. But if the present seems unfavourable for the appraisal of Victorian literature from a purely artistic standpoint, it is especially adapted to an historical estimate. We have few of the disadvantages of the contemporary observers of life in the days of Peel and Disraeli. We are at last familiar with the new world which was born with industrial organization. We have less prejudice against it. We can take a more detached view of the women who were hustled about in mill and workshop. Conventional morals are more likely to be regarded as convenient short-cuts to efficiency in a machine age which permits little waste of energy than as material for literary sermons. The science of investigation, largely a development of our century, has assisted the impartiality of the perfect critic. An increasing number of contemporary books helping to interpret the preceding age are appearing. We are at last far enough away from the nineteenth century to see the effects of some of the changes which bewildered contemporaries.

For a study of working women all these advantages have combined to make possible a more impersonal view than ever before. The woman who supports herself by her own labour is a familiar part of our industrial and social structure. She is no longer a pitiable or tragic figure, to be admired or senti-mentalized. She is merely accepted. The women who have become her historians are not ladies sheltered from the world, who make their observations by means of charity missions or books. They are themselves workers, differentiated only in their scientific equipment for observation, proud of their financial independence, pleading no cause of their own. Women will always be most zealous in the investigation of questions pertaining to their own sex. An improved education has removed much of their emotional bias and sex prejudice. But the modern woman has perhaps a tendency to over-emphasize the advantages which Victorian working women had over the idle, fretful lady, and the ruined girl over the starved old maid. Some forceful reformers, in their desire to eliminate all women whose time is not taken up with a definite occupation, totally disregard the possibility that a woman with both leisure and freedom might become a definite cultural force in modern life. But with these exceptions, women are at last qualified to take an historic point of view toward their own sex as workers.

From the vantage ground of the present, one can look back upon the period of 1832–50 as a time of gradual gains for the working woman. By 1850 writers were beginning to realize that it was not the entrance of women into industry which degraded them. "Probably it is too much to expect that society will ever be without a large thriftless and squalid class", admitted one critic, "but its number will be decreased, not by withdrawing the female sex from industry, but by bettering their position there. . . . The woman that is squalid and thriftless when working ten hours a day, and earning 5s. a week, would be much more so if she could earn nothing."[1] The observer discerns a recognition of the working woman as an integral part of the new machine age. One more step in the development of urban civilization was thus taken and the Industrial Revolution completed when women gained an honoured place in it. On the whole, the new age has been good for woman. Although she was temporarily enslaved by the factory, the final result has been her emancipation, since as a wage-earner outside of her own home she has been much freer than she was as a household drudge, with the added burdens of spinning, hand-sewing, and the care of cow and pigs feeding on the village common.

At the same time that she gained economic recognition, she acquired social individuality. Woman is now considered apart from the family, just as man gradually became separate from the feudal organization of the estate. Although Mary Woll-stonecraft had a sense of woman's political individuality, hers was a romantic view, inferior to that which was to come later. The triumph of woman as an individual was up to 1850, however, only for the worker. The lady of the upper class was, as Meredith showed in *The Egoist*, still regarded as a chattel.

The result of this changed attitude, this new economic and social individuality, manifested itself at once in a determined effort to throw off all the forces which shackled woman as an individual. The agitation for reform of the divorce laws, property laws, the custody of children, which was begun by Mrs. Norton, was to become more and more the concern of literature. Meredith, who used Mrs. Norton in the making of his heroine Diana, and Thomas Hardy in *Jude the Obscure*, have been advocates of a freer system of marriage. Women were quick to see that for their own legal protection they needed the vote, and agitation for political rights, begun feebly before 1850, became more insistent when John Stuart Mill led the early suffragists in their campaign of 1866–67. Mrs. Humphrey Ward, in selecting her series of novels portraying women's interest in politics, recorded a growing consciousness of the need of participation in State affairs.

As the question of women's rights came to the front about 1850, a new point of view was gradually adopted toward the struggles of working women to have justice. The Factory Law of 1847 had been a triumph for Government interference; Parliament passed legislation for women as apart from men, who had fought their battles through labour unions, even though they enjoyed the benefits of the laws designed to protect women. In every branch of women's work this same principle of protecting the weaker sex by parliamentary interference had been recognized. The Government agents had investigated all employments open to women. Parliament had next passed laws to safeguard women in textile mills and mines and had attempted some relief n workshops. In dressmaking, the spasmodic efforts at reform through private organization had been largely the result of Government investigation. Even the governess received relief from the belated official examination of schools, although private concerns first agitated her wrongs. But with the growing consciousness of woman's importance, feminist agitators became hostile to shielding themselves behind parliamentary gentlemen. In 1878, and again in 1895, there was a temporary desertion of the principle of Government assistance for the men's method of gaining protection through labour unions.[2] With the spread of Socialism and the growing strength of the Labour Party, however, men as well as women are going back to the idea of Government protection which was triumphant in 1850.

A new development of woman's independence has come through birth-control, also foreshadowed by Richard Carlile and Francis Place early in the preceding century. When women are voluntary mothers they become free to develop a less haphazard programme of occupation. They also have the same chance for adventure as men. What the results of this new freedom will be is still uncertain. The new adventuress has, however, occupied the centre of the stage in contemporary literature. Hardy, Mr. Shaw, Mr. Galsworthy, Mr. Wells, and Mr. Aldous Huxley have been concerned with the woman of independent spirit, although none has yet succeeded in doing anything of importance with her newly discovered energy.

Side by side with the growing consciousness of individuality which resulted from women's participation in the Industrial Revolution developed a new sense of sex solidarity. A social sympathy has grown up which has been powerful in breaking down class barriers. The author of *The Industrial and Social Position of Women* was one of the first writers to comment on the unfortunate segregation of women from one another, and to emphasize the need of mill women for some contact with those of the middle class. Miss Merryweather's welfare work referred to in Chapter II was a pioneer attempt to fulfil this need. In modern industry women factory inspectors and the welfare workers employed by the larger mills have carried on this modest beginning. In the agitation for the reform of dressmaking shops the women of the aristocracy and the upper middle class, who joined the early closing movement, widened the sympathies of leisure women for those who toil for them. This kind of class association has continued. Both the governess and the mother of the children she teaches have been able to meet on the common ground of educational policy as both have increased their mental equipment. This was begun before 1850, and has since then increased. In the fight for suffrage and the reform of laws affecting women, especially divorce laws, women have been further united. The start made by 1850 has steadily continued.

In the general improvements affecting working women, no change has been of greater importance than that brought about through the application of science to domestic comfort.

Mechanical inventions, practically all of them by men, have done more to dignify the home than Victorian sentiment. The factory woman in the year 1832, who lived in a house without window-glass, washed clothes without soap, sewed by hand, if she could sew at all, and at night dropped down upon a bed, if she owned a bed, in the clothes she had worn during the day, seems now to belong to a period as remote from modern domestic comfort as the Elizabethan Age. Modern plumbing and general education in sanitation have made crowded cities healthful. The sewing-machine, which began the Industrial Revolution in the home, has been followed by a steady succession of improvements to relieve household toil. Ready-made clothing, laundries, canning on a large scale, shops where food ready for the table can be bought at moderate prices, have made it possible for wives to work in factories and still secure the comforts of life for their families. Although the electric washing-machine, mangle, and vacuum sweeper, which are common in working-class homes in the United States, are not yet widely used in Great Britain, their adoption belongs, we hope, to the near future. The telephone, the gramophone, and the radio have also been great inventions for women in relieving lonely domestic drudgery. In the application of science to social schemes, working women have also gained both mental and spiritual emancipation. Municipal housing schemes, dreamed of in the days of Sir James Kay-Shuttleworth, who lived to see the improvements in housing between 1832 and 1850 in the neighbourhood of Manchester, are more and more popular. Neighbourhood nurseries and schools for babies; the general improvement in education, including extension classes for pupils who work during the day; working-girls' clubs, especially well organized in London; night classes in domestic science for working mothers, have all been a boon to the large number of women who both before and after marriage are wage-earners. In most respects, then, the Industrial Revolution has been good for women of the lower classes. Factory work has brought comfort to families dependent upon a family wage, and the application of science to housekeeping will more and more enable women to work in factories without being denied the compensations of wifehood and motherhood. By 1850 factory women were better off than working women had ever been before. The greatest disadvantage of the factory has been that it has given women little chance to rise to positions of trust. But men have suffered the same handicaps, since machines are the brains of industry.

By 1850 women had started agitation for practically all of the professions now open to them. Nursing and teaching were becoming then, as they are now, the two important occupations for middle-class women. From nursing they advanced to medicine, but as yet they suffer tremendous sex discrimination. Teaching since 1850 has steadily risen in dignity through the reforms of secondary schools and the opening of university degrees to women. In 1872 the Girls' Public Day School Company was created to provide good, cheap, dayschools for girls; in 1878 the Maria Grey Training College was founded. The University of London has given a B.A. Degree to women since 1878; Cambridge opened the triposes to women in 1881; Oxford allowed women to pass the examinations in 1884, and in 1920 gave them the B.A. The women's colleges at Oxford, Cambridge, and the University of London all have women on their teaching staff, among them distinguished scholars; professorships are now open to women, in the universities of both London and Oxford. With this educational reform were introduced such sports as hockey, lacrosse, tennis, in both preparatory schools and colleges. Their influence upon health, dress, and morals cannot be overestimated. But women in the universities have not escaped some of the evils which Tennyson saw clearly in *The Princess* (1847). Although women's colleges, following closely in educational policy those of the men, have maintained an intellectual dignity far in advance of similar institutions in the United States, they have suffered far more from sex antagonism. The counterparts of Princess Ida, too powerful in the pioneering days of university education for women, have left their mark. Women in England, as in the United States, have almost no intellectual co-operation with men, and their studies have suffered from female isolation. The record of professional women is discouraging, since by 1850 they were in sight of the gains they have made since then. In business they have achieved no definite place as they have in the United States. The clerk class is largely masculine. The feminine stenographer has seldom advanced to a secretarial position of confidential trust. Banks have not given openings to women, nor have they been sufficiently employed in various investigating economic capacities for which their training has fitted them. Englishwomen of the middle class still have most of their professional struggles before them.

One would expect that the literature since 1850 would do for the working women of the middle class what that earlier accomplished for those of the lower ranks. The significant social phenomenon of this later period has been the emergence of middle-class women as workers. An improved education, an even larger number of women writers, and an overflow of women into new occupations, are circumstances favourable to literary recognition. We could reasonably expect that Charlotte Brontë's independent new heroine should have had legions of successors. Yet an examination of British *belles-lettres* since 1850 reveals no real change in the picture which was drawn in the early reign of Queen Victoria. What fiction and poetry were either unwilling or unable to do then, is still left undone. Such novelists as Mr. Arnold Bennett, Mr. Frank Swinnerton, and Mr. Somerset Maugham, continue to use working women of the lower classes to serve the traditional modes of fiction. Workers from the middle class are neglected. In actual life women as doctors, lawyers, preachers, university lecturers, in the face of stubborn masculine opposition, have gained recognition. Where are the novels chronicling this determined fight against the barrier of sex? We have as yet no literary presentation of the woman whose romance is her success in her work. Novelists, both men and women, continue to depict only the emotional history of their heroines, in spite of the fact that there is a large army of women into whose lives love and passion enter little or none at all. This literary concentration upon a love life, intensified by the present interest in psycho-analysis, has had an unfortunate social influence. Useful women are deceived into thinking they have been cheated. The truth is that many women find plenty of compensation, as do men, in an absorbing job. Literature, however, is reflecting the popular attitude. If a woman says her work satisfies her, few women believe her, and even fewer men. Not until she learns to accept a job as play, as emotional outlet, as children, will she have advanced beyond the Victorian point of view. The feminists preach this doctrine, but as yet few of them practise it. Women writers, perhaps more than men, have kept the novel tied to love and courtship. Only when it becomes the handmaid of ideas, as Miss Rebecca West trusts it will, can one reasonably expect an extension of the fictional function. With such an intellectualizing of the novel, an author who is herself a working woman might be able to write novels whose heroines portray their creator's employment, her struggles, her success. One prophesies less stereotyped women characters for the novel of this genre. The biographies of scientists, painters, musicians, would seem to prove that a record of work can be made as enthralling as one of amours. But novelists have as yet failed to make this simple discovery. We beg for a heroine who is a worker whether she marries or not. But until she appears, the study of working women in literature is completed by the year 1850, and needs at present no postscript.

NOTES

(All the references to standard novels are made to chapters, not pages. The complete American edition of Mrs. Tonna's tales in two volumes, 1849, is used.)

CHAPTER I

1. Jameson, Mrs. Anna: Memoirs and Essays, ch. v.
2. Jameson, Mrs. Anna: Sisters of Charity at Home and Abroad, p. 94.
3. Trevelyan, G. M.: British History in the Nineteenth Century, 1782–1901, p. 129.
4. Trevelyan, G. M.: British History in the Nineteenth Century, 1782–1901, p. 188.
5. Austen, Jane: Emma, ch. x.
6. A few of the magazines of this class were:
    The Christian Lady's Friend and Family Repository, 1832, 1834.
    The Christian Lady's Library, 1850.
    The Christian Lady's Magazine, 1834–49.
    The Christian Mother's Magazine, 1844, 1845, edited by Mrs. Milner.
    The Englishwoman's Magazine and Christian Mother's Miscellany, edited by Mrs. Milner, 1846–54, and continued as The Christian Lady's Magazine, 1855–57.
    The Ladies' Cabinet of Fashion, Music, and Romance, 1832–38, 1839–43, 1844–52, 1852–70.
    The Ladies' Companion at Home and Abroad, edited by Mrs. Loudon, 1850, 1851, 1852–70.
    The Ladies' Gazette of Fashion, 1842–74, 1874–94.
    The Ladies' Journal, 1847.
    The Ladies' Magazine of Gardening, edited by Mrs. Loudon, 1842.
    The Ladies' Own Magazine and Mirror of the Months, 1843.
    The Ladies' Penny Gazette, 1832–33.
    The Ladies' Pocket Magazine, 1825–39.
    The Ladies' Portfolio, 1853.
    The Ladies' Album of Fancy Work, 1850.
    The Ladies' Gazette of Fashion, 1834–35.
    The Ladies' Magazine and Museum of the Belles-Lettres, 1832–37.
7. Gaskell, Elizabeth Cleghorn: The Life of Charlotte Brontë, p. 364.

CHAPTER II

1. Gaskell, Elizabeth Cleghorn: Mary Barton, ch. i.
2. Lipson, E.: History of the Woollen and Worsted Industries, pp. 34, 35, 57.
3. Clark, Alice: Working Life of Women in the Seventeenth Century, pp. 95, 113, 114.
4. Parliamentary Papers, 1835, Vol. XIII; 1839, Vol. XLII; 1840, Vols. XXIII, XXIV; 1841, Vol. I.
5. Wordsworth, William: The Excursion, Book VIII, ll. 165–185.
6. Hutchins, B. L.: Women in Modern Industry, p. 93.

7. Parliamentary Papers, 1833, Vol. XXI, A3, p. 53 and A1, p. 84; 1831–32, Vol. XV, pp. 236, 535.
8. Tonna, Charlotte Elizabeth: Works, Vol. I, p. 537.
9. Tonna, Charlotte Elizabeth: Works, Vol. I, p. 538.
10. Ure, Andrew: The Philosophy of Manufactures, pp. 466, 473. Gaskell, Peter: Artisans and Machinery, p. 173.
11. Parliamentary Papers, 1842, Vol. XXII, p. 365.
12. Hansard, Vol. 73, p. 1088.
13. Hansard, Vol. 73, p. 1092.
14. Parliamentary Papers, 1847, Vol. XLVI, pp. 610–621. For United Kingdom:

	Males above 18	Females above 18
Cotton	85,533	117,667
Woollen ..	27,610	16,215
Worsted ..	7,366	22,133
Flax	10,430	25,978
Silk	7,359	16,238

15. Hansard, Vol. 74, p. 666.
16. Hutchins: Women in Modern Industry, pp. 40–43. P.P., 1833, Vol. XX, pp. 644, 645.
17. P.P., 1834, Vol. XIX, p. 508.
18. Gaskell: Manufacturing Population of England, p. 127. Kay-Shuttleworth, Sir James: Four Periods of Public Education, pp. 151–153.
19. Disraeli, Benjamin: Sybil, Book II, ch. x. Hansard, Vol. 73, pp. 1147, 1148.
20. Hansard, Vol. 73, pp. 1147, 1148.
21. Hansard, Vol. 74, p. 970. Clapham, J. H.: An Economic History of Great Britain, Vol. I, pp. 582–583. Edmund Ashworth's letter quoted that immigration "would have a tendency to equalize wages, as well as prevent, in a degree, some of the 'turns out' which have of late been so prevalent".
22. Taylor, W. Cooke: Notes of a Tour in the Manufacturing Districts of Lancashire in a Series of Letters to his Grace the Archbishop of London, p. 195. In a letter to the Morning Chronicle from Lancashire, June 20,1842, Dr. Cooke Taylor reports a death by starvation, the deceased refusing to apply for relief because it meant being sent back to his own parish. "They had rather endure anything in the hope of some manufacturing revival than return to the condition of farm labourers from which they had emerged." Also Fay, Charles Ryle: Life and Labour in the Nineteenth Century, p. 174.
23. Tickner, F. W.: Women in English Economic History, pp. 136–137. Clapham gives a modifying opinion, pp. 98–117. He states that the importance of enclosures in this connection has been exaggerated.
24. Ure: Philosophy of Manufactures, pp. 474–477.
25. Edinburgh Review, Vol. 89, p. 417.
26. Fraser's, Vol. 37, pp. 1–16.
27. P.P., 1833, Vol. XX, p. 58.
28. P.P., 1833, Vol. XX, pp. 694, 860. Wood, George Henry: History of Wages in the Cotton Trade, passim.
29. P.P., 1834, Vol. XIX, p. 292.
30. P.P., 1833, Vol. XX, pp. 336–338.
31. P.P., 1833, Vol. XX, pp. 336–338.

32. P.P., 1834, Vol. XIX, p. 292.
33. P.P., 1834, Vol. XIX, p. 644.
34. P.P., 1834, Vol. XIX, pp. 33–35 and p. 292.
35. P.P., 1834, Vol. XIX, pp. 33–35, for average wages of men and women at different ages in all textile industries.
36. Ure: Philosophy of Manufactures, p. 475. P.P., 1834, Vol. XIX, p. 39 (Dr. Mitchell's Report).
37. P.P., 1833, Vol. XXI, p. 53.
38. Sybil, Book II, ch. ix.
39. P.P., 1833, Vol. XX, p. 502.
40. Hansard, Vol. 73, p. 1497.
41. P.P., 1844, Vol. XXVIII, p. 557.
42. P.P., 1833, Vol. XX, p. 84.
43. Hansard, Vol. 73, p. 1084.
44. P.P., 1844, Vol. XXVIII, p. 556.
45. P.P., 1834, Vol. XIX, pp. 404, 405. Hansard, Vol. 74, p. 976.
46. For difference of opinion about women in spinning, see Gaskell: Artisans and Machinery, p. 269; and Hutchins: Women in Modern Industry, p. 93.
47. Hutchins: Women in Modern Industry, p. 82.
48. Roebuck, J. A.: Political Pamphlets on the Means of Conveying Information to the People. See Francis Place's Letter to James Turner, Cotton Spinner, Brompton, London, September 29, 1835.
49. Hutchins: Women in Modern Industry, p. 92 and Appendix 271 note; ch. iv. contains good material on unions.
50. Hammond, J. L. and B.: The Town Labourer, p. 262.
51. Drake, Barbara: Women in Trade Unions, p. 4.
52. Webb, B. and S.: History of Trade Unionism, p. 105.
53. Wade, John: History of the Middle and Working Classes, pp. 570, 571.
54. Drake, Barbara: Women in Trade Unions, p. 5.
55. Hammond: The Town Labourer, p. 318.
56. London Times, April 19, 1834.
57. Baernreither, J. M.: English Associations of Working Men, p. 225. Cole, G. D. H.: Life of William Cobbett, pp. 252, 253.
58. Drake: Women in Trade Unions, Appendix.
59. Hutchins: Women in Modern Industry, p. 94.
60. Drake: Women in Trade Unions, p. 9.
61. Hammond: The Skilled Labourer, p. 80: "The women are, if possible, more turbulent and mischievous than the men," p. 105.
62. P.P., 1831–32, Vol. XV, p. 236.
63. Gaskell: Artisans and Machinery, p. 271.
64. Disraeli: Sybil, Book VI, ch. viii.
65. Household Words, Vol. VIII, p. 555.
66. Tonna: Works, Vol. II, p. 444. Hansard, Vol. 73, p. 1096.
67. Baernreither: *op. cit.*, pp. 225–227.
68. Lovett, William: Autobiography, Vol. I, p. 174.
69. Hansard, Vol. 73, p. 1097.
70. Hansard, Vol. 98, p. 290. Slosson, P. W.: Decline of the Chartist Movement, p. 207.
71. Punch, Vol. XV, p. 3.
72. Sybil Book VI, ch. iii.
73. Sybil, Book VI, ch. viii.

74. Drake: Women in Trade Unions, Table II in Appendix for information about what unions admitted women to membership, and dates.
75. P.P., 1831-32, Vol. XV, p. 236.
76. Hansard, Vol. 73, p. 1081.
77. Hansard, Vol. 73, pp. 1078, 1079.   Vol. 74, p. 671.
78. P.P., 1833, Vol. XXI, p. 25; 1847-48, Vol. XXVI, p. 128; 1831-32, Vol. XV, p. 474. Hansard, Vol. 73, p. 1095. P.P., 1833, Vol. XX, p. 659.
79. P.P., 1843, Vol. XXVII, pp. 19, 307.
80. P.P., 1843, Vol. XXVII, p. 19, 307; P.P., 1833, Vol. XXI, p. 33.
81. Household Words, Vol. IX, p. 224; Vol. XI, pp. 241, 337, 494, 605.
82. P.P., 1833, Vol. XX, p. 645.
83. P.P., 1833, Vol. XXI, p. 30.   Hansard, Vol. 74, p. 679.
84. Hansard, Vol. 73, p. 1082.
85. P.P., 1833, Vol. XXI, pp. 33-35.   Hansard, Vol. 73, pp. 1081-1082; Vol. 74, p. 679.
86. P.P., 1834, Vol. XIX, p. 141.
87. Hansard, Vol. 89, p. 488.
88. Taylor: Notes of a Tour, pp. 260-261.   Fraser's, Vol. 37, pp. 1-16.
89. Ure: Philosophy of Manufactures, p. 392.
90. Hansard, Vol. 73, p. 1113.
91. P.P., 1833, Vol. XXI, p. 121.
92. Taylor: Notes of a Tour, pp. 263-264.   Hansard, Vol. 73, p. 1113.
93. Hansard, Vol. 73, pp. 1133-40.   P.P., 1834, Vol. XIX, p. 497.
94. Hansard, Vol. 73, p. 1092.   Vol. 74, p. 679.   One case of the danger of continued labour upon a pregnant woman was reported at a meeting at Blackburn, April 22, 1844.   A woman far advanced in pregnancy was removed from a mill bleeding profusely from the bursting of a blood-vessel in the leg.   P.P., 1833, Vol. XXI, p. 141.   A midwife of a lying-in hospital testified to the frequent miscarriages among a class of women who worked in the mill after breakfast and gave birth to children at noon. See Gaskell: Artisans and Machinery, p. 192.
95. P.P., 1834, Vol. XIX, p. 296.
96. P.P., 1833, Vol. XXI, p. 70.
97. Hansard, Vol. 73, p. 1145.
98. P.P., 1833, Vol. XXI, pp. 58, 69.
99. P.P., 1833, Vol. XX, p. 5.
100. P.P., 1833, Vol. XXI, p. 133.
101. P.P., 1833, Vol. XXI, p. 102.
102. Hansard, Vol. 73, p. 1091.
103. Hansard, Vol. 73, p. 1093.   P.P., 1833, Vol. XXI, p. 141.
104. P.P., 1833, Vol. XXI, pp. 58, 69.   Hansard, Vol. 73, p. 1116.
105. P.P., 1833, Vol. XX, p. 860.   Vol. XXI, pp. 139-141.   Hansard, Vol. 73 p. 1093.
106. P.P., 1833, Vol. XXI, pp. 139, 140.
107. Sybil, Book II, ch. ix.
108. Jewsbury, Geraldine: Marian Withers, p. 52.   Gaskell: Manufacturing Population, ch. iii and vi.
109. Hansard, Vol. 89, p. 488.   P.P., 1833, Vol. XX, p. 658.
110. Life and Letters of Roebuck, p. 120.
111. Life and Letters of Roebuck, p. 618.
112. Senior, Nassau: Letters on the Factory Act.
113. Fraser's, Vol. 37, p. 5.

114. Taylor: Notes of a Tour, p. 32.
115. Ure: Philosophy of Manufactures, pp. 350, 423.
116. Taylor: Notes of a Tour, pp. 23, 24.
117. Kay-Shuttleworth: Four Periods of Public Education, pp. 19, 20.
118. Kay-Shuttleworth: Four Periods of Public Education, p. 83.
119. Gaskell: Manufacturing Population, ch. v. P.P., 1833, Vol. XX, D1,
    p. 36.
120. Gaskell, E. C.: Mary Barton, ch. vi. Douglas Jerrold's Shilling Magazine,
    Vol. I, pp. 117, 443.
121. Trollope, Frances: Michael Armstrong, ch. iv and xvi. Sybil, Book II,
    ch. ix.
122. Kay-Shuttleworth: Four Periods of Public Education, pp. 21-22.
123. Gaskell: Manufacturing Population, ch. iv. Fraser's, Vol. 29, pp. 617-628.
    Hansard, Vol. 73, p. 1093.
124. Kay-Shuttleworth: Four Periods of Public Education, pp. 7, 8.
125. Gaskell: Manufacturing Population, ch. vi. Michael Armstrong, ch. xix.
126. P.P., 1831-32, Vol. XV, p. 374; 1833, Vol. XX, pp. 649, 812.
127. P.P., 1833, Vol. XXI, p. 141.
128. The Excursion, Book VIII, ll. 267-275.
129. Mary Barton, ch. x.
130. Gaskell, E. C.: Libbie Marsh's Three Eras, Era I.
131. Mary Barton, ch. x.
132. P.P., 1833, Vol. XX, p. 644. Notes of a Tour, Taylor, pp. 29, 32.
133. Gaskell: Manufacturing Population, ch. iii and vi. Artisans and Machi-
    nery, p. 174.
134. P.P., 1843, Vol. XXVII, p. 299. Stubborn Facts from the Factories by a
    Manchester Operative, p. 12.
135. P.P., 1833, Vol. XX, p. 644.
136. Mary Barton, ch. xiv.
137. Sybil, Book II, ch. ix. Mary Barton, ch. i.
138. Sybil, Book II, ch. ix.
139. Mary Barton, ch. i.
140. Hansard, Vol. 73, pp. 1096, 1097. Bodichon, Barbara: A Brief Summary
    in Plain Language of the Most Important Laws concerning Women,
    pp. 14, 15.
141. Tonna: Works, Vol. I, p. 554.
142. Tonna: Works, Vol. I, p. 538.
143. Tonna: Works, Vol. I, p. 531.
144. Household Words, Vol. I, p. 184.
145. P.P., 1831-32, Vol. XV, pp. 99-100.
146. P.P., 1833, Vol. XXI, p. 133.
147. P.P., 1831-32, Vol. XV, p. 132.
148. P.P., 1833, Vol. XX, p. 648; 1834, Vol. XIX, p. 345; 1834, Vol. XIX,
    p. 479. Cooke Taylor: Tour, p. 257. Gaskell: Artisans and Machinery,
    pp. 98-101.
149. P.P., 1831-32, Vol. XV, pp. 89, 100; 1833, Vol. XX, pp. 659, 687.
150. Gaskell: Manufacturing Population, p. 117. Engels, Frederick: Condition
    of the Working Class in England in 1844, p. 126. Hansard, Vol. 73,
    p. 1094.
151. Fraser's, Vol. 37, pp. 1-16. Ure: Philosophy of Manufacturers, pp. 374,
    398, 399. Notes of a Tour, Taylor, p. 256.
152. Gaskell: Artisans and Machinery, ch. iv. P.P., 1831-32, Vol. XV, p. 474.

153. P.P., 1831–32, Vol. XV, pp. 218, 229, 320, 374. Hansard, Vol. 72, p. 278.
154. Tonna: Works, Vol. I, pp. 554, 555.
155. Sybil, Book I, ch. x.
156. Schulze-Gaevernitz: Social Peace, pp. 18, 19.
157. Wade: History of the Middle and Working Classes, p. 582.
158. Tonna: Works, Vol. I, p. 641.
159. P.P., 1831–32, Vol. XV, p. 474. Engels, p. 181.
160. Schulze-Gaevernitz: Social Peace, p. 57. P.P., 1842, Vol. XXII, p. 365.
161. P.P., 1833, Vol. XX, D2, p. 8; D1, p. 49.
162. Binns, H. Bryan: A Century of Education, p. 137.
163. Kay-Shuttleworth: Four Periods of Public Education, pp. 102, 103.
164. P.P., 1833, Vol. XX, D2, pp. 21, 23, 45; Vol. XXI, A3, p. 53. Dobbs,
     A. E.: Education and Social Movements, p. 165.
165. Gaskell: Artisans and Machinery, p. 245. P.P., 1833, Vol. XX, D1,
     pp. 45, 85.
166. Dickens, Charles: Great Expectations, ch. vii.
167. P.P., 1833, Vol. XX, D2, p. 8.
168. Porter, G. R.: Progress of the Nation, Vol. II, p. 281.
169. P.P., 1833, Vol. XXI, pp. 3, 365. Gaskell: Artisans and Machinery, p. 248.
170. Gaskell: Artisans and Machinery, p. 253.
171. Kay-Shuttleworth: Four Periods of Public Education, p. 109.
172. Sybil, Book I, ch. xi.
173. Cooke Taylor: Notes of a Tour, p. 293.
174. Tonna: Works, Vol. I, p. 575.
175. Mathieson, W. L.: English Church Reform, pp. 32, 33. Tonna: Works,
     Vol. I, pp. 575, 576.
176. Tonna: Works, Vol. I, pp. 564, 605.
177. Fay: Life and Labour in the Nineteenth Century, p. 200.
178. Gaskell: Artisans and Machinery, p. 255. Kay-Shuttleworth, p. 39, op. cit.
179. Kay-Shuttleworth: op. cit., p. 109.
180. Scoresby, William: American Factories and their Female Operatives,
     p. 110.
181. Gutch, Charles: A Sermon on a Recent Mill Accident.
182. Tonna: Works, Vol. I, p. 608.
183. Fay: op. cit., p. 202.
184. P.P., 1833, Vol. XXI, pp. 184–189; 1834, Vol. XIX, p. 498.
185. Ure: op cit., p. 298. Senior, Nassau: Letters on the Factory Act, p. 19.
     P.P., 1847, Vol. XV, p. 128.
186. Hansard, Vol. 79, p. 1120.
187. P.P., 1847, Vol. XLVI, p. 623.
188. P.P., 1847–48, Vol. XXVI, p. 153.
189. P.P., 1842, Vol. XXII, pp. 361, 366. Leonard Horner, a factory inspector,
     in 1841 prepared elaborate tables to show the loss that would follow
     upon short time. He contended that a mill-owner to receive profit must
     get as much work as possible out of his machinery. He estimated that
     a loss of £850 from working 11 hours would be increased to £1,530
     from working 10 hours. In 1847 and 1848 he was still greatly agitated
     over the loss of capital sunk in buildings and machinery.
190. Senior: op. cit., p. 12. P.P., 1842, Vol. XXII, p. 366. Hansard, Vol. 73,
     p. 1112.
191. Miles, Sibella: Essay on the Factory Question.
192. Hansard, Vol. 73, p. 1487; also p. 1102.

193. Hansard, Vol. 74, p. 622.
194. P.P., 1842, Vol. XXII, p. 366.   Hansard, Vol. 73, p. 1109.
195. Hansard, Vol. 73, p. 1488; Vol. 89, p. 1143.
196. Hansard, Vol. 89, pp. 1127–1130.
197. Ure: *op. cit.*, p. 297.
198. Hansard, Vol. 73, p. 1110–1111.
199. Life and Letters of John Arthur Roebuck, p. 617.
200. Hansard, Vol. 73, p. 1088–1097.
201. P.P., 1831–32, Vol. XV, p. 533.
202. P.P., 1842, Vol. XXII, p. 443.
203. P.P., 1842, Vol. XXII, p. 448.
204. P.P., 1842, Vol. XXII, p. 448.
205. P.P., 1844, Vol. XXVIII, pp. 536, 545.
206. Hansard, Vol. 73, p. 1098.
207. Hansard, Vol. 90, p. 770.
208. P.P., 1842, Vol. XXIII, p. 346.
209. P.P., 1845, Vol. XXV, p. 445.
210. Hansard, Vol. 90, p. 135.
211. P.P., 1857, Vol. III, p. 590.   The percentage of women workers above 13 is
     55·2 per cent.; of men above 18 is 22·8 per cent.; of youths 13–18 is
     16·1 per cent.   This makes a total of men above 13 of 38·9 per cent., to
     compare with the 55·2 per cent. of women above 13.   See also P.P., 1843,
     Vol. XXVII, p. 355.
212. Hansard, Vol. 73, p. 1099.   P.P., 1843, Vol. XXVII, p. 353.
213. P.P., 1844, Vol. XXVIII, p. 536.
214. Hansard, Vol. 89, p. 1112.
215. P.P., 1842, Vol. XXII, p. 366; 1844, Vol. XXVIII, p. 536.   Hansard,
     Vol. 90, p. 815.
216. P.P., 1845, Vol. XXV, pp. 449–451, 456, 457.
217. Hansard, Vol. 74, p. 911. A letter from a mill-owner published in the Bolton
     Free Press, April 1844, and read by Lord Ashley in the House of Com-
     mons, dwelt upon the spoiled work of the last hour.
218. P.P., 1842, Vols. XV, XVI, XVII.
219. P.P., 1842, Vol. XV, p. 39.
220. P.P., 1842, Vol. XV, p. 38.
221. Hodder, Edwin: Life of the Earl of Shaftesbury, Vol. I, p. 421.
222. Tonna: Works, Vol. II, p. 194.
223. Bodichon, Barbara: *op. cit.*   P.P., 1849, Vol. XXII, p. 240.
224. Hansard, Vol. 89, p. 1134.   Figures for Bright's mill.
225. Wood, George Henry: History of Wages in the Cotton Trade, pp. 14,
     134, 138.
226. Hansard, Vol. 89, p. 1135.
227. Halifax Guardian, June 5 and 19, 1847.   Manchester Guardian, June 5,
     1847.
228. London Times, May 4, 1847.
229. P.P., 1849, Vol. XXII, p. 225.
230. P.P., 1849, Vol. XXII, pp. 135, 239.
231. Hutchins, B. L., and Harrison, A.: A History of Factory Legislation,
     p. 107.
232. Von Plener, E.: History of English Factory Legislation, p. 41.
233. P.P., 1849, Vol. XXII, p. 236.
234. P.P., 1850, Vol. XXII, p. 236.   P.P., 1850, Vol. XLII, p. 183.

235. P.P., 1849, Vol. XXII, p. 217 (Horner, December 1, 1848).
236. P.P., 1849, Vol. XXII, p. 217 (Horner, December 1, 1848).
237. P.P., 1850, Vol. XIII, p. 183.
238. Wood: *op. cit.*, p. 133.
239. Wood: *op. cit.*, p. 138; also p. 135.
240. P.P., 1852, Vol. XXI. For year ending October 31, 1851.
241. P.P., 1845, Vol. XXV, p. 461.
242. P.P., 1845, Vol. XXV, p. 461.
243. P.P., 1849, Vol. XXII, p. 209.
244. P.P., 1850, Vol. XLII, p. 265.
245. P.P., 1850, Vol. XLII, p. 221.
246. P.P., 1849, Vol. XXII, p. 186.
247. P.P., 1850, Vol. XLII, pp. 224, 225.
248. Household Words, Vol. V, p. 85.
249. Carlyle: Past and Present, Book IV, ch. viii.
250. Ure: *op. cit.*, pp. 343–455. P.P., 1833, Vol. XXI, p. 133.
251. P.P., 1850, Vol. XLII, pp. 221, 224, 225.
252. P.P., 1846, Vol. XX, pp. 574–577.
253. P.P., 1846, Vol. XX, p. 579. An equally amusing periodical is the Christian Magazine, published from 1841–43 in Manchester, to which clergymen in the manufacturing districts contributed. It described itself as "an antidote to the blasphemous and unprincipled publications circulated among the labouring population", and was "adapted to the reading of the manu-facturing poor". One number contained the story of a factory girl who, when weakened by a cold on the lungs and advised to go out to service, could not get work on account of her gaudy clothes. Another recorded the tragedy of Jane Phillips, also forced to leave the mill for domestic service because of poor health. She proved unsatisfactory, however, be-cause humility was not developed in mill girls. She went back to the unhealthy mill and died, a victim to a "headstrong and wilful temper".
254. In 1847, the year of the ten-hour bill, one employer gave 160 volumes to the mill library, and the workers subscribed one penny weekly for newspapers and periodicals. P.P., 1849, Vol. XXII, pp. 148–152. In another mill, with a school made up of 109 men and 39 women members, lectures were held; there were a library, a medical fund, a burial society, and a cow club. P.P., 1849, Vol. XXII, p. 151.
255. Merryweather, Mary: Experience of Factory Life.
256. Tonna: Works, Vol. II, p. 434.
257. Gutch: A Sermon on a Recent Mill Accident.
258. Carlyle: Past and Present, Book IV, ch. v. Gaskell: North and South, ch. xlii.
259. P.P., 1849, Vol. XXII, p. 186.
260. P.P., 1847–48, Vol. XXVI, p. 152.

CHAPTER III

1. Hansard, Vol. 73, p. 1133.
2. Hansard, Vol. 73, p. 1254.
3. Hammond: The Skilled Labourer, p. 221.
4. Hammond: The Skilled Labourer, p. 252.
5. Voice of the People, 1848.
6. P.P., 1845, Vol. XV.

7. Tonna: Works, Vol. II, p. 495.
8. Hammond: The Skilled Labourer, p. 253.
9. Hutchins and Harrison: Factory Legislation, p. 156. P.P., 1845, Vol. XV, p. 909.
10. Household Words, Vol. I, p. 126.
11. P.P., 1844, Vol. XXVII, Preface, p. 16.
12. Hammond: The Skilled Labourer, note p. 222.
13. P.P., 1833, Vol. XX, p. 554.
14. P.P., 1834, Vol. XIX, p. 364.
15. P.P., 1845, Vol. XV, p. 997.
16. P.P., 1845, Vol. XV, p. 997.
17. P.P., 1863, Vol. XVIII; 1864, Vol. XXII.
18. P.P., 1844, Vol. XXVII, Preface, p. 20. In 1844 in Great Britain, 4,401 women over 20 and 1,689 girls under 20 were engaged in glove-making, as compared with 2,803 men and 332 boys.
19. Hammond: op. cit., pp. 254–256.
20. Hammond: op. cit., pp. 238–240.
21. P.P., 1843, Vol. XIV, pp. 569–575. Tonna: Works, Vol. II, p. 477.
22. P.P., 1861, Vol. XXII, p. 8.
23. P.P., 1844, Vol. XXVII, Preface, p. 12.
24. P.P., 1833, Vol. XX, p. 554.
25. P.P., 1834, Vol. XIX, p. 294.
26. P.P., 1843, Vol. XV, pp. 559, 607.
27. P.P., 1843, Vol. XV, p. 611.
28. P.P., 1843, Vol. XV, p. 611.
29. In one instance the first agent allowed a "runner" 5s. 9d. for working a wedding-veil. Another offered 11s. The Wrongs of Women. Tonna: Works, Vol. II, p. 501.
30. Tonna: Works, Vol. II, p. 488.
31. P.P., 1843, Vols. XIV, XV, for material on lace and hosiery.
32. In all branches of nail manufacture, 2,692 women over 20 and 1,369 under 20 were employed out of a total of 20,311 male and female workers. P.P., 1844, Vol. XXVII, p. 38.
33. In the making of steel pens, 128 women over 20, 104 under 20, out of a total of 327, and in the making of hooks and eyes, 33 women over 20 and 34 under 20, out of a total of 115, were employed. P.P., 1844, Vol. XXVII, p. 38.
34. In pin-making in 1844, 478 women over 20 and 360 under 20, out of a total of 1,330 workers, were employed. P.P., 1844, Vol. XXVII, p. 38.
35. In some places fixed hours from 8 a.m. to 7 p.m. with no overtime were the rule, although a working day of from 12 to 14 hours was usual. The wages ranged from 1s. a week, earned by a woman of 56, to 6s., which was stated as the average wage for young women. P.P., 1843, Vol. XV, p. 383.
36. In screw-making and screw-cutting, 279 women over 20 and 122 under 20 were employed out of a total of 745. P.P., 1844, Vol. XXVII, p. 38.
37. Tonna: Works, Vol. II, pp. 421, 425.
38. Household Words, Vol. IV, p. 141.
39. Household Words, Vol. V, pp. 192–197.
40. In the brass foundries in 1840 only 112 women over 20 and 10 under 20 were employed out of a total of 6,672 workers. P.P., 1843, Vol. XV, p. 274.

41. In burnishing there were 86 women over 20 and 48 girls out of a total of 255. P.P., 1843, Vol. XV, p. 274.

42. Household Words, Vol. IV, p. 449.

43. P.P., 1843, Vol. XIV, pp. 821-823. Government figures for women and girls include match-makers and sellers together, so they are of little use. P.P. 1844, Vol. XXVII.

44. Household Words, Vol. V, p. 152.

45. P.P., 1850, Vol. XXVII. 918 women over 20 and 354 under 20, out of a total number of fustian cutters of 3,558.

P.P., 1850, Vol. LXXXVIII. 1,455 women over 20, 751 under 20, out of a total of 5,511.

P.P., 1843, Vol. XV, p. 413. One witness, a woman of 29, by working 13 hours daily earned 7s. weekly.

46. P.P., 1843, Vol. XV, p. 274.

47. P.P., 1840, Vol. XXVII. Out of a total of 7,407 workers in glass works in 1840, only 222 were women over 20 and 73 under 20.

48. Household Words, Vol. II, pp. 433-437.

49. Household Words, Vol. V, p. 36.

50. P.P., 1843, Vol. XV, p. 303.

51. P.P., 1843, Vol. XIV, p. 701.

52. Household Words, Vol. V, p. 106.

53. In 1840, out of a total number of 3,955 button-makers, 1,034 were women over 20 and 613 were girls under 20.

54. Dickens: Bleak House, ch. xxxv.

55. Dickens: Bleak House, ch. xxi.

56. Household Words, Vol. V, p. 33.

57. Household Words, Vol. V, p. 120.

58. Household Words, Vol. VI, p. 519.

59. Owen, Harold: The Staffordshire Potter, p. 70.

60. Owen, Harold: The Staffordshire Potter, p. 38.

61. Drake, Barbara: Women in Trade Unions, p. 6.

62. Owen, Harold: op. cit., p. 70.

63. Wages for pottery have never been given with any scientific exactness. Owen, op. cit., p. 318. In 1833 the Chamber of Commerce give workmen a weekly average of from 17s. to 21s., women from 6s. to 11s., children of 14 from 3s. to 3s. 6d. In 1836-37 men 21s. to 28s., women from 10s. to 15s., children 3s. 6d. to 4s. to 4s. 6d. Government figures: men from 16s. to 28s., women 8s. P.P., 1834, Vol. XIX, p. 294.

64. P.P., 1844, Vol. XXVII. In paper mills total workers 7,160: women over 20, 1,387, and 641 girls under 20. Out of 57 mills examined there was a proportion of 180 females to 256 males, with 168 of the latter between 13 and 18. P.P., 1843, Vol. XIII, pp. 340-343.

65. In a busy season one witness, a girl of 17, stated that she worked continuously day and night, but this is an isolated case. P.P., 1843, Vol. XV, p. 990.

66. Household Words, Vol. I, p. 529.

67. Dickens: Our Mutual Friend, ch. vi.

68. Bradshaw's Manchester Journal, Vol. 3, 1841-43, pp. 33-39, 50-55.

69. P.P., 1843, Vol. XIV, pp. 806-813.

70. Satisfactory figures for the number of women employed in 1840 are lacking, however, since book-binding, selling, and publishing were given together. In 1850, out of a total of 11,029 book-binders, 2,451 were women over 20 and 1,703 under 20. P.P., 1850, Vol. LXXXVIII.

71. MacDonald, J. Ramsay: Women in the Printing Trades, p. 30 f.
72. MacDonald, J. Ramsay: Women in the Printing Trades, p. 24.
73. P.P., 1843, Vol. XIV, XV.
74. P.P., 1843, Vol. XIV, p. 629.
75. P.P., 1843, Vol. XIV, p. 740.
76. Westminster Review, Vol. LIII, pp. 448–506.
77. P.P., 1843, Vol. XIV, p. 738.
78. P.P., 1843, Vol. XIV, p. 733.
79. P.P., 1843, Vol. XIV, p. 763.
80. P.P., 1843, Vol. XV, p. 622.
81. Sybil, Book III, ch. v.
82. P.P., 1843, Vol. XV, pp. 571, 575.
83. P.P., 1843, Vol. XV, p. 579.
84. P.P., 1843, Vol. XV, p. 639.
85. P.P., 1843, Vol. XV, pp. 596, 640.
86. P.P., 1843, Vol. XIV, pp. 565, 566.
87. Sybil, Book II, ch. iv.   P.P., 1843, Vol. XV, 639.
88. Edinburgh Review, Vol. 79, p. 143.
89. P.P., 1843, Vol. XIV, p. 515.
90. Tonna: Works, Vol. II, p. 420.
91. Tonna: Works, Vol. II, p. 445.
92. Pendennis, Vol. I, ch. xv, xxiii.
93. Household Words, Vol. IV, pp. 488, 490.
94. Household Words, Vol. IV, p. 577.
95. P.P., 1850, Vol. XLII, p. 60.
96. Household Words, Vol. II, p. 577.
97. P.P., 1850, Vol. XLII, pp. 5, 72.
98. P.P., 1850, Vol. XLII, p. 9.
99. P.P., 1850, Vol. XLII, p. 72.
100. P.P., 1850, Vol. XLII, p. 31.
101. P.P., 1850, Vol. XLII, p. 34.
102. P.P., 1850, Vol. XLII, p. 23.
103. P.P., 1850, Vol. XLII, p. 33.
104. P.P., 1850, Vol. XLII, p. 38.
105. P.P., 1850, Vol. XLII, p. 39.
106. P.P., 1850, Vol. XLII, p. 27.
107. Household Words, Vol. VI, p. 18.
108. P.P., 1843, Vol. XIV, p. 721.
109. Gutch: *op. cit.*, Appendix.
110. P.P., 1843, Vol. XV, pp. 576, 625.

CHAPTER IV

1. Clark, Alice: Working Life of Women in the Seventeenth Century, p. 176.
2. P.P., 1833, Vol. XXI, p. 102.
3. P.P., 1833, Vol. XXI, p. 189.
4. P.P., 1833, Vol. XXI, p. 862.
5. P.P., 1844, Vol. XXVII, pp. 31–44.
6. Speeches delivered at the Great Meeting held under the Auspices of the Early Closing Association, July 11, 1856, p. 7.

7. Eliot, George: Mill on the Floss, Book VI, ch. ii.
8. P.P., 1843, Vol. XIV, p. 555.
9. Hansard, Vol. 73, p. 1135.
10. Fraser's, Vol. 33, p. 308.
11. Dickens: David Copperfield, ch. xxx.
12. P.P., 1843, Vol. XIV, p. 555.
13. Gaskell: Mary Barton, ch. iii.
14. Dickens: Nicholas Nickleby, ch. xi.
15. Tonna: Works, Vol. II, p. 402.
16. Tonna: Works, Vol. II, p. 408.
17. P.P., 1843, Vol. XIV, p. 556.   Tonna: Works, Vol. II, p. 416.
18. Tonna: Works, Vol. II, p. 409.
19. P.P., 1843, Vol. XIV, p. 555.
20. P.P., 1843, Vol. XIV, p. 556.   Tonna: Works, Vol. II, p. 416.
21. P.P., 1843, Vol. XIV, p. 772.
22. P.P., 1843, Vol. XIV, p. 556.
23. P.P., 1843, Vol. XIV, p. 547.
24. P.P., 1843, Vol. XIV, p. 358.
25. P.P., 1843, Vol. XIV, p. 776.
26. Tonna: Works, Vol. II, p. 404.
27. Tonna: Works, Vol. II, p. 416.
28. Tonna: Works, Vol. II, p. 404.
29. Tonna: Works, Vol. II, p. 404.
30. Tonna: Works, Vol. II, p. 407.
31. Dickens: Our Mutual Friend, Book II, ch. i.
32. Gaskell: Ruth, ch. i.
33. Thackeray: Pendennis, Vol. II, ch. xliv
34. Mary Barton, ch. iii.
35. Nicholas Nickleby, ch. xi.
36. P.P., 1843, Vol. XIV, p. 556.
37. Tonna: Works, Vol. II, p. 416.
38. Ruth, ch. i.
39. P.P., 1843, Vol. XIV, p. 556.
40. Tonna: Works, Vol. II, p. 416.
41. Tonna: Works, Vol. II, p. 402.
42. Tonna: Works, Vol. II, p. 404.
43. Tonna: Works, Vol. II, p. 409.
44. Ruth, ch. i.
45. Mary Barton, ch. xii.
46. Nicholas Nickleby, ch. xvii.
47. P.P., 1843, Vol. XIV, p. 559.
48. P.P., 1843, Vol. XIV, p. 776.
49. Tonna: Works, Vol. II, p. 411.
50. Ruth, ch. iii.
51. P.P., 1843, Vol. XIV, p. 556.   Tonna: Works, Vol. II, p. 416.
52. Tonna: Works, Vol. II, p. 402.
53. Tonna: Works, Vol. II, p. 410.
54. Ruth, ch. i.
55. Mary Barton, ch. xiii.
56. P.P., 1843, Vol. XIV, p. 9.
57. Tonna: Works, Vol. II, p. 404.
58. Ruth, ch. iii.

59. P.P., 1834, Vol. XIX, p. 510.
60. P.P., 1843, Vol. XIV, p. 556.
61. Fraser's, Vol. 12, p. 278.
62. P.P., 1843, Vol. XIV, p. 772.
63. P.P., 1843, Vol. XIV, p. 776.
64. Illustrated London News, January 22, 1844.
65. Nicholas Nickleby, ch. xi.
66. Nicholas Nickleby, ch. xvii.
68. Tonna: Works, Vol. II, p. 404.
69. Tonna: Works, Vol. II, p. 402.
70. Tonna: Works, Vol. II, p. 406.
71. Tonna: Works, Vol. II, p. 416.
72. Ruth, ch. i.
73. Tonna: Works, Vol. II, p. 416.
74. P.P., 1843, Vol. XIV, p. 556.
75. P.P., 1843, Vol. XIV, p. 559.
76. Vanity Fair, ch. xiii.
77. Vanity Fair, ch. xxx.
78. Pendennis, Vol. I, ch. xv.
79. Mary Barton, ch. xiv.
80. Fraser's, Vol. 33, pp. 308–316.
81. Mary Barton, ch. xiii.
82. Tonna: Works, Vol. II, p. 407.
83. P.P., 1843, Vol. XIV, p. 556.
84. Hall, S. C.: Oppressed Condition of the Dressmakers' and Milliners
    Assistants, p. 15.
85. Fraser's, Vol. 33, p. 310.
86. Ruth, ch. i.
87. Tonna: Works, Vol. II, p. 410.
88. Mary Barton, ch. xix.
89. Mary Barton, ch. xxv.
90. Tonna: Works, Vol. II, p. 404.
91. Mary Barton, ch. vii.
92. Fraser's, Vol. 33, p. 308.
93. Tonna: Works, Vol. II, p. 406.
94. Fraser's, Vol. 33, p. 310.
95. Ruth, ch. iv.
96. Tonna: Works, Vol. II, p. 406.
97. Ruth, ch. iii.
98. Fraser's, Vol. 33, p. 308.
99. Dickens: Little Dorrit, ch. v.
100. Christian Lady's Magazine, Vol. IV, p. 535.
101. Fraser's, Vol. 41, pp. 4, 5.
102. P.P., 1843, Vol. XIV, p. 833.
103. P.P., 1843, Vol. XIV, pp. 446–448.
104. Punch, Vol. XV, p. 76.
105. Carlyle: Latter-Day Pamphlets, p. 29, N.Y., 1898.
106. Shaw, William: An Affectionate Pleading for England's Oppressed
    Female Workers.
107. Hill, Frederic: National Education, pp. 154, 158.
108. Punch, Vol. XV, p. 140.
109. Kingsley, Charles: Alton Locke, ch. viii.

110. Fraser's, Vol. 41, pp. 1–18.
111. Alton Locke, ch. viii.
112. Shaw, William: *op. cit., passim.*
113. Shaw, William: *op. cit.*, p. 30.
114. Shaw, William: *op. cit.*, pp. 24–30.
115. Good Words, Vol. 4, p. 687.
116. Fraser's, Vol. 12, p. 277.
117. P.P., 1843, Vol. XIV, F. 209.
118. Edinburgh Review, Vol. 79, p. 145.
119. Hansard, March 15, 1844, p. 1135.
120. Hansard, March 15, 1844, p. 1075.
121. P.P., 1843, Vol. XIV, F. 218.
122. All the Year Round, Vol. 10, p. 36.
123. Punch, Vol. VII, p. 32.
124. Hall, S. C.: Oppressed Condition of the Dressmakers' and Milliners' Assistants, p. 16.
125. Hodder: Life of Shaftesbury, Vol. II, p. 76.
126. Hodder: Life of Shaftesbury, Vol. II, p. 79.
127. Hall: *op. cit.*, p. 6.
128. Hodder: *op. cit.*, Vol. II, p. 523.
129. All the Year Round, Vol. 10, p. 37.
130. Fraser's, Vol. 33, p. 314.
131. Hall: *op. cit.* Hansard, House of Lords, Vol. 138, p. 1943.
132. Hansard, Vol. 138, p. 1946.
133. Hodder: *op. cit.*, Vol. II, p. 524.
134. Hall: *op. cit.*, p. 7.
135. Hodder: *op. cit.*, Vol. II, p. 2.
136. Hall: *op. cit.*, p. 17.
137. Hall: *op. cit.*, p. 4. All the Year Round, Vol. 10, p. 36.
138. Tonna: Works, Vol. II, p. 406.
139. Christian Lady's Magazine, Vol. XV, p. 417.
140. All the Year Round, Vol. 10, p. 36.
141. Good Words, Vol. 4, p. 684.
142. Tuckwell, Gertrude M., and Others: Woman in Industry, p. 72.
143. Once a Week, Vol. 3, p. 399.
144. Industrial and Social Position of Women, p. 186.
145. Edinburgh Review, Vol. 79, p. 152.
146. Edinburgh Review, Vol. 93, p. 19.
147. Fraser's, Vol. 41, p. 16.
148. St. James Magazine, Vol. 3, p. 474.
149. Edinburgh Review, Vol. 93, p. 26.
150. Edinburgh Review, Vol. 93, p. 20.
151. Lamb, Mary: On Needlework, Lamb's Works, Vol. I, pp. 176–180.
152. Good Words, Vol. 4, p. 688.
153. Edinburgh Review, Vol. 83, p. 24.
154. Industrial and Social Position of Women, p. 186.
155. Industrial and Social Position of Women, p. 183.
156. Latter-Day Pamphlets, p. 28.
157 Household Words, Vol. IV, p. 409.
158. Illustrated London News, Vol. 15, p. 370.
159. Household Words, Vol. VIII, p. 42.
160. Illustrated London News, Vol. 16, p. 115.

161. Household Words, Vol. I, pp. 19–24, 514, 515; Vol. III, p. 228; Vol. IV, p. 531.
162. Household Words, Vol. I, p. 515.
163. Household Words, Vol. IV, p. 530.
164. Household Words, Vol. IV, p. 531.
165. Fraser's, Vol. 41, p. 13.
166. Household Words, Vol. VIII, p. 575.
167. Alton Locke, ch. viii.
168. Shaw, William: *op. cit.*, p. 38.
169. Once a Week, Vol. 3, p. 596.
170. Household Words, Vol. VIII, p. 575.
171. Good Words, Vol. 4, p. 684.
172. Tickner: Women in English Economic History, p. 158.
173. Burdett, Charles: The Elliot Family, or the Trials of New York Seamstresses.
174. Douglas Jerrold's Shilling Magazine, Vol. I, p. 160.

CHAPTER V

1. Reynolds, Myra: The Learned Lady, p. 195.
2. Tickner, F. W.: Women in English Economic History, pp. 68, 69.
3. P.P., 1844, Vol. XXVII, pp. 31–44. P.P., 1852–53, Vol. LXXXVIII.
4. P.P., 1867–68, Part IV, Vol. 13, p. 944.
5. P.P., 1867, Part III, Vol. XXVIII, p. 693; 1867–68, Part IV, Vol. 13, p. 246.
6. Quarterly, Vol. 84, p. 176.
7. Fraser's, Vol. 30, p. 572.
8. Christian Lady's Magazine, Vol. II, p. 39.
9. Quarterly, Vol. 84, p. 180.
10. Emma, ch. xxiv.
11. Mill on the Floss, Book III, ch. xii.
12. Janet's Repentance, in Scenes of Clerical Life.
13. Middlemarch, ch. xi.
14. Middlemarch, ch. xvi.
15. Emma, ch. xx.
16. Wives and Daughters, ch. xi.
17. Gaskell: Life of Charlotte Brontë, p. 122.
18. Gaskell: Life of Charlotte Brontë, p. 135.
19. Gaskell: Life of Charlotte Brontë, p. 117.
20. Jameson, Anna: Memoirs and Essays, p. 254.
21. Industrial and Social Position of Women, p. 130.
22. Fraser's, Vol. 30, p. 577.
23. Quarterly, Vol. 84, p. 182.
24. Quarterly, Vol. 84, p. 180.
25. Fraser's, Vol. 30, p. 577.
26. Fraser's, Vol. 37, p. 412.
27. Once a Week, Vol. 3, p. 270.
28. Gaskell: Life of Charlotte Brontë, p. 135.
29. Punch, Vol. VII, p. 11.
30. Quarterly, Vol. 84, p. 182.

31. Once a Week, Vol. 3, p. 271.
32. Punch, Vol. XV, p. 78.
33. Fraser's, Vol. 30, p. 578.
34. Christian Lady's Magazine, Vol. II, p. 45.
35. Vanity Fair, ch. xi.
36. Wives and Daughters, pp. 104, 105.
37. Brontë, Anne: Agnes Grey, p. 146.
38. Thackeray: The Book of Snobs, ch. xxvi.
39. Fraser's, Vol. 37, p. 413.
40. Wives and Daughters, ch. viii.
41. Jameson: Memoirs and Essays, p. 261.
42. Jameson: Memoirs and Essays, p. 284.
43. Gaskell: Life of Charlotte Brontë, p. 38.
44. Vanity Fair, ch. ii.
45. Quarterly, Vol. 84, p. 181.
46. Industrial and Social Position of Women, p. 130.
47. Thackeray: The Newcomes, Vol. I, ch. xx.
48. Gaskell: Life of Charlotte Brontë, p. 115.
49. Gaskell: Life of Charlotte Brontë, pp. 137, 186.
50. Gaskell: A Dark Night's Work.
51. Christian Lady's Magazine, Vol. II, p. 42.
52. Jameson: Memoirs and Essays, p. 257.
53. Brontë, Charlotte: Jane Eyre, ch. xxx.
54. The Book of Snobs, ch. xxv.
55. Once a Week, Vol. 3, p. 267.
56. Wives and Daughters, ch. x.
57. Punch, Vol. X, p. 159.
58. Vanity Fair, ch. vi.
59. Fraser's, Vol. 30, p. 575.
60. Gaskell: Life of Charlotte Brontë, p. 115.
61. Quarterly, Vol. 84, p. 177.
62. Shirley, ch. xxi.
63. The Newcomes, Vol. I, ch. xx.
64. Shorter, Clement: The Brontës and their Circle, p. 395.
65. Gaskell: Life of Charlotte Brontë, p. 135.
66. Agnes Grey, ch. iii.
67. Jane Eyre, ch. xvii.
68. Pendennis, Vol. II, ch. xliv.
69. Gaskell: Life of Charlotte Brontë, p. 135.
70. The Newcomes, Vol. I, ch. vii.
71. Gaskell: Life of Charlotte Brontë, p. 159.
72. Gaskell: Life of Charlotte Brontë, p. 115.
73. Gaskell: Life of Charlotte Brontë, p. 114.
74. Gaskell: Life of Charlotte Brontë, p. 114.
75. Pendennis, Vol. I, ch. xxiii.
76. Pendennis, Vol. I, ch. xxiv.
77. Fraser's, Vol. 30, p. 573.
78. Ruskin, John: Queen's Gardens, p. 81.
79. Gaskell: Life of Charlotte Brontë, p. 115.
80. Middlemarch, ch. xxxvi.
81. Vanity Fair, ch. x.
82. Quarterly, Vol. 84, pp. 180–181.

83. Jameson: Memoirs and Essays, p. 253.
84. Jameson: Memoirs and Essays, p. 290.
85. Martineau, Harriet: Industrial and Social Position of Women, p. 131.
86. Martineau, Harriet: Society in America, p. 150.
87. Jameson: Memoirs and Essays, pp. 275–277.
88. Fraser's, Vol. 30, p. 582.
89. Christian Lady's Magazine, Vol. IV, p. 45.
90. Once a Week, Vol. 3, p. 270.
91. Martineau, Harriet: Deerbrook, Vol. I, p. 23.
92. Fraser's, Vol. 37, p. 412.
93. Jameson: Memoirs and Essays, p. 32.
94. Quarterly, Vol. 84, pp. 176–185.
95. Quarterly, Vol. 84, p. 183.
96. St. James Magazine, Vol. IV, pp. 505–507.
97. Quarterly, Vol. 86, pp. 364–383.
98. P.P., 1861, Vol. XXI, Part I, p. 643.
99. P.P., 1867–68, Part IV, Vol. 13, p. 238.
100. P.P., 1867–68, Part IV, Vol. 13, p. 625.
101. P.P., 1867–68, Part IV, Vol. 13, p. 240.
102. P.P., 1867–68, Part IV, Vol. 13, p. 718.
103. P.P., 1867–68, Part IV, Vol. 13, p. 246.
104. P.P., 1850, Vol. XLII, p. 28.
105. Quarterly, Vol. 84, p. 184.
106. P.P., 1867–68, Part IV, Vol. 13, p. 676.
107. P.P., 1867–68, Part IV, Vol. 13, p. 706.
108. Once a Week, Vol. 3, p. 271.
109. Quarterly, Vol. 84, p. 179.
110. Once a Week, Vol. 3, p. 272.
111. Once a Week, Vol. 3, p. 269.

CHAPTER VI

1. Tickner, F. W.: Women in English Economic History, pp. 30, 31.
2. Illustrated London News, Vol. 14, p. 405.
3. Shirley, ch. xii.
4. Jameson: Sisters of Charity, note p. 37.
5. The Newcomes, Vol. I, ch. xxiii.
6. Vanity Fair, ch. i.
7. In Pendennis the Misses Finucane's establishment for young ladies, and in The Newcomes Madame Latour's school, followed the general pattern.
8. The Newcomes, Vol. I, ch. xxiii.
9. Vanity Fair, ch. xxxiv.
10. Vanity Fair, ch. xxxix.
11. Vanity Fair, ch. i.
12. Vanity Fair, ch. i.
13. Vanity Fair, ch. xli.
14. Pendennis, Vol. I, ch. xxii.
15. Middlemarch, ch. xvi.
16. Shirley, ch. xi. Also Janet's Repentance, ch. iii, in Scenes of Clerical Life. Miss Linnet had "spent a great deal of time in acquiring flower-painting,

according to the ingenious method then fashionable, of applying the shapes of leaves and flowers cut out in cardboard, and scrubbing a brush over the surface thus conveniently marked out; but even the spill-cases and hand-screens which were her last half-year's performances in that way were not considered eminently successful, and had long been consigned to the retirement of the best bedroom". Margaret Hale, when Henry Lennox visited her home, took him on an expedition to draw picturesque labourers' cottages. North and South, ch. iii. Rosamond Vincy sketched "landscapes and market-carts and portraits of her friends". Middlemarch, ch. iii. Amelia, long after her schooldays were over, on a trip down the Rhine "drew crags and castles". Vanity Fair, ch. lxii.

17. Pendennis, Vol. I, ch. xxii.
18. Jane Eyre, ch. xiv. Mill on the Floss, Book III, ch. ii.
19. North and South, ch. xviii.
20. Vanity Fair, ch. xviii.
21. Op. cit., ch. iv. Jane Eyre, ch. xvii. Celia Brooke was engaged with her tapestry frame. Rosamond Vincy and Lucy Deane filled their empty hours with embroidery. Nancy Lammeter worked on her sampler.
22. Sybil, ch. xii. Jane Eyre, ch. xxi. Lizzie Potter in The Newcomes also embroidered an altar-cloth. Vol. II, ch. xix. Blanche Amory started one in Tunbridge Wells, but no record was made of her finishing it. Pendennis, Vol. II, ch. lxiii.
23. Mill on the Floss, Book III, ch. ii. Vanity Fair, ch. lxvii. Shirley, ch. x, xxiii.
24. Caroline Helstone, to find relief for a sick heart, and Ellinor Wilkins (A Dark Night's Work), to beguile the tedium of a long engagement, sought such employment.
25. Pendennis, ch. xxxix. The Newcomes, Vol. I, ch. xi.
26. Pendennis, ch. xxxix.
27. Shirley, ch. xv. Also Pendennis, ch. vii. Blanche Amory took a temporary interest in the village school and visiting the poor, but her energies were soon turned into other channels.
28. Middlemarch, ch. i, iii. Vanity Fair, ch. xxxiii.
29. Vanity Fair, ch. iv.
30. Jane Eyre, ch. xxi, xviii. Middlemarch, ch. xvi, xxvii, xxxii. Janet's Repentance, ch. iii. Foker's cousin, Lady Ann, also got novels from the circulating libraries. Pendennis, ch. xxxix, xxiii.
31. Pendennis, ch. xxxix. Vanity Fair, ch lxii. Middlemarch, ch. iii.
32. Pendennis, ch. xxii, xxxix. Sybil, ch. vi.
33. Margaret Hale (North and South), Phyllis (Cousin Phyllis), and Ellinor Wilkins (A Dark Night's Work) read Dante. See Mary Barton, ch. xviii. Vanity Fair, ch. x. Janet's Repentance, ch. iii.
34. Lubbock, Percy: Elizabeth Barrett Browning in her Letters, p. 9.
35. Jane Eyre, ch. xviii. Vanity Fair, ch. xxxiv, xii.
36. Middlemarch, ch. iii. Jane Eyre, ch. xxi.
37. Westminster Review, 1849–50, p. 371.
38. Pendennis, ch. lix. The Newcomes, Vol. I, ch. xxviii. Vanity Fair, ch. xxxiv, xxxix, lx.
39. Vanity Fair, ch. xxxiii. Newcomes, Vol. I, ch. xxviii; Vol. II, ch. xxxv.
40. Vanity Fair, ch. x. Shirley, ch. xxii. The Newcomes, Vol. II, ch. xxi, xv.

41. The Newcomes, Vol. I, ch. xv., xxviii. Pendennis, ch. xliv. " 'And what,' continued Miss Amory, musing, 'what are the men who we see about at the balls every night—dancing guardsmen, penniless Treasury clerks—boobies! If I had my brother's fortune, I might have such an establishment as you promise me, but with my name, and with my little means, what am I to look to? A country parson, or a barrister in a street near Russell Square, or a captain in a dragoon regiment, who will take lodgings for me, and come home in from the mess tipsy and smelling of smoke like Sir Francis Clavering. That is how we girls are destined to end life.' " See also Vanity Fair, ch. xii.

42. Vanity Fair, ch. x. Middlemarch, ch. xvi. Vanity Fair, ch. xii.

43. Silas Marner, ch. xi. Pendennis, ch. lxvi. Shirley, ch. vii. The Newcomes, ch. xv. David Copperfield, ch. xxxvii. North and South, ch. ix.

44. Jane Eyre, ch. xvi. The Newcomes, Vol. I, ch. xxiv. Jane Eyre, ch. xvii. The Newcomes, Vol. I, ch. xxiv. Vanity Fair, ch. xliii. Villette, ch. xxxvii. Vanity Fair, ch. lxvii. Pendennis, ch. xxi, xxii.

45. Jane Eyre, ch. vii, x, xii, xvii, xxxi. Becky Sharp in a white frock and blue sash looked the "image of youthful innocence". Vanity Fair, ch. xxv, lix. Dora Spenlow wore a white chip bonnet and a dress of celestial blue. David Copperfield, ch. xxiii.

46. The Newcomes, Vol. I, ch. xxiii; Vol. II, ch. xii. The Misses Baines, "those young sirens of Regent's Park, sang numberless songs to enchant Clive Newcome". Foker thought that Blanche Amory sang "like a mermaid". Pendennis, ch. xxxix. Mill on the Floss, Book VI, ch. i. Pendennis, ch. xxxviii. Vanity Fair, ch. iv, xliii. Janet's Repentance, ch. iii.

47. The Newcomes, Vol. I, ch. xxv. Vanity Fair, ch. xxxviii.

48. The Newcomes, Vol. I, ch. x. Shirley, ch. vi. Pendennis, ch. lxvi. Shirley, ch. xviii. Mill on the Floss, Book VI, ch. ii, i. The Newcomes, Vol. I, ch. xxiv, xxx. Middlemarch, ch. xi.

49. Silas Marner, ch. xi. Pendennis, ch. xxxvii, xxiii. Middlemarch, ch. xxvii. Shirreff, Emily: Intellectual Education, p. 167. David Copperfield ch. xxiv. Vanity Fair, ch. lix. The Newcomes, Vol. I, ch. xxvi. Vanity Fair, ch. vi.

50. Shirley, ch. xxxi. Gaskell: Life of Charlotte Brontë, p. 203.

51. Shirreff: op. cit., p. 408. The Newcomes, Vol. II, ch. xxv.

52. Shirreff: op. cit., p. 409. Shirley, ch. xxii. The lack of books is seen in the case of Caroline Helstone, who had nothing to read but "some venerable Lady's Magazines", "some mad Methodist Magazines", "the equally mad Letters of Mrs. Elizabeth Rowe from the Dead to the Living, a few old English Classics. From these faded flowers Caroline had in her childhood extracted the honey. They were tasteless to her now." Vanity Fair, ch. xlii, xlvi. The Newcomes, Vol. I, ch. x.

53. Shirreff: op. cit., p. 406. Grey and Shirreff: Thoughts on Self-Culture, Vol. I, p. 33.

54. Shirreff: Intellectual Education, p. 410. David Copperfield, ch. xliv. Vanity Fair, ch. xli. Silas Marner, ch. xvii. Lady Marney in Sybil, Mrs. Carson in Mary Barton, Rosamond and Dorothea in Middlemarch were all suffering from a combination of mental and bodily idleness.

55. The Newcomes, Vol. II, ch. xxvii; Vol. II, ch. xxix, xli, xxx, iii. Letters and Memoirs of Sir William Hardman, footnote p. 45. Vanity Fair, ch. xxxii. Catherine Crowe in Lilly Dawson observed that a woman was treated "like a full-grown baby, to be flattered and spoilt on the one hand, and

coerced and restricted on the other, vibrating between royal rule and slavish serfdom". The Newcomes, Vol. II, ch. xiv. Middlemarch, ch. ix. Jane Eyre, ch. xvii. Shirley, ch. xviii. Middlemarch, ch. xxxvi. Shirley, ch. iv. Middlemarch, ch. viii. The Newcomes, Vol. II, ch. xiv. Vanity Fair, ch. ix.

56. Westminster Review, Vol. X, pp. 343, 344. Reid, Mrs. Hugo: Plea for Woman, p. 159. Industrial and Social Position of Women, p. 297. Hard Times, Book I, ch. xi. See also Mrs. Caroline Norton's English Laws for Women.

57. Babenroth, Charles A.: English Childhood, pp. 194–195. Gregory, Allene: The French Revolution and the English Novel, p. 199. Mansfield Park, ch. ii. De Quincey: Reminiscences of English Lake Poets (Temple edition), p. 153.

58. Edinburgh Review, Vol. 15, pp. 299–315. Gregory: *op. cit.*, p. 269.

59. P.P. 1833, Vol. xx, p. 577. Fraser's, Vol. 31, pp. 703–712. Christian Lady's Magazine, Vol. xix, p. 509. Westminster Review, 1849–50, p. 376.

60. Vanity Fair, ch. i. The Newcomes, Vol. I, ch. viii. Vanity Fair, ch. xxix, xxxix, iv, i, ii. The Newcomes, Vol. I, ch. xx; Vol. II, ch. xv; Vol. I, ch. xx. Vanity Fair, ch. iii.

61. Sketches by Boz, ch. iii of Tales of Minerva House. Little Dorrit, ch. v, xi. Great Expectations, ch. xv. The Old Curiosity Shop, ch. viii. Bleak House, ch. iv.

62. Hardy, Thomas : Mayor of Casterbridge, ch. xv.

63. Jane Eyre, ch. x. Shirley, ch. x, v, xxvi.

64. Amos Barton. Janet's Repentance. Middlemarch, ch. xi, xliii, xi, xvi. Shirley, ch. xxxi. Middlemarch, ch. v, vii. See also Gaskell: North and South, ch. ix, xviii.

65. Of what Dorothea and Celia got in the way of education George Eliot gave this general description: "They had both been educated, since they were about twelve years old and had lost their parents, on plans at once narrow and promiscuous, first in an English family and afterward in a Swiss family at Lausanne." Ch. i. Middlemarch, ch. ii, vii, x, xx, ix.

66. Mill on the Floss, Book I, ch. v.

67. Grey and Shirreff, Vol. I, p. 54.

68. P.P., 1867–68, Part IV, Vol. 13, pp. 744, 743. Parents opposed anything but a showy education, and wished their daughters to study English literature but to omit grammar (p. 698). According to Miss Buss (same volume, p. 254) most parents wanted "some knowledge of music and drawing, music especially". Time spent on fancy work was preferred to hours devoted to Latin (p. 743).

69. P.P., 1867–68, Part I, Vol. XXVIII, p. 546.

70. P.P., 1867–68, Part IV, Vol. 13, p. 256.

71. P.P., 1867–68, Part IV, Vol. 13, p. 945.

72. P.P., 1867–68, Part I, Vol. XXVIII, p. 559.

73. P.P., 1867–68, Part IV, Vol. 14, p. 233. Miss Buss stated that girls left school with only such education as was "almost entirely showy and superficial; a little music, a little singing, a little French, a little ornamental work, and nothing else, because many girls come to us who fancy they can speak French and play the piano, but have comparatively no knowledge of English and arithmetic" (p. 258). P.P. 1867–68, Part IV, Vol. 13, p. 742.

74. P.P., 1867–68, Part I, Vol. XXVIII, p. 558. To compare with these actual

figures we have Dickens's mention of £50 yearly for the boarding schoo
Kate Nickleby attended (ch. xxvi), and Thackeray's of £93 for Amelia.

75. P.P., Part I, Vol. XXVIII, p. 548; Part IV, Vol. 13, p. 236; Part I, Vol.
XXVIII, pp. 552, 11; Part IV, Vol. 13, pp. 260, 239, 261, 707.
76. Shirreff: Intellectual Education, pp. 414, 417, 423, 45.
77. Grey and Shirreff: Thoughts on Self-Culture, Vol. II, ch. i; Vol. I, p. 37.
78. Industrial and Social Position of Women, pp. 21, 22.
79. Morley, Henry: Defence of Ignorance, p. 33. Industrial and Social Position
of Women, pp. 59, 74, 75, 98, 99, 88.
80. Reid, Mrs. Hugo: A Plea for Woman, p. 177.
81. Clough, Arthur Hugh: Bothie of Tober-na-Vuolich (Selections from
Poems), pp. 99, 100, 15.
82. Shorter, Clement: The Brontës and their Circle, pp. 355, 367, 368.
83. Shorter, Clement: The Brontës and their Circle, pp. 220, 228, 232, 239.
84. Shorter, Clement: The Brontës and their Circle, p. 352. Martineau, Harriet:
Deerbrook, Vol. II, ch. xv.
85. Bleak House, ch. xxx. Parkes, Bessie Rayner: Essays on Woman's Work,
p. 37.
86. Davies, Emily: Higher Education of Women, p. 92.
87. Industrial and Social Position of Women, pp. 212, 206, 289.
88. Fraser's, Vol. 37, pp. 539–542.
89. Jameson, Anna: Communion of Labour, p. 28. Sisters of Charity, p. 102.
90. Strachey, Lytton: Eminent Victorians, p. 138.
91. Fraser's, Vol. 37, pp. 539–542; Vol. 41, p. 18; Vol. 42 (October 1850).
Edinburgh Review, Vol. 87, pp. 430–451.
92. Shirreff: op. cit., p. 418.
93. Trevelyan, G. M.: British History in the Nineteenth Century, pp. 306, 307.
94. Fraser's, Vol. 42, pp. 397–399.
95. Jameson: Sisters of Charity, p. 62.
96. Edinburgh Review, Vol. 87, pp. 430–451.
97. Industrial and Social Position of Women, p. 279. Household Words, Vol. IX,
p. 158; Vol. VI, p. 18. Hill, Georgiana: Women in English Life,
p. 103. P.P., 1867–68, Part IV, Vol. 13, p. 719. Edinburgh Review,
April 1859.
98. Brontë, Charlotte: The Professor, ch. xxiii. Shorter, Clement: op. cit.,
p. 356.
99. Edinburgh Review, Vol. 73, pp. 189–209. Reid: op. cit., pp. 55, 56.
100. Bleak House, ch. xxx. The Comic Almanac, First Series, p. 159; 1852,
p. 358.
101. Jameson: Sisters of Charity. Martineau, Harriet: Autobiography,
pp. 301, 302. Perkins: Life of Mrs. Norton, p. 149.
102. Fraser's, Vol. 19, pp. 205–215.
103. Perkins: op. cit., p. 247.
104. Shirley, ch. xxii.

CHAPTER VII

1. Industrial and Social Position of Women, p. 155.
2. Hutchins and Harrison: History of Factory Legislation, p. 187.

BIBLIOGRAPHY

I. NON-LITERARY MATERIALS (MISCELLANEOUS)

ALFRED (pseudonym for Samuel Kydd): History of the Factory Movement. 2 vols. London. 1850.

ARNOLD, MATTHEW: Reports on Elementary Schools, 1852–82. London. 1889.

BABENROTH, CHARLES: English Childhood. New York. 1922.

BAERNREITHER, J. M.: English Associations of Working Men. Translated from the German by Alice Taylor. London. 1893.

BAINES, EDWARD: History of the Cotton Manufacture in Great Britain. London. 1835.

BESANT, ANNIE: The Trades Union Movement. London. 1890.

BINNS, HENRY BRYAN: A Century of Education. London. 1908.

BOWDEN, WITT: Industrial Society in England towards the End of the Eighteenth Century. New York. 1925.

BOWLEY, ARTHUR L.: Wages in the United Kingdom. Cambridge. 1900.

BREMNER, C. S.: Education of Girls and Women in Great Britain. London. 1897.

CAZAMIAN, LOUIS: Le roman social en Angleterre. Paris. 1904.

CHEYNEY, EDWARD P.: Introduction to Industrial and Social History of England. New York. 1920.

CLAPHAM, J. H.: An Economic History of Modern Britain. Vol. 1, The Early Railway Age. Cambridge. 1926.

CLARK, ALICE: The Working Life of Women in the Seventeenth Century. New York. 1919.

CLEVELAND, ARTHUR: Woman under English Law. London. 1896.

COLE, G. D. H.: Life of William Cobbett. New York. 1924.

COOPER, ANTHONY ASHLEY, EARL OF SHAFTESBURY: Speeches upon Subjects having relation chiefly to the Claims and Interests of the Working Classes. London. 1868.

CUNNINGHAM, W.: Growth of English Industry and Commerce. 3 vols. Cambridge. 1912.

DAVIES, EMILY: The Higher Education of Women. London. 1866.

DILKE, EMILIA: Trade Unionism among Women. London. 1893.

DOBBS, A. E.: Education and Social Movements, 1700–1850. London. 1919.

DODD, G.: Days at the Factories. London. 1843.

DRAKE, BARBARA: Women in Trade Unions (Trade Union Series No. 6). London. No date.

ENGELS, FREDERICK: Condition of the Working Class in England in 1844. Translated from the German by Florence K. Wischnewetzky. London. 1892.

E. W.: The Distressed Needlewomen and Cheap Prison Labour. London. No date.

FAY, C. R.: Life and Labour in the Nineteenth Century. Cambridge. 1920.

FELKIN, W.: History of Machine-Wrought Hosiery and Lace Manufacture. London. 1867.

FIELDEN, J.: Curse of the Factory System. London. 1836.

GASKELL, PETER: Artisans and Machinery. London. 1836.
Manufacturing Population of England. London. 1833.

GRANT, PHILIP: The Ten-Hours Bill: A History of Factory Legislation. London. 1866.

GREENOUGH, JAMES C.: Evolution of the Elementary Schools of Great Britain. New York. 1903.

GREG, R. H.: The Factory Question. London. 1837.

GREG, W. R.: Why are Women Redundant? London. 1869.

GREGORY, AILEEN: The French Revolution and the English Novel. New York. 1915.

GREY, MARIA G., and SHIRREFF, EMILY: Thoughts on Self-Culture. 2 vols. London. 1850.

GUTCH, CHARLES: A Sermon on a Recent Mill Accident. London. 1853.

HALE, SARAH JOSEPHA: Woman's Record. London. 1853.

HALÉVY, ÉLIE: A History of the English People in 1815. Translated from the French by E. I. Watkin and D. A. Barker. New York. 1924.

HALL, S. C.: Oppressed Condition of the Dressmakers' and Milliners' Assistants. London. No date.

HAMMOND, J. H. and BARBARA: Lord Shaftesbury. London. 1923.
Rise of Modern Industry. New York. 1926.
Skilled Labourer. London. 1919.
Town Labourer. London. 1917.
Village Labourer. London and New York. 1913.

HANSARD: Debates of the House of Commons. Third Series. Vols. 73–90.

HILL, FREDERIC: National Education. 2 vols. London. 1836.

HILL, GEORGIANA: Women in English Life. London. 1896.

HIRST, W.: History of the Woollen Trade during the Last Sixty Years. London. 1844.

HODDER, EDWIN: Life and Work of the Seventh Earl of Shaftesbury, K.G. 3 vols. London. 1888.

HUGHES, JAMES L.: Dickens as an Educator. New York. 1903.
HUTCHINS, B. L.: Conflicting Ideals of Woman's Work, London. 1916.
The Girl in Industry. London. 1918.
Statistics of Women's Life and Employment. Reprinted from the Journal of the Royal Statistical Society. Vol. LXXII. Part II.
Women in Modern Industry. London. 1915.
HUTCHINS, B. L., and HARRISON, H.: History of Factory Legislation. London. 1903.
INDUSTRIAL and Social Position of Women in the Middle and Lower Ranks. (Anon.) London. 1857.
JAMESON, ANNA BROWNELL: Communion of Labour. Boston. 1857.
Memoirs and Essays. London. 1846.
Sisters of Charity at Home and Abroad. Boston. 1857.
KAY-SHUTTLEWORTH, SIR JAMES: Four Periods of Public Education. London. 1862.
KNOWLES, LILIAN: Industrial and Commercial Revolutions in Great Britain in the Nineteenth Century. London. 1921.
LIPSON, EPHRAIM: History of the Woollen and Worsted Industries. London. 1921.
McCULLOCH, J. R.: Dictionary of Commerce and Commercial Navigation. London. 1832.
MACDONALD, J. RAMSAY: Women in the Printing Trades. London. 1904.
MALLET, MRS. C.: Dangerous Trades for Women. London. 1893.
MARTINEAU, HARRIET: The Factory Controversy. Manchester. 1855.
Society in America. New York. 1837.
MATHIESON, WILLIAM LAW: English Church Reform, 1815–40. London. 1923.
MERRYWEATHER, MARY: Experience of Factory Life. London. 1862.
MILES, SIBELLA: Essay on the Factory Question. London. 1844.
MORLEY, HENRY: Defence of Ignorance. London. 1851.
NEFF, EMERY: Carlyle and Mill. Revised edition. New York. 1926.
NORTON, CAROLINE: English Laws for Women. London. 1854.
Oppressed Condition of the Dressmakers' and Milliners' Assistants. London. 1856.
OWEN, HAROLD: The Staffordshire Potter. London. 1901.
PARKES, BESSIE RAYNER: Essays on Woman's Work, London. 1865.
PARLIAMENTARY PAPERS (Reports of various Commissions and factory inspectors). 1831–32, Vol. XV through 1867–68, Vol. 13.

PENNY, VIRGINIA: Remarks on the Education of Girls. London. 1854.
Five Hundred Employments adapted to Women. Philadelphia. 1868.
PERKINS, JANE GREY: Life of Mrs. Norton. London. 1909.
PLENER, ERNEST VON: History of English Factory Legislation. Translated from the German by Frederick Weinmann. London. 1873.
PORTER, G. H.: The Progress of the Nation. 3 vols. London. 1838.
PRATT, EDWIN A.: Pioneer Women in Victoria's Reign. London. 1897.
REDGRAVE, ALEXANDER: The Factory Truck and Shops Acts. London. 1916.
REICH, EMIL: Woman through the Ages. London. 1908.
REID, MARION (Mrs. Hugo): Plea for Woman. London. 1845.
REYNOLDS, MYRA: The Learned Lady. Boston and New York. 1920.
ROBERTS, R. D. (editor): Education in the Nineteenth Century. Cambridge. 1901.
ROEBUCK, J. A.: Autobiography and Letters. Edited by R. Eadon Leader. London. 1897.
Political Pamphlets. London. 1835.
SCHULZE-GAEVERNITZ, G. VON: Social Peace. Translated from the German by G. M. Wicksteed. London. 1893.
SCORESBY, WILLIAM: American Factories and their Female Operatives. London. 1845.
SENIOR, NASSAU: Letters on the Factory Act. London. 1837.
SHAW, SIR C.: Manufacturing Districts: Replies to Lord Ashley. London. 1843.
SHAW, WILLIAM: Affectionate Pleading for England's Oppressed Female Workers. London. 1850.
SHIRREFF, EMILY: Intellectual Education. London. 1858.
SHORTER, CLEMENT: The Brontës and their Circle. London. 1914.
SLANEY, R. A.: Reports of the House of Commons on Education and on Health of the Poorer Classes. London. 1841.
SLATER, GILBERT: Making of Modern England. London. 1913.
SINCLAIR, CATHERINE: Modern Accomplishments. Edinburgh. 1836.
SLOSSON, P. W.: Decline of the Chartist Movement. New York. 1916.
SMITH, BARBARA LEIGH (Madame Bodichon): A Brief Summary of the Most Important Laws concerning Women. London. 1854.

SPEECHES delivered at the Great Meeting held under the Auspices of the Early Closing Association. July 11, 1856.

STODART, M. A.: Female Writers. London. 1842.

STRACHEY, LYTTON: Eminent Victorians. 7th impression. New York. No date.

STUBBORN FACTS from the Factories. By a Manchester Operative. London. 1844.

TAYLOR, W. COOKE: Notes of a Tour in the Manufacturing Districts of Lancashire. London. 1842.

THORNDIKE, ASHLEY H.: Literature in a Changing Age. New York. 1920.

TICKNER, F. W.: Women in English Economic History. London. 1923.

TORRENS, R.: On Wages and Combinations. London. 1834.

TOYNBEE, ARNOLD: Lectures on the Industrial Revolution in England. London. 1908.

TRAILL, H. D. (editor): Social England. New York. 1899.

TREVELYAN, G. M.: British History in the Nineteenth Century, 1782–1901. London. 1925.

TUCKWELL, GERTRUDE, and Others: Woman in Industry. London. 1908.

TUFNELL, EDWARD C.: Character, Objects and Effects of Trades' Unions. London. 1834.

URE, ANDREW: Philosophy of Manufactures. 2 vols. London. 1835.

VILLARD, LÉONIE: La femme anglaise au XIXᵉ siècle et son évolution aprés le roman anglais contemporain. Paris. 1920.

WADE, JOHN: History of the Middle and Working Classes. London. 1835.

WALLAS, GRAHAM: Life of Francis Place. London. 1898.

WEBB, SIDNEY and BEATRICE: History of Trade Unionism. London. 1894.

WILLIAMS, JANE: Literary Women of England. London. 1861.

WINCHESTER, C. T.: Life of John Wesley. New York. 1906.

WING, CHARLES: Evils of the Factory System. London. 1837.

WOOD, GEORGE HENRY: History of Wages. London. 1910.

YOUNG WOMEN of the Factory. London. 1845.

ZIMMERN, ALICE: Renaissance of Girls' Education in England. London. 1898.

ADDENDUM.—Since this book was sent to the press there has appeared "*The Cause,*" *A Short History of the Women's Movement in Great Britain,* by Ray Strachey (London, 1928), which contains valuable material on women's education, professional training, and development in political consciousness.

II. LITERARY MATERIALS

AUSTEN, EMMA:
   Emma.
   Mansfield Park.
BAMFORD, SAMUEL: Passages in the Life of a Radical and Early
   Days. 2 vols. London. 1893.
BLESSINGTON, MARGARET POWER, COUNTESS OF: The Governess.
BRONTË, ANNE: Agnes Grey.
BRONTË, CHARLOTTE:
   Jane Eyre.
   The Professor.
   Shirley.
   Villette.
BROWNING, ELIZABETH BARRETT: Aurora Leigh.
BROWNING, ROBERT: Poetical Works.
BURDETT, CHARLES: The Elliott Family.
CARLYLE, THOMAS:
   Latter-Day Pamphlets.
   Past and Present.
CLOUGH, ARTHUR HUGH: Poetical Works.
COOPER, THOMAS: Life of Thomas Cooper. Written by himself.
   London. 1873.
CROWE, CATHERINE: Lilly Dawson.
DE QUINCEY, THOMAS: Reminiscences of the English Lake Poets.
DELONEY, THOMAS: Pleasant History of John Winchcombe.
DICKENS, CHARLES:
   Bleak House.
   Christmas Books.
   David Copperfield.
   Great Expectations.
   Hard Times.
   Little Dorrit.
   Martin Chuzzlewit.
   Nicholas Nickleby.
   Old Curiosity Shop.
   Oliver Twist.
   Our Mutual Friend.
   Sketches by Boz.
DISRAELI, BENJAMIN: Sybil.
ELIOT, GEORGE:
   Adam Bede.
   Felix Holt.

Middlemarch.
Mill on the Floss.
Scenes of Clerical Life.
Silas Marner.
GASKELL, ELIZABETH CLEGHORN:
A Dark Night's Work.
Cousin Phyllis.
Cranford.
Libbie Marsh's Three Eras.
Life of Charlotte Brontë (Temple edition).
Lizzie Leigh.
Mary Barton.
North and South.
Ruth.
Wives and Daughters.
GORE, CATHERINE: Men of Capital.
HALL, ANNA MARIA:
Stories of the Governess.
Tales of Woman's Trials.
HARDY, THOMAS: Mayor of Casterbridge.
HOOD, THOMAS: Poetical Works.
INCHBALD, ELIZABETH: The Simple Story.
JEWSBURY, GERALDINE: Marian Withers. London. 1851.
KINGSLEY, CHARLES: Alton Locke.
LAMB, CHARLES: Works. (Mary Lamb: On Needlework.)
LETTERS and Memoirs of Sir William Hardman. Edited by S. M.
Ellis. New York. 1925.
LOVETT, WILLIAM: Life and Struggles of William Lovett. New
York. 1920.
LUBBOCK, PERCY: Elizabeth Barrett Browning in her Letters.
MARTINEAU, HARRIET: Deerbrook.
NORTON, CAROLINE:
Child of the Islands.
Stuart of Dunleath.
Voice from the Factories.
OWEN, ROBERT DALE: Threading My Way.
RUSKIN, JOHN: Sesame and Lilies.
TENNYSON, ALFRED: Poetical Works.
THACKERAY, WILLIAM MAKEPEACE:
Book of Snobs.
Newcomes.
Pendennis.
Vanity Fair.

TONNA, CHARLOTTE ELIZABETH: Works, with an Introduction by
Harriet Beecher Stowe. 2 vols. New York. 1849.
TROLLOPE, FRANCES: Michael Armstrong.
WOLLSTONECRAFT, MARY: Vindication of the Rights of Women.
WORDSWORTH, WILLIAM: The Excursion.

III. PERIODICAL LITERATURE

All the Year Round. Vol. 10.
Bradshaw's Journal. Vol. III.
Christian Lady's Magazine. Vols. II–XIX.
Comic Almanac, First and Second Series.
Douglas Jerrold's Shilling Magazine. Vol. I.
Edinburgh Review. Vols. 15–93.
Fraser's Magazine. Vols. 12–42.
Good Words. Vol. 4.
Halifax Guardian. June 5 and 19, 1847.
Household Words. Vols. I–XI.
Illustrated London News. Vols. 4–18.
London Times. May 4, 1847.
Manchester Guardian. June 5, 1847.
Morning Chronicle. 1850.
Once a Week. Vol. 3.
Punch. Vols. V–XV.
Quarterly Review. Vol. 84.
Saint James Magazine. Vols. 3, 4.
Voice of the People. 1848.
Westminster Review. Vols. X–LIII.

INDEX